THE FINANCIERS

THE

FINANCIERS

*The World of the Great Wall Street
Investment Banking Houses*

Michael C. Jensen

WEYBRIGHT and TALLEY
New York

Weybright and Talley
750 Third Avenue,
New York, New York 10017.

LIBRARY OF CONGRESS CATALOGING IN PUBLICATION DATA

Jensen, Michael C
The financiers.

Includes bibliographical references and index.
1. Investment banking—United States. 2. Capital-
ists and financiers—United States. 3. Wall Street.
I. Title.
HG4930.J45   332.1   76–9808
ISBN 0–679–40075–3

MANUFACTURED IN THE UNITED STATES OF AMERICA

*Dedicated to the memory
of my Father*

CONTENTS

CONTENTS

THE FINANCIERS

INTRODUCTION:
The Money Monarchs

They are the elite of Wall Street. Their offices are furnished with expensive antiques and original works of art. They dress in conservatively cut $500 suits, and are as quick to place a telephone call to Rome or Zurich or Frankfurt as most Americans are to call their next-door neighbor. They give $50,000 or $100,000 gifts to Presidential candidates to help finance their campaigns. They shuttle between high-level cabinet jobs in Washington and their private positions on Wall Street, finding it easy to sacrifice for a few years a business income that may exceed $1 million a year for the $40,000 or $50,000 they are paid for their government service. They engineer multi-million-dollar transactions and, although they render middleman services only, enough money remains in their hands to make them the richest wage earners in the world.

They are the investment bankers of Wall Street; the men who raise billions in cash for America's giant corporations; the men who bring together or accomodate the chief executive officers who want to buy someone else's company, or sell their own, or fight off a corporate raider. Unknown to the general public, as dissimilar to the neighborhood savings banker as Harold Geneen of ITT is to the owner of a neighborhood delicatessen, the investment banker is an invisible man. Most Americans have only the vaguest notion of what he does.

In a country that has grown from largely agrarian beginnings to become the industrial giant of the world, the investment banker functions in the manner of the rainmaker of an earlier generation. He comes and goes quietly, surfacing only to perform his sometimes spectacular task. His art is arcane. But just as the rainmaker promised to draw from the sky the drops that nourished the farmers' crops, so these latter-day rainmakers draw from the people and institutions around them the dollars that are needed to build the nation's factories and department stores; its roads and schools; indeed, the very fabric of all our lives.

What is investment banking? Simply the art of raising money for a client. There are many ways to borrow money in the United States. The individual consumer can borrow from his bank. He can get a loan from his stockbroker, his retail merchant, a gasoline company, or an airline. Almost anyone who sells a service or product is willing to loan money—and collect interest on the loan at a handsome rate.

Most of us are familiar with those methods of borrowing. We get our monthly mortgage statements, our credit card bills, our department store revolving credit statements. And we know we are paying a premium for the privilege of buying now and paying later.

There is also a popular but less publicized way to borrow. If a poor man borrows money from a loan shark to buy his wife a washing machine or to cover a losing bet on the horses, he gives

2

a "marker." He then must make regular payments, which often add up to more than the original loan. Part of that money goes to the loan shark and part of it goes to the shark's own source of money.

Investment banking works the same way, except that the customer is a corporation or a government. For example, assume the American Telephone and Telegraph Company needs money to finance a new factory, new cables, or switchboards—or just because it doesn't have enough money to meet next Friday's payroll. It can raise its rates; it can go to a neighborhood commercial bank for a loan, or it can issue pieces of paper called stock, or bonds, or "commercial paper" which are simply "markers" promising to repay the buyer at a certain rate over a specified period of time.

The investment banker is the middleman in the great world of corporate borrowing. He tells the company treasurer what sort of plan would work best for his company. Should there be a simple offering of stock? Or is there already enough stock outstanding? Should it be a bond offering? And, if so, what should the interest rate be? Should something more be involved; for example, a bond offering with warrants attached, which give the buyer an opportunity to buy future shares of stock at a specified price? When should the offering be made? Should it be done all at once, or staggered over a longer period of time? These are just a few of the most basic questions for which the investment banker must provide answers. This part of his job is straightforward, if sometimes complex.

"Investment banking puts money behind ideas," proclaim the industry's spokesmen. "It aids in the economic process which creates jobs, schools, and new products. If a corporation needs capital funds to manufacture a new device, the investment banker arranges for it. If a town needs money to build a new high school or pollution control center, the investment banker finds it. In a nation that depends upon individual enterprise to make its economy work, the investment banker brings together people who need money with people who have savings to invest."

In recent years, American industry has needed over $100 billion in new capital each year for growth and replacement. Much of this has been provided by individuals and institutional investors who bought newly issued stocks and bonds. The investors earned income through interest or dividends. In some cases, they made even more money because their securities increased in price as the market rose. In other cases, they lost money as markets fell.

"Investment bankers are the people who help shape the financing plans of industry and government, so that the securities being sold satisfy long-term investors and long-term users of capital," explains a prominent industry spokesman. "The investment banker is a risk-taking middleman linking the two sides of the process. He risks his capital, often in large amounts, such as the billions needed to pay for California's huge water development program or New York State's rapidly growing university system, or for expansion of public utility systems serving our mushrooming population. His efforts may be little noticed, but they are pivotal in the expansion of new industry."

All quite true, but there is another side to investment banking as well, and this book attempts to explore both. The more traditional and less controversial aspect of investment banking is described in the first six chapters. They tell the story of the tiny, privately owned company that is discovered by investment bankers and transformed into a larger, publicly held corporation with stock on the nation's exchanges. These opening chapters discuss the raising of hundreds of millions of dollars for giant corporations; the necessity of dealing with politicians when fund-raising efforts have national economic repercussions; international transactions that involve not only finances but also foreign policy considerations; and the relationship of investment bankers with some of the most powerful and wealthy individuals in the world.

The other side of investment banking is described in the subsequent six chapters. There the darker and less clearly defined areas of the profession emerge: the high-level wheeling and dealing that surrounds financial transactions inside a major corporation; the rise and fall of reputations on Wall Street when scandal enters the picture; the sensitive and often murky role of the investment banker in persuading government officials that arcane practices should be allowed; the role of the financier as a corporate conscience; the parallels between the investment banker and the self-confessed thief; and, finally, the role of the government's watchdogs and how well or poorly they keep financiers ethically accountable.

This second section of *The Financiers* also examines the contention of critics who allege that investment banking is simply the art of insuring that the rich get richer; that well-informed insiders stay ahead of the public tide of information; that the wheels of finance are lubricated with the kind of convoluted financial dealing that only an investment banker can handle.

Investment bankers, like members of any other profession, come in all forms. Some are brilliant, others merely average. Some are altruistic and giving, others venal and grasping. Some are family men, others retirees from the hearth. *The Financiers* attempts to provide the reader with some of the diversity in an important if obscure corner of the larger financial world. It is not intended as a textbook on investment banking, nor as an exhaustive survey of the investment banking world. Rather it is an anecdotal exploration into some of the fascinating financial deals devised by the nation's financiers. While virtually all the investment bankers described in the book have been interviewed, much of the information about them, their firms, and the transactions they wrought has come from other sources—often from obscure government documents filed away in courthouses or at the Securities and Exchange Commission, sometimes from competitors, occasionally from friends. Although an attempt has been made to keep *The Financiers* nonjudgmental, in the end, whatever judgments are made are perforce the author's.

On Wall Street, as nowhere else in the world, the business of making money is stripped to its essentials. Wall Streeters don't have to worry about some of the things that concern others: huge personnel rosters or assembly lines, or the sort of massive capital investment that is required in, say, steel. On Wall Street, the product is money. And the aim is simple: Make all you can as fast as you can.

An old adage of Wall Street has it that you can sometimes be a bear, sometimes a bull, but never, never a hog. Don't you believe it! Every morning, as the subway unloads at the corners of Wall Street and Broadway, the oinks can be heard loud and clear. Wall Street is the quintessential heart of capitalism—the great maximizer of profits. And in the forefront of this omnipotent cash connection is our friend the investment banker, with his contacts, his inside information, his ability to invest millions as easily as most men place a $2 bet at a race track window.

It is gospel on Wall Street that the way to make money is to be in on the ground floor. The investment banker builds the ground floor. He knows before anyone else whether a merger is going to be attempted, and whether it is likely to be successful. He knows what securities offerings are going to be hot. He has both the knowledge and the capital to be the archetypal ground floor resident; virtues which, in many cases, result in his becoming a millionaire in a very short time.

The work of the investment banker generally is carried out behind the closed doors of private offices, carefully screened from public view. One purpose of this book is to look behind those closed doors into the world of powerful financiers who seldom emerge as public figures. Although they are often well known in financial circles, their names mean nothing to most Americans. How many of your neighbors can identify Charles Allen, Gustave Levy; Julius Sedlmayr or Richard Coons? Occasionally, however, names like Felix Rohatyn (see Chapter 6) begin to make headlines, and as they appear on the six o'clock news, their faces and voices become a part of our consciousness.

One spectacular example of an investment banker virtually surfacing overnight from the anonymity of Wall Street to become a national figure occurred in late 1973 when William Simon became, for a time, the energy czar of the United States. Later he would be promoted to Secretary of the Treasury, and although his prestige would be greater with his new position, his visibility would not.

As energy czar, Simon was transformed into the country's authority figure, sternly telling 200 million citizens that they must lower their thermostats; cajoling them to stop driving their automobiles; pushing Congress to pass new laws; holding an endless stream of press conferences.

At the age of forty-six, he had stepped from his role as a Wall Street bond trader and underwriter into the national spotlight. Ironically, he became known for the first time to the nation as the $42,500-a-year-chief of the Nixon administration's Federal Energy Office. But Wall Street, which measures performance by a dollar yardstick, had made an earlier assessment of his capabilities. Before he left Manhattan for Washington, Simon had been earning as much as $3 million in a single year as a partner of the investment banking firm of Salomon Brothers.

What had the investment banker done to earn that much money? Basically, he had sold bonds. Simon dealt in millions, sometimes billions of dollars in bonds. At times his firm had as much as $2 billion in securities, mostly U.S. Government bills, notes, and bonds for sale. At that level, the bond business becomes something totally foreign to the average investor. It involves an intricate knowledge of who can buy the enormous volumes of paper spewed out by the government; which institutions can absorb a particular type of security at any given moment. It also means that the top men in the field must use their expertise to help the government decide what shape its money-raising program will take. Soon after he became a partner, Simon was invited to join a securities industry committee that advised the Treasury how to refinance the national debt.

To reach the top ranks of investment banking, a man (and the term man is used deliberately: at the moment, there are no women filling key jobs at investment banking firms) must have extraordinary energy, a mind that is geared to problem solving, and an instinct to reach for the jugular. In this respect, it is instructive to look more closely at Simon, because he is somewhat typical of ambitious financiers.

Simon began his Wall Street career at the age of twenty-five as a trainee at the Union Securities Company, a firm that later merged successively with the firms of Dillon & Co. and Blyth &

Co. Already behind him when he went to Wall Street was a bachelor's degree from Lafayette College in Pennsylvania where he had been an indifferent student, followed by a stint in the army where he served as a private first class and swam in the Pacific Olympics in Japan. Simon stayed with Union for five years, learning the tax-exempt bond business, and then moved to Weeden & Co., the successful maverick of Wall Street. After seven years at Weeden, Simon moved again, this time to the up-and-coming firm of Salomon Brothers. Riding the crest of one of the most profitable periods in the bond market's history—in the late 1960s and early 1970s—Simon solidified his reputation as one of the bright young men of Wall Street. Then, demonstrating an instinct for timing, he left Salomon Brothers in late 1972, to become Deputy Secretary of the Treasury, a job he had held for only a year when he was tapped to become energy czar.

Simon was known as a tough administrator who worked long hours. In the government, as in his private jobs, he was accustomed to putting in fourteen-hour days. He was as demanding of his staff as of himself, and one widely circulated story of his days on Wall Street focused on his penchant for efficiency, if not for tact. It is told that Simon once ordered a trainee to clean up his desk, but the next time he passed the desk, it still was cluttered. Whereupon Simon swept his arm across it, knocking its contents onto the floor. Such actions led associates to give Simon the title "Vince Lombardi of the financial world."

As a result of his appointment as head of the nation's energy office, Simon's life became a whirlwind of activity. One day early in January 1974, for example, he delivered an address at the Americana Hotel in New York, received a "Good Scouting" award, completed a roundtable interview at *The New York Times,* finished contributing to a major energy speech the President was to make the following day, and arranged to discuss the Middle East oil embargo with Secretary of State Henry Kissinger the following day. It was the same sort of hectic schedule he had also kept as an investment banker.

While Simon represents one type of investment banker—the

man who earns a fortune, goes to Washington, establishes a national reputation, and ultimately either returns to Wall Street or enters elective politics—there is another type of financier who follows a reverse path. He makes his initial mark as a businessman or industrialist, wins recognition and makes contacts in Washington, and then arrives on Wall Street to take advantage of his earlier experience. Peter G. Peterson typifies the public man who turned to investment banking in mid-career.

Peterson had been a rising young star in both the private and public affairs of the country since the early 1950s. A vice president of McCann-Erickson, an advertising agency, at the age of twenty-seven, he was tapped for the presidency of Bell & Howell, the big camera company, only seven years later. He later moved up to the chairmanship of that company, and then, early in 1971, he was named to Nixon's White House staff. In Washington, Peterson was a flamboyant exception to the men who surrounded the President. He was a favorite guest at Georgetown cocktail and dinner parties, and counted among his close friends such liberal enemies of the administration as newspaper columnist Mary McGrory.

Although he was somewhat of a maverick, Peterson's prestige and power in Washington grew. After serving as the President's expert on foreign trade, he was named Secretary of Commerce in January 1972. However, as his political enemies multiplied, he was eased out of the Cabinet and given an assignment as a roving trade envoy. The problem, insiders said, was that he had run afoul of Nixon's two key advisors, H.R. Haldeman and John W. Ehrlichman.

Peterson, who had been a business protégé of Illinois Senator Charles Percy at Bell & Howell, also was a close friend of Secretary of State Henry Kissinger. With such good connections, he had many offers in business and finance.

It did not surprise Wall Street that he decided to take the investment banking route. Despite his termination from the Nixon administration, he had a successful record, and his leaving Washington at the precise moment he did, before Watergate began to sink the administration, would later seem to be excellent timing.

So Peterson went to Wall Street, joining the venerable but financially troubled firm of Lehman Brothers as a partner and vice chairman, and was named chairman shortly thereafter. Before long, he was presiding over the firm's eleven-storied edifice, its series of partners' dining rooms, known as Wall Street's best, and the partners' gymnasium on the top floor.

For a few months, Peterson was the object of massive doses of publicity, as he began reorganizing the troubled firm, paring its staff and reordering its priorities. Then, gradually, he disappeared from public view. The same thing had happened to two men who preceded him as partners at Lehman Brothers—General Lucius D. Clay, the organizer of the 1948 Berlin airlift, and George W. Ball, Undersecretary of State and Ambassador to the United Nations in the Kennedy and Johnson administrations. For Wall Streeters, however, there was little doubt that now, for the first time, Peterson had really reached the big leagues. Neither the White House, the world of industry, nor anything in his past would automatically qualify Peterson for success as an investment banker. And so, Wall Street watched curiously and often skeptically. One rival banker, perhaps more cynical than most, told Marylin Bender of *The New York Times,* "Peterson will be devoured by the wolves in the street."

Not every investment banker finds Wall Street a congenial place to earn his living. Some become disenchanted and leave. One was Alan Silverstone, a graduate of Columbia University's law and business schools, who had been earning $50,000 a year as a fledgling investment banker while still in his twenties. He forsook Wall Street to become the proprietor of a Beverly Hills, California, toy store and penny arcade.

Silverstone had all the credentials to become a successful investment banker. There was the Ivy League background, the set of advanced degrees, the family history of accomplishment (his father was a physician who lectured all over the world on radiology, his mother held a law degree, and a brother was a professor of chemistry at Johns Hopkins University).

Somehow, though, the life of an investment banker didn't agree with Silverstone. One sleepless night, while playing a pinball machine in his living room, he concluded that he was not happy and had to do something about it. So, he packed up his family and moved to California where he loosened up his life style, while continuing to work in investment banking. All the while, he was preparing to earn a living with his first love—pachinko machines, gumball dispensers, old coins from Nevada bawdy houses, and other funky gadgets.

By early 1974, Silverstone had successfully built his new enterprise, which included three stores located in Hollywood, Beverly Hills, and San Francisco, and a plant in Pasadena to manufacture some of the goods he sold.

Why did he leave investment banking?

"I think," he said, "I got bored solving other people's problems. I wasn't getting anything personal out of it. There was no satisfaction. My life was oriented around bringing my firm into other people's lives."

From the anonymity of Wall Street, Silverstone became something of a celebrity himself. By the age of thirty-one, which is still postpuberty for investment bankers, he had rubbed shoulders with movie and television stars, and had been the subject of splashy write-ups by the *Los Angeles Times* and United Airlines' *Mainliner* magazine. The Associated Press had sent his picture across the country to hundreds of newspapers. Silverstone's new life seemed to fit him so perfectly that it prompted Les Gilbert of Fairchild News Service to pin on him the title, "the antihero of investment banking."

While there are those who, like Silverstone, do not flourish as investment bankers, others blossom. Attracted by the variety, the challenge, and above all, by the opportunity to earn vast sums of money, they eschew more prosaic fields to enter investment banking.

What exactly do they do, these highly paid, enigmatic financial wizards?

Unlike the savings banker or commercial banker, the investment banker makes his big money not from the public, but from the client. He earns massive fees and commissions for telling his customer, be it a government body or a corporation, whether to issue common stock, preferred shares, debentures, first mortgage bonds, notes, equipment trust certificates, convertible bonds, debentures with warrants attached, and so on.

Just as various financiers become known for a particular specialty, so some Wall Street financial houses are better known for handling one type of deal over another. Merrill Lynch, Pierce, Fenner & Smith, the behemoth of the financial world, has the world's largest and most successful chain of retail brokerage houses. As a result, it can market virtually any sort of public offering. This gives the firm enormous leverage in attracting investment banking business. It also means it is a much sought-after partner in syndicates organized by other investment bankers. Merrill Lynch also has another advantage. There are certain types of individuals and companies who are comfortable dealing only with the biggest, most highly regarded institutions in their field, regardless of the competitive situation. Howard Hughes, for example, found dealing with Merrill Lynch preferable to doing his investment banking business with some other Wall Street house.

Another investment banking house that enjoys the reputation of being a blue-chip firm is Morgan Stanley & Co. Traditionally, it has had the most top-heavy roster of "Fortune 500" clients of any Wall Street concern, and it does everything it can to enhance and publicize that position. Its sumptuous offices and aggressive young financiers wheeling and dealing in the back room scarcely detract from the firm's image as a gold-plated financier.

Some firms, Goldman, Sachs or Lehman Brothers, for example, are often thought of as specialists in some particular industry such as airlines or retailing. Some of them have connections with large companies that go back for several generations. Still other firms, like Allen & Company, are considered to be essentially opportunistic. They recognize investment opportunities and seize them, with the principals becoming extraordinarily wealthy along the way. Then there are the establishments like Salomon Brothers, best known for their ability to handle large blocks of stock.

One popular method of assessing an investment banking firm is to count the amount of cash at its disposal. To underwrite an offering of securities in the traditional fashion, a firm must buy the securities from the client and then resell them to customers. That takes vast amounts of money.

At the beginning of 1975, Merrill Lynch stood in first place among the big investment banker-brokers in terms of total capital available, with a capital position of over $540 million, more than four times as great as the second-place firm of Salomon Brothers, which had $124 million. A firm's capital position is not always a definitive indicator of its power in the world of investment banking, where participation in a massive underwriting may be limited by the amount of capital a company can raise. Some firms have unreported money available that belongs to its partners, or to big customers, or to former partners who have dropped into the limited partner category. Still, there is no escaping the significance of reported capital, and Merrill Lynch clearly led the pack. In the twelve-month period ending January 1, 1973, Merrill Lynch managed or comanaged 212 equity and debt issues worth over $8 billion, and participated in another 315 issues worth $12 billion.

By contrast, Salomon Brothers managed or comanaged 137 issues worth over $6 billion, and had participated in 486 additional issues worth about $1 billion. However, Salomon had only 1,000 employees and 11 offices, as against Merrill Lynch's 20,000 employees and 247 offices.

After Bache & Co.'s total capital of $120 million at the beginning of 1975, the list fell off sharply. Rounding out the top ten firms were the E.F. Hutton Group with $100 million; Dean Witter & Co., $86 million; Paine, Webber, Jackson & Curtis Inc., $84 million; Loeb, Rhoades & Co., $78 million; Goldman, Sachs & Co., $76 million; Allen & Company, $70 million; Shearson Hayden Stone Inc., $66 million.

Not that capital position is preeminently significant. Lazard Frères & Co., with capital of only $17 million, was considered one of the more imaginative investment banking firms on the Street. Walston & Co. and duPont Glore Forgan, which between them had capital of over $130 million at the beginning of 1973, found after their merger that capital alone was not enough to forestall a rapid slide into a sea of red ink. The firms announced early in 1974 that they were going out of business, and selling off their costly chain of branch offices.

In addition to capital, the investment banker needs clients. And, after he finds the client, the banker must decide which of many methods available is the most appropriate for raising money. Which will provide his customer with the amount of money he needs, at the precise time he needs it? The banker also must be sure the offering will find a market, either with the public or with private investors. He might have devised the most imaginative deal in the world, but if market conditions are wrong, or the financiers have misjudged the public's mood, the offering can be a disaster.

After the financier has decided what form the offering will take, which of the myriad types of securities he should offer, a method of distribution must be selected. It might be decided to offer the securities directly to a group of institutional investors, like pension fund or mutual fund operators. Or, it might seem more profitable to let the public have a chance to buy the securities. If the latter is the case, a syndicate must be formed. A syndicate is simply a group of investment banking and brokerage houses who will underwrite the issue and offer it to the public. Underwriting the issue means the members of the syndicate actually purchase the securities from the corporation or government body, assuming the risk if they are not sold.

An example of how a public offering operates is found in Chapter 2, which describes Morgan Stanley's role in creating the biggest such offering in history for the American Telephone and Telegraph Company (although in this case, the syndicate did not underwrite the offering). In most instances, each member of the syndicate agrees to buy part of the new stock or bond issue and to distribute it at an offering price to syndicate customers.

One way investment bankers solidify their positions as syndicate managers and consultants to giant corporations is to win a place on that company's board of directors. They then are in a position not only to stay abreast of the company's long-range plans, but also to influence those plans, often to their own advantage. Chapter 9, which describes the role of Lazard Frères & Co. in the expansion of ITT, includes such a situation. In other cases, public companies are literally created by investment bankers for their own personal gains. The birth of Syntex in the late 1950s, with Charles Allen of Allen & Company serving as the midwife, is an excellent example (see Chapter 1).

If the investment banker in an underwriting has done his job well and perceptively gauged market conditions, the securities will sell out quickly at the offering price. However, if the public response has been misjudged, or if the market suddenly deteriorates, the underwriters must reduce the price to a level that will attract buyers. It is this possibility that brings the greatest element of risk. In most cases, the corporation or government body is protected. Sometimes, however, arrangements are made which shift the risk back to the company. One such case, involving the Penn Central Railroad, is described in Chapter 7.

Vincent P. Carosso, professor of history at New York University whose book, *Investment Banking in America,* is considered one of the definitive works in the field, offered his assessment of investment bankers and their profession.

"My impression," Carosso said, "is that while they hate to be called middlemen, they *are* middlemen. They're a kind of professional middlemen who provide advisory services. They like to think of themselves as 'professional,' and I suppose that's all right, but it depends on how you define professional.

"They certainly are the most influential of the people on Wall Street, and I have the feeling they regard themselves as the elite. They may deny it, but have you ever seen Morgan Stanley's name appear anywhere else except at the masthead or the head of the syndicate in the underwriting ads? There is evidence to show that sometimes they're in a syndicate anonymously, but if their name can't appear on the top, then it doesn't appear at all. Judge Harold R. Medina said a curious thing in the antitrust trial during the

1950s. He said he thought it was only the prima donnas and Hollywood movie starlets who were worried how their names appeared on the marquee. But he was flabbergasted when he saw these investment bankers jockeying for position."

As for the future, Carosso foresees a gradual shift in the types of business that will engage the nation's financiers.

"More and more, investment bankers are going to raise money for governments," he said. "Municipalities, states, foreign governments. The investment houses are also beginning to get interested in the underdeveloped countries that want issues. The corporations are getting bigger and bigger, and wealthier and wealthier. In a sense, they are becoming less dependent upon money from investment bankers, whereas municipalities and states, the public authorities like the TVA, that's the kind that will be the investment bankers' big thing."

Another area that will become increasingly important, he said, is advisory financial service. "For a long time, I never could understand why a large corporation, let's say duPont, needed the investment banker to place a private issue. But apparently there are a lot of technical details that have to be worked out, and the corporation isn't willing to maintain a staff to do all this work. So, the investment banker does it for them, and becomes important. What the investment bankers have to offer in these private placements is that they know how to do it, who wants to buy the issue, why they want it, and how they want it packaged."

Change also seems certain in the patterns of employment and advancement within the investment banking profession.

During the post-World War II period, there was a tradition of young men becoming entrenched at a firm and then spending an entire career there. In the early 1970s, however, an unusually heavy move of ambitious and talented young investment bankers from one firm to another took place. It was caused partly by a desire to move ahead faster in what had become an increasingly competitive business, and partly by anxiety that the fortunes earned by their predecessors might not be so easy to accumulate today.

Not only did investment bankers shift from firm to firm, they also took the traditional alternate route of government service. At about the same time William Simon of Salomon Brothers was beginning to make a reputation in Washington, another Wall Street investment banker, William Donaldson, also moved to the nation's capitol to serve as Undersecretary of State. A look at both the man and his firm illustrates the flavor of the period.

Donaldson, a cofounder of the young, successful firm of Donaldson, Lufkin & Jenrette, had in fourteen years parlayed an investment of $20,000, much of it borrowed, into a personal fortune of about $8 million. His salary when he left DLJ was $185,000 a year, but most of his fortune came from deals he helped fashion and investments that skyrocketed in value.

Donaldson's career was aided by his personality. He exuded a quality that is characteristic of many of Wall Street's top investment bankers: an air of forced sincerity. Many investment bankers have it, just as many industrialists don't. Industrialists often are guarded and seldom outgoing. Their world is a closed one, peopled with obedient subordinates and suppliers, prying regulators, and intractable legislators. Investment bankers, however, live by their wits. They have no large factories, no slowly altering markets for their physical products. Each time they bring in a new customer, they must employ not only the arts they have learned, but also a knowing approach. Look your client in the eye and tell him what's best. Does he know the money markets? Not likely. Do you question your doctor when he says your appendix needs removing?

Donaldson came from modest circumstances, and it was at Yale that he picked up the patina and connections that would later serve him so well as an investment banker. In this regard, Donaldson is reasonably typical of young men who enter investment banking. There is a social cachet that goes with success in the field. Either consciously or unconsciously, many investment bankers move upward along the social scale at a rate that roughly parallels their business progress. For a man like Donaldson, who became a multimillionaire at an early age, it was easy to afford the accouterments of society.

One of the reasons why Donaldson became rich so quickly was

that DLJ was the first financial house in the country to sell its own stock to the public. Traditionally, such firms had been closely held partnerships. When a successful partnership goes public, and the market for its stock is good, it means the shares retained by the partners become extraordinarily valuable. In many cases, instant fortunes are created.

In addition, DLJ was a highly profitable firm. It was the first on Wall Street to become a financial holding company, a move which broadened its base of operations, and enabled it aggressively to take advantage of the growing demand in the middle sixties for thorough investment research from institutional investors such as mutual funds, insurance companies, and banks.

For many investment bankers, however, money is not enough. That is one reason why Wall Streeters like Donaldson accept government jobs. As young men in a highly competitive field, their immediate goal is usually money. The money itself, however, is only an indicator, not an absolute goal. After all, any man who earns $30,000 a year is among the top 5 percent of the nation's wage earners. Money is more of a barometer for Wall Streeters. What is important is whether they have done their job well. Have they outsmarted their competitors? Have they devised a more ingenious way to do business, or to fill a developing need? At DLJ, the answer was yes. Donaldson and his partners had seen a trend and had capitalized on it. They recognized that the stock market in the 1960s would come to be dominated by institutions rather than individuals. However, a decade is a long time on Wall Street. With some of the nation's shrewdest and most ambitious young men arriving each year to match themselves against their predecessors, an investment banker can be young at thirty but old at forty. Donaldson had made his fortune, had outsmarted the competition. His interests had broadened. When the opportunity came to work at the side of Henry Kissinger, he grabbed it. Later, when the government infighting palled, and the spot at Kissinger's side became less glamorous, Donaldson returned to Wall Street. His tenure in Washington was shorter than most, but it is not unusual for investment bankers to shuttle back and forth between government and private enterprise.

Although the people in the world of investment banking make fascinating studies, the complex deals they fashion are more interesting, and are the substance of this book.

Late in 1973, *Institutional Investor* magazine published a list of some of investment banking's toughest deals. Investment bankers themselves were asked to single out the most difficult of the last few years. Their selections told a great deal about the emergence of new firms in the investment banking community, and the fading of others, but most important, they revealed the diversity of the profession.

In the listing of investment banking's toughest transactions, Morgan Stanley, which ranked forty-first at the beginning of 1974 in total capital, appeared twice. First, it was cited for its $1 billion private placement for AT&T, which took place a year after it issued $1.3 billion in convertible preferred securities for "Ma Bell," and two years after the offering of $1.6 billion in debentures and warrants that is described in Chapter 2.

The other operation which involved Morgan Stanley was the biggest single project financing in history, involving the development of the hydroelectric resources of Churchill Falls, in Labrador, by a company called Brinco Ltd. So intimately was Morgan Stanley involved, that when several Brinco executives, including its chief executive, were killed in an air crash in 1969, William D. Mulholland, the Morgan partner in charge, took up the reins at Brinco.

Perhaps the most intriguing of the "tough" deals was one that brought Merrill Lynch into personal contact with Howard Hughes, the elusive billionaire. After Merrill Lynch was told in 1972 that Hughes wanted to sell the tool division of his vast empire, it set up a series of meetings with Hughes representatives to arrange for a public offering. At the time, Hughes was living in Nicaragua. Although Hughes prefers not to participate directly with outsiders in his business dealings, Merrill Lynch had other plans. Julius Sedlmayr, a group vice president of the securities firm, accompanied by an attorney from Brown, Wood, Fuller & Ivey, flew to Nicaragua to make sure the offering had Hughes's personal blessing. At 5 A.M. on a Monday morning, after waiting for two days, the Merrill Lynch men finally saw the elusive Hughes, who signed a document they had brought with them indicating that he personally approved of the negotiation (see Chapter 5).

Notwithstanding the size and complexity of the Morgan Stanley deals involving AT&T and Churchill Falls, and the mystery surrounding Merrill Lynch's negotiation with Howard Hughes, perhaps the most startling of all, from a get-rich-quick point of view, was Donaldson, Lufkin & Jenrette's role in creating Envirotech, a company in the field of pollution control equipment. Envirotech was an amalgam of several other existing companies, or divisions of other companies, as well as a number of smaller entities that were later absorbed.

The company had made its first public offering of stock in 1971, and DLJ, which had been involved in the project from the beginning, managed to parlay an investment of $60,000 into a stock participation which at one point was worth $15 million.

While the uniqueness of its transactions is one way of ranking investment banking houses, another is by the number of major clients they have. In a recent list of the one hundred largest industrial companies, Morgan Stanley had twenty-four, and Goldman, Sachs was second with nineteen. Lehman Brothers had sixteen; Blyth Eastman Dillon and First Boston had twelve each; Merrill Lynch and Kuhn Loeb had nine each; Dillon Read had eight; Smith Barney had seven; and Kidder Peabody, six.

Another traditional indicator of an investment banking house's prestige is the number and quality of directorships the partners hold. For an investment banker to be named to a board of directors of a major corporation generally means either that his firm holds considerable stock in that company, or that it handles most of the company's securities issues. Either way, the investment banker is positioned to keep an eye on internal developments at the company, and to best serve the interests of his firm. On the darker side, he also is in a position to keep other partners at his firm abreast of developments in a company that have not yet been made public. Such information can prevent investment banking firms from making costly mistakes. Although the use of significant inside information for such purposes violates the nation's securities laws, it is extraordinarily difficult to prove (see Penphil in Chapter 7), and inordinately difficult to resist. Indeed, some investment bankers maintain privately that the lifeblood of Wall Street is inside information.

It was hardly surprising that in the mid 1970s, at a time when the fashions of the United States were undergoing sweeping change, the world of the investment banker stood relatively unaltered. There were few concessions to longer hair styles, to modish clothing, or to the incursion of the drug culture. Investment bankers, like most people over 30, still preferred martinis to marijuana and scotch to "uppers" and "downers." For the most part, investment bankers continued to wear the same dark, pin-striped suits and modestly patterned ties; the same highly polished, low-heeled, wing-tipped brown or black shoes that their predecessors for generations had worn. Early in 1974, *Business Week* magazine published a full-page, color photograph showing more than two dozen partners at Morgan Stanley & Co. standing on a staircase. The picture looked as though it might have been posed for at a mortician's convention.

In 1973, an advertisement appeared in *New York* magazine. "Do you have an exciting personality?" it asked. "Are you looking for a job that will not only afford you a good life, but a happy one? Would you like to be associated with fun and beautiful people who deal with each other on a human level?" The job? Assistant to the bond trading desk manager of a small financial house. But the ad copy, plus the headline "Wall Street Investment Banking" drew a clutch of responses from people who had been conditioned to believe that investment banking was an entrée to the seemingly glamorous world of money and power.

By the middle of the 1970s, investment bankers were earning starting salaries of $20,000 or more per year, with the prospect of increasing their earnings to the six-figure range within a decade if they performed up to expectations. However, the demands on them were great.

Naneen Neubohn, first in her class at the Columbia University Graduate School of Business, joined Morgan Stanley & Co. in 1974 with a starting salary of about $22,000, and immediately plunged into ten- to twelve-hour workdays. If she stays the course at Morgan Stanley, she can expect to become a vice president within about five years and, if all goes well, perhaps become a partner after about ten years. Although Morgan Stanley is not required to make public either its profits or the salaries of its key officials, it is estimated by some Wall Streeters (and Morgan does not quarrel with the estimate) that partners earn $150,000 in a slow year, and as much as $500,000 in a very good year.

Many of the so-called "support" employees, such as securities salesmen, research analysts, and professional traders, also earn upwards of $100,000 a year at investment banking houses.

At many firms, social background and business and political connections count heavily. Some firms prefer to bring in older partners who have recently retired from key jobs in industry or government. Consider the mix of partners at Lazard Frères & Co. in the early 1970s. One partner was Guy Sauvage deBrantes, a thirty-four-year-old French count, and brother-in-law of France's finance minister, Valéry Giscard d'Estaing. Another partner was Eugene R. Black, Jr., an amateur playwright and son of the former president of the World Bank. Also sitting at the partners' table was Robert F. Ellsworth, former ambassador to NATO, who had close connections in the Nixon White House. Still another partner was James S. Adams, the seventy-four-year-old former chairman of Standard Brands, Inc.

Andre Meyer, senior partner of the firm, counted among his friends such politicians as Senators Edward M. Kennedy, Jacob K. Javits, and Charles H. Percy, also Lyndon B. Johnson, David Rockefeller, and Giovanni Agnelli, the Italian industrialist. Meyer's connection with the Kennedy family was especially close, and in some Wall Street circles the marriage between Jacqueline Kennedy and Aristotle Onassis was jokingly referred to as a "Lazard Frères merger," partly based on a rumor, which Meyer would deny when asked, that he had helped draft a marriage contract between the two that spelled out any future property settlement.

While many of the old guard investment bankers had little formal education, and got their start as Wall Street runners, new arrivals in the 1970s came bearing a host of diplomas. Charles Allen, the founder of Allen & Company, was a high school dropout. But his son, C. Robert Allen III, attended the Hill School and earned a bachelor's degree from Lafayette College before becoming a partner in his father's firm. Allen's nephew, Herbert A. Allen, graduated from Williams College after attending the Hackley School in Tarrytown, New York, and then assumed his partnership.

Many financiers had other careers before turning to the world of investment banking. For example, Richard Coons, who in his middle forties was serving as director of international operations at Kidder Peabody, started as a commercial banker, then attended Harvard's Graduate School of Business Administration where he majored in production. He spent a few years as an industrial engineer for such companies as Bridgeport Brass and Fairchild Engine and Airplane, but liked the challenge of investment banking and took a paycut to $3500 a year to work at Kidder Peabody in 1955. By the mid 1970s Coons was a millionaire and his duties had become nearly as much social as financial. He had an apartment on the East Side of Manhattan, a home in Oyster Bay, belonged to the New York Yacht Club, sailed a forty-four-foot ocean sloop, wore $300 suits, drank Dewars scotch, and considered himself to be a member of an elite profession.

"It's the reshuffling of wealth," he said by way of explaining his commitment to his profession. "I don't mean individual, personal wealth. Sure, that's part of the system, but it's a byproduct. It's not raison d'être."

1 / The Fabulous Package

I n the early 1960s, there was hardly a stock market buff in the country who didn't know about Syntex, a small pharmaceutical company headquartered in Mexico that had cashed in on the U.S. birth control boom. One Wall Streeter, though, knew more about Syntex than anyone. He was Charles Allen, a secretive investment banker who preferred to risk his own money on speculative investments rather than underwrite the stocks and bonds of giant corporations. Allen bought Syntex when it was little more than a faltering back-country drug company, expanded it, and took it public. For months it was at the center of the Wall Street vortex, helping spark one of the most explosive growth periods in the stock market's history. As for Allen, with the peculiar combination of shrewdness,

*timing, manipulation, and luck that characterized his investment
banking style, he became a multimillionaire.*

It was April 1958, and a perfect day for a New York coming-out
party. The skies over Manhattan were cloudless and the tempera-
ture was a balmy sixty-eight degrees. At the Plaza Hotel, final
arrangements were being made for the debuts of two dozen young
ladies who would be formally introduced to society the following
evening at the Tenth Annual Presentation Cotillion.

Meanwhile, at the downtown tip of Manhattan, another debut
was taking place—one that was to have a profound influence on
thousands of Americans and create one of the most amazing
phenomena in the history of the nation's securities markets. It was
the introduction on the stock exchange of Syntex, a tiny, Mexican-
based drug company, that in the months ahead would parlay a
knowledge of the manufacture of birth control pills into one of the
most sensational investment gains of all time.

Syntex's coming-out party was also to be the climactic venture
of Charles Allen's career as an investment banker. Working
mostly in the shadows of Wall Street, investing his own cash,
Allen was a man with an eye for a bargain. When Allen was
through giving Syntex the full treatment, it would be transformed
from a poorly managed, struggling concern into the hottest item
on Wall Street. In an amazingly short time its stock's performance
would eclipse most of the blue bloods of the nation's stock exchanges, providing Allen, his firm, and members of his family with
nearly half a million shares of the tiny drug company for just $2
a share. During the mid 1960s, Syntex would become a household
word, its stock soaring to more than $100 a share, splitting six for
one. It was a 300-to-1 payoff that had to be considered a financial
coup in investment circles. Yet despite the hoopla caused by Syntex, Charles Allen would remain relatively unknown, sitting un-
heralded in his cluttered, downtown Manhattan offices, pulling
the strings in other entrepreneurial ventures, searching for another Syntex.

In Allen's hands, Syntex became the quintessential example of the most glamorous and profitable type of investment banking deal. Although complex in execution, it was simple in theory: Discover a tiny, privately held company with potential. Buy it. Take it public. Oversee its development. Then reap the benefits as it is discovered by other investors who, in the process, bid up the price of its stock.

In the sixties, as now, Allen was an enigma to much of Wall Street. He shunned membership on the stock exchanges, where most Wall Streeters gained the advantage that made their fortunes secure. He avoided sitting on the prestigious committees where senior partners of Wall Street firms rubbed shoulders and swapped high-level gossip. Unlike many successful Wall Streeters, Allen was not Ivy League nor high society; in fact, he hardly fit the traditional investment community mold. About the only thing Allen and other investment bankers had in common was a thirst for making money.

At the age of fifteen, Allen quit high school and became a Wall Street runner—a messenger for a brokerage house. Four years later, he started his own firm with less than $1,000 in savings. At first, it was a one-room operation, with only a few employees no older than Allen himself. But Allen & Company rode the crest of a booming market, and by 1929 had played the over-the-counter market in securities so successfully that Allen, at the age of twenty-six, and his firm were worth nearly $1 million. Then came the crash.

While Wall Streeters were leaping out of windows and filing for bankruptcy, Allen, who by then had been joined in the firm by his brother, Herbert, reached his financial low point. His company found itself a quarter of a million dollars in the red. However, when the Depression ended, he bounced back, making a killing in large blocks of over-the-counter stocks and setting the stage for the big speculations of the next four decades that were to make Allen & Company one of the more profitable firms on the Street. Indeed, by 1954, the partners would have taken out more than $12 million in profits.

The *modus operandi* that Allen adopted after his brush with failure during the Depression was this: Invest your own cash. Keep a hand in on the investment. Remember that long term is better than short term. Follow your instincts. It also included the following dicta: Leave stock trading to the rest of Wall Street. Invest in companies that (1) need help, (2) want to go public, or (3) where the owner simply wants to get out.

How successful did Allen & Company become by following those guidelines? Investment bankers are ranked in many ways, but the rule of thumb most often applied is their capital position, that is, the amount of cash and securities they have amassed to back up any venture they wish to try.

In 1975 the Allen firm ranked ninth with over $70 million in stated capital. (The dollar figure was actually substantially higher, since securities were carried for capital purposes at their purchase price, not at their current market value.) That put them ahead of such well-known Street names as Reynolds Securities, First Boston, Kidder Peabody, Lehman Brothers, and Morgan Stanley.

Although Allen & Company had been involved in numerous transactions over the years, it was Syntex that was mentioned most often by Wall Streeters when they talked about the firm. Even Allen himself considered Syntex to be his "number one deal." The maneuvers that Allen performed after buying Syntex turned it into one of the most profitable transactions of his career. First he bought the tiny drug company on behalf of a larger holding company called Ogden, which he controlled. Then he split Syntex off from Ogden so it could be traded by itself on the American Stock Exchange. Then, as previously mentioned, Allen & Company kept nearly 500,000 of the 1.2 million shares issued, for $2 a share.

By mid 1973 the stock was selling for $100 a share, and Allen and his family still held close to 900,000 shares, about one-third of their original purchase. Their holdings at that time were valued at $90 million, and they made many millions more by selling some of their shares.

As for Charles Allen himself, after his successful start at the age of nineteen, he never faltered. At a time of life when many men are puttering in a garden, Allen was still engaged in a seemingly endless flow of correspondence and telephone calls, as he participated in one venture after another. His fortune, estimated by some at over half a billion dollars, was secure. In addition, he had won the grudging acknowledgement of entrenched Wall Streeters who, on occasion, had viewed him as a quick-witted speculator with a hand in too many marginal deals. By 1974, with the price of seats on the New York Stock Exchange dropping nearly as fast as the Dow-Jones industrial average, the Street was inclined to admit that Allen had chosen a profitable way to run his business. However, it was clear from talking to some of Allen's critics that he did not develop one of Wall Street's more successful investment banking houses without stepping on a few toes.

The most useful tool in Allen's career as a corporate rejuvenator was the Ogden Corporation. It served as a sort of catchall for his interests. Control of a publicly held corporation like Ogden gives acquisitive financiers both a cash flow to finance their purchases of other companies and access to public money through the stock market.

Ogden had been formed in 1935 for the sole purpose of liquidating the assets of a bankrupt company called the Utilities & Light System. In time, the various pieces of the firm were sold off and Ogden, its function served, was to be dissolved. However, recognizing the opportunity provided by a corporate shell, Allen decided to buy Ogden, even though it contained only about $1.6 million in cash and a few securities. But it did have its attractions. First, there was $20 million in capital-loss tax carryover. That could be used by Allen to lower his tax bill on other enterprises that were subsequently acquired by Ogden. Second, Ogden was listed on the Curb, the predecessor of the American Stock Exchange. That gave Allen entrée to investors on a public exchange.

Allen bought 80 percent of Ogden and was immediately confronted with a massive problem—keeping the company alive. The difficulty was that Ogden's shareholders had already voted to dissolve the company. Under state law in Delaware, where the company was incorporated, such a vote was irreversible. However, much of Allen's financial success resulted from his ability to deal effectively with government bodies.

He sent his attorney to Delaware and was successful in getting a new law passed which allowed a two-thirds vote of shareholders to cancel a corporate dissolution. Such a vote was taken by Ogden's shareholders, and the dissolution was cancelled. It was the beginning of the fifties, and Allen had succeeded in acquiring the corporate shell that would later be so important to him in the Syntex deal.

Syntex came to Allen's attention in 1956 from a business friend in New York who, from time to time, would bring him word of prospective deals. Syntex needed money, so a meeting in Manhattan with the company's principals was arranged. Allen went to the Sherry-Netherland hotel suite of Dr. Emeric Somlo, the principal owner of Syntex. Dr. George Rosenkranz, the company's chief scientist and moving force, also was present.

The New York meeting was fruitful and was quickly followed by another in Mexico—one of the few times that Allen had flown to an out-of-town conference with principals. It was an indication of the importance of the transaction.

In Mexico City he conferred with Dr. Somlo at his home, and with Dr. Rosenkranz. Dr. Somlo seemed eager to sell Syntex, partly because he was facing an antitrust suit and had income tax problems.

Allen negotiated for two days, commuting between his hotel and Dr. Somlo's home. Finally, he felt he knew enough. The company seemed attractive, and it could be his for $2 million in cash, plus another $2 million to be paid later in cash and notes.

Allen returned to New York and consulted with Maurice Sindeband, then executive vice-president of Ogden. Ogden put up the $2 million to acquire Syntex, with a personal assurance from Allen that he would make good if the deal went sour.

For a total payment of $4 million, three-fourths of it in cash, and the rest in promissory notes, the deal was struck. Ironically, Somlo never shared in the immense financial success that was to befall Syntex. Allen recalled meeting Dr. Somlo in a restaurant outside Paris a decade after the original arrangement was consummated. "He was trying to establish a frozen food business over there," Allen said, "and it seemed as if he had really let this company go by."

One reason why Syntex had been so appealing as an investment was its virtual monopoly on the barbasco root, which was dug from parasitic vines that grew wild in the Mexican jungle. Most of the drug sales of Syntex at the time it was bought by Allen were dependent upon the root, which Syntex used as the raw herbal material in the production of steroid hormones. Previously such hormones had been derived from such substances as cattle glands and spinal cords, sows' ovaries, and the urine of pregnant women. It was this control over barbasco that made it possible for the company to become the leader in the birth-control-pill boom that was to follow.

By the early 1960s, the Pill was being marketed commercially, and by the middle of that decade it was being made by at least seven U.S. companies under such trade names as Enovid, Norlestrin, and C-Quens. Sales of the Pill in the United States had soared to $65 million. A new industry had developed.

Although Syntex's own pill, Norinyl, held a relatively small share of the market, the company supplied the basic ingredients to three other major pharmaceutical houses: Eli Lilly, Johnson & Johnson, and Parke Davis.

In 1956, the year Allen and his associates had bought Syntex, total sales had been a meager $6.8 million, and profits only $1.4 million. By 1963, sales had jumped to $16 million and earnings had nearly tripled. Then the quantum leap began. With the manufacture of the Pill, sales rose to $67 million by 1967, and earnings to $19 million. By 1969, steroids for oral contraceptives accounted for 41 percent of Syntex's gross profits and over one-third of its sales. By 1972, sales had reached $140 million, and earnings were over $30 million, about twenty times as high as they had been when Allen & Company first laid eyes on Syntex fifteen years earlier.

Although Allen did not play an active role in the management of Syntex, he occasionally did step in. There was the time, in the early 1960s, when negotiations for a joint research project with Eli Lilly, the big pharmaceutical firm, had bogged down because the Eli Lilly management wasn't sure who they were dealing with.

"Syntex didn't have the standing," Allen recalled, "and Eli Lilly wanted to know, if they made the contract, who the owners were. I imagine when Dr. Somlo was the owner he was not very communicative with different companies. Where we could do them some good was to show them how the owner of a large block of the stock felt." Allen flew to the Eli Lilly offices, toured the labs, conferred with the company's officers, and came home with the contract.

Millions of dollars were made in speculations on the company. There were some skeptics, however, who missed their golden chance. At one point, for example, the company issued $2.5 million worth of preferred shares at $10 each, convertible to common stock at a later date. Allen recalled that a million dollars worth was offered to a friend, who in turn offered it to a branch of the Whitney family of New York. They turned it down. That million dollars would have been convertible into 100,000 shares of Syntex common, which later split six for one. The stock was worth $70 million in subsequent years.

One of Allen's intermediaries in guiding Syntex's fortunes was young Howard M. Holtzmann, who, like his father before him, earned a good part of his livelihood as Allen's lawyer. Young Holtzmann had been on the Syntex board of directors from the beginning. He was also on the Ogden board, and was an original participant in the Syntex deal.

Holtzmann said that in the early Syntex days, he would go home with the smell of the factory on his clothes. "I know my wife didn't like that smell," he said. "But she was very sympathetic about it and we used to sing the song from *Carousel* that went: 'The first time I saw him, the smell of his clothes knocked me flat on the floor of my room. But now that I love him, my heart's in my nose, and fish is my favorite perfume.' Syntex was our favorite perfume." Holtzmann observed that Syntex, which he considered

Allen & Company's most important venture, lacked many of the essential elements of a classic investment banking arrangement.

"It wasn't a story of pumping money into a company, or raising money for a company," he said. It wasn't a story of finding merger partners for a company. It wasn't a story of the investment banker going out and finding a manager to run the company, as some have, or the investment banker sitting on the board and making policy.

"On the other hand, the investment banking input elements to Syntex were very crucial. I'd be unwilling to say to you that if there hadn't been investment bankers, there wouldn't have been some kind of a Syntex. I suppose there would have been. But I can't imagine that it would have been this big."

The inputs, according to Holtzmann, were: (1) the identification of an industry by the investment bankers—the spotting of a concept of high technology early in the game when it wasn't yet fashionable; (2) the decision that Syntex was a company that would be better with its own stock, rather than being part of a conglomerate; (3) the decision that management should have a major stake in the company.

How many millionaires were created by Syntex? "Clearly, a lot," Holtzmann said. "I suspect the true figure must be close to twenty-five."

Among the men who profited greatly were the five directors of Syntex, three of them Allen men. One was Marvyn Carton, a pivotal figure in the Syntex arrangement, who served as the company's secretary and treasurer. He had been associated with Allen & Company for more than five years and was later to become a large financial contributor to President Richard Nixon. The others were Holtzmann and Maurice Sindeband. The two directors who were at Syntex when Allen bought it were Dr. George Rosenkranz, who was to become president, and Dr. Alejandro Zaffaroni, the research scientist.

Fifteen years later, both Carton and Holtzmann would still be serving on the board of Syntex. Carton's holdings by then had risen to 15,000 shares, and Holtzmann's to 20,250. Neither man, however, came close to the holdings of Rosenkranz, who held nearly 180,000 shares, valued at over $18 million in mid 1973.

All that was inside the company, of course. Outside, the excitement surrounding Syntex stock was incredible. In the mid 1960s, Syntex stock was the darling of the Wall Street plungers. It was almost unthinkable not to take a spin on Allen's Syntex merry-go-round, and millions of investors and speculators did.

In 1963 the stock started at $5.75, its low for the year, but by the end of the same year it had soared to $67.50, after a 3-for-1 split. In 1964 the market went the other way. Starting the year at $95.25 a share, Syntex plummeted to $25.50 as the year neared its end. However, by 1965, believers in Syntex began smiling again. After dawdling along for the first half of the year at $30 to $35 a share, Syntex took off, ending the year at almost $110 a share. The ranges in 1966 and 1967 showed how speculators could make a fast killing, while unwary investors could be ravaged if they sold at the wrong time. In 1966, for example, the high was $125 a share and the low was $57. In 1967 the high was $108 and the low was $70.

The market crash of 1970 took a terrible toll of investors, as Syntex dove to $18, after starting the year at $70. It then staged a long recovery, and rose to the $119 mark in early 1972, before again falling victim to a long bear market that took it down to the $65 range.

Although the annual fluctuations of Syntex stock were indeed spectacular, the stock also had single days that would qualify it for entry into the stock market record books. For example, on November 1, 1963, in the most flamboyant single-day price gain of the year on any major exchange, Syntex soared $21 amid turbulent trading. The opening for the stock was delayed twenty-nine minutes so orders could be matched, and even when trading was begun, it had to be halted twice more during the day so that the specialists on the floor could catch up with trading activity.

January 17, 1964, another single day of trading, showed that Syntex could be a devastating two-way street for investors. On that day, Syntex dropped $18.75 a share and was responsible for almost 5 percent of the volume on the American Stock Exchange, where 763 stocks were traded. One problem was that many investors had bought the stock on margin, that is, by putting up only a percentage of the purchase price. When a stock bought in such fashion declines sharply, it triggers a call for more money; if the investor doesn't have the cash available, he has to sell some of his stock to provide it. That, in turn, helps to push the price of the stock down further, and sets off a vicious cycle.

One thing that made Syntex so appealing to investors and institutions alike was that they didn't have to wait long for a reversal in the action. For instance, on January 22, 1964, less than a week after the dramatic one-day drop of $18.75, Syntex stock soared nearly $17.50, and was the most actively traded stock on the Exchange, with 130,300 shares turning over. It was like a slot machine that might gobble up silver dollars, but would send them spewing out again at any moment.

It was not surprising that amid all this wildly fluctuating price activity, investors outside the company could make fortunes as well as those on the inside. In the spring of 1964, for example, the Lehman Corporation, an investment company managed by the investment banking firm of Lehman Brothers, sold 30,000 shares of Syntex stock for a profit of about $4.2 million. Lehman sold at an average price of $152 a share. It retained half of its original 60,000 shares, which it had bought for only $725,126, or $12 a share.

The fantastic trading volume in Syntex—some days more than 100,000 shares of it were bought and sold on the American Stock Exchange—called for unusual measures. Early in 1964, the Exchange created, for the first time in its history, a special trading post on the floor solely for Syntex stock. The key men who kept the trade flowing smoothly at the post were David Jackson, Warren Winter, Andrew Segal, and Frank Graham.

Unlike other posts on the floor, trading in Syntex was so hyperactive that some of the specialists handled only round-lot buying —transactions of 100 shares, or multiples of 100 shares. Odd-lot transactions, consisting of orders to buy or sell less than 100 shares, were handled by other specialists.

Frank Graham compared the Exchange floor in those hectic days to the front wall of the Green Bay Packers. At times there were forty or fifty people milling around in an area no larger than a small livingroom, all trying to get into the middle of the action. The specialists had to yell and scream above the voices of the people trying to make bids and offers. The problem was to control the bidders, to keep the general noise level down. Graham recalled the time when Cary Middlecoff, the professional golfer, came to the floor of the Exchange to see how it operated.

"They brought him over and I talked to him for awhile and explained to him what was going on. I told him Syntex had closed the night before at $110, and then some news had come out. It looked about nine points lower. I told him what I thought would happen immediately after we opened it—that it was going to go lower because of the first rush to get it open. As I went through the exercise with him, and he observed for awhile, his comment to me was: 'And I used to think coming down the eighteenth one-up was tough.' "

Tough. It also was a word often used to describe Charles Allen's business tactics. Even before Syntex came to dominate the attention of traders on the American Stock Exchange Allen had fashioned enough deals to insure his place in the annals of Wall Street.

Nearly twenty years ago, Robert Sheehan, a *Fortune* writer, said that Allen had emerged as "one of the few investment bankers with the old-time creative flair for buying and merging companies." He bought control of the slumbering Colorado Fuel & Iron Corp. from the Rockefellers, for example, quadrupled its sales, and raised it to the ninth spot in the steel industry.

Allen also had helped build such companies as Data Processing Financial & General Corp., and Benguet Consolidated, which owned a gold mine in the Philippines that had been shut down by the Japanese during World War II. When General Douglas MacArthur, who was a Benguet shareholder, retook the Philippines, the mine went back into production and Allen & Company made its profit. Other companies that Allen bought and rehabilitated included the Arma Corporation, a precision instruments company; a number of large real estate developments; two small railroads, and a steamship company.

The techniques employed by Allen and his firm in fashioning such deals were mostly shrouded in secrecy, but occasionally the veil was lifted.

In 1973 the Securities and Exchange Commission filed suit against a number of defendants including Allen & Company, and Allen & Company, Inc., an affiliated concern with many of the same principals as Allen & Company.

The suit alleged that the General Host Corporation, with the help of Allen & Company, Inc. and others, had secretly formed a syndicate to illegally manipulate the market in General Host and Armour & Company stock. The action was taken, the suit said, at a time when General Host was trying to take control of Armour. As a result of the SEC suit, Allen & Company, Inc. agreed to "disgorge" $300,000—about half the fee it had earned. The money would be used in any settlement of private lawsuits against Allen & Company, Inc. in the case, including a class action that was pending on behalf of Armour stockholders.

The General Host deal was not the only controversial transaction Allen had had a hand in. His firm made millions on a venture that involved the Grand Bahama Port Authority and Benguet Consolidated. It meant dealing with a former Wall Street stock promoter who had served a jail term for mail fraud and was involved in making secret payments to Bahamian officials, leading to a conflict-of-interest scandal that toppled the Bahamian government. But that did not deter Allen.*

---

*In June 1974, a federal district judge ruled that Allen & Company, Inc. had committed fraud in a 1969 private offering of $7.5 million in securities. The judge said financial statements issued by Firestone Group Ltd., a California real estate company, were false and misleading, and that Allen & Company, Inc. "encouraged" dissemination of the statements. Allen & Company, Inc. appealed the ruling. The case was the most recent of several in which the firm's reputation was brought into question.

In addition to the firm's questionable dealings, there were the occasional Allen failures and the missed opportunities. One such incident occurred when H. Ross Perot, the Texas computer millionaire, was taking his own company public, and he talked to Allen & Company about handling the transaction.

Perot wanted to keep most of his company's stock for himself, with smaller blocks for his key employees, selling just enough to establish a market on the stock exchange. That's precisely what he did with Pressprich & Co., quickly becoming an instant billionaire when the public bid up the price of the stock. Perot said he had discussed the underwriting with Allen, but Allen had wanted to own the stock, not distribute it.

Perot recalled, "He [Allen] said, 'if you're going to sell 650,000 shares, I'll match your best offer. I'll buy it, and at a later point in time, I'll distribute it.'

"I liked his style, because that's an underwriter. He was saying, 'I will underwrite you. I will take the risk. I will put my money on the line.' But I wanted distribution."

The result was that Allen lost out on the deal and Perot went on to become even richer than Allen.

You win some and you lose some. For Allen that had become a way of life. And while none of his winners in the years following Syntex were quite as dramatic as his "number one" deal, the firm continued to prosper at a time when larger, more prestigious investment banking houses were ailing.

Indeed, as investment bankers confronted the challenges of the 1970s with a variety of strategies, Allen & Company continued to follow its founder's basic philosophy: Find an investment opportunity that nobody else wants, and run with it.

2 / The Giant Bond Sale

I n the spring of 1970, a group of brokerage houses, led by Morgan Stanley & Co., offered for sale an unprecedented $1.6 billion worth of American Telephone and Telegraph bonds, known technically on Wall Street as debentures with warrants. For weeks it appeared that the nation's credit markets might be toppled by the sheer enormity of the offering. The story of how the transaction was conceived, arranged, and executed is a classic in the history of investment banking. It required split-second timing and a rewriting of the rule book at the New York Stock Exchange. There were moments when it appeared that the arbitrageurs, those Wall Street insiders who make their profits by bucking prevailing trends, might scuttle the offering. But in the end the bonds were sold, and as a result, the offering took its place in the financial hall of fame.

Sitting in his vice-presidential office at Morgan Stanley, Robert Hayes Burns Baldwin leaned back in his easy chair and smoothed his dark blue patterned tie. On a table near him was an impressive foot-high bronze reproduction of an announcement that appeared in financial publications across the country on April 13, 1970. In the understated, nearly indecipherable jargon of Wall Street, it told the story of Baldwin's efforts.

> Thirty Year 8¾% Debentures, due May 15, 2000 with Warrants Expiring May 15, 1975 to Purchase 31,386,540 Common Shares at $52 a share.
>
> A.T.& T. shareholders of record April 10, 1970 are being issued rights (one for each share held) to subscribe at a price of $100 for $100 principal amount of Debentures (together with Warrants to purchase two Common Shares of the Company) for each 35 shares held. The rights are evidenced by transferable Rights Certificates and will expire on May 18, 1970.
>
> From time to time during and after the subscription period, Debentures with Warrants may be offered to investors by members of the Dealers Group at prices, determined as set forth in the Prospectus, related to the market prices of the Debentures with Warrants on the New York Stock Exchange.

Peering over his half-moon glasses, Baldwin reflected on the highlights of the record-breaking financial deal he fashioned, a transaction so immense in size and complexity that it set Wall Street on its ear for several weeks in mid 1970, and made millions of dollars in profits for at least two banking firms directly involved.

"You're playing a part in financial history, and trying to advise the biggest company in the world on what the right course is— and then contemplating going with a device that had been used mainly in much smaller, more speculative situations and with the biggest amount in history. There was a lot of oil burned, and a lot of consideration. It was an exciting period."

The excitement had begun to build in 1969, at a time when

American Telephone and Telegraph was painfully short of cash to shore up its faltering communications empire. Between 1966 and 1968, its construction expenses had grown at a normal rate of about eight or nine percent, and Bell System financing to cover it, arranged in small chunks, averaged just over $1.5 billion for each of those three years.

In 1969, Bell System assets amounted to nearly $44 billion and its total operating revenues, the money it took in from local and toll service, topped $16 billion.

Suddenly, in 1969, construction costs leaped by 21 percent. Financing totaled almost $2.5 billion as the operating companies rushed to sell more bonds and went to the banks for increasingly larger loans. But it wasn't until the 1970 projections were made that the enormity of the problem became apparent. The company would need to spend $7 billion on new construction and would need $4 billion in new money to handle it. What to do?

The operating companies would have to push their bond issues to $2 billion—a level 60 percent higher than the previous record. That meant offering about $125 million in bonds for sale at least every three weeks. It was decided that the market probably couldn't digest much more telephone company debt than that. Increasing the amount of short-term loans from local banks wasn't considered to be a serious possibility because of the enormous expense in high interest rates. So, by the summer of 1969, AT&T's financial vice-president, John J. Scanlon, was staring at a $1.5 billion deficit in his financing plans for 1970, and was beginning to sound out investment bankers for ideas, including his old friend Bob Baldwin of Morgan Stanley.

Scanlon cleared his throat almost reflexively as he recalled the situation. Even the thought of it was discomfiting. "We were convinced we had to do something major," he said.

AT&T was faced with several alternatives in raising the cash it needed. It could simply increase its bond issues and short-term debt. It could go to its three million shareholders with an offering of stock or bonds as it last had in 1964, or, and this was something the company never had tried, it could make some sort of stock or bond offering to its customers. After all, there were tens of millions of them out there, and they all had enough money to pay their telephone bills, so maybe they'd like to own a piece of the company? The idea was given serious consideration.

"We have a mailing list of about 57 million customers that we might have approached," Scanlon explained, "and it did have some intriguing aspects. We went quite far in exploring it, but what finally turned us against it was that (1) the interest rate would have had to be pretty attractive vis-à-vis a Series E Bond or a thrift institution rate. And (2) we would have to be ready to redeem it if interest rates went still higher and everybody flocked back to the thrift or savings institutions or to Series E Bonds."

An added drawback, Scanlon continued, was simply the expense of mailing prospectuses, the detailed description of the transaction, to 57 million people. Furthermore, when a company is as big as AT&T, with more assets, income, stockholders' equity, and employees than any other private corporation, it has to worry about the impact of anything it does on the economy as a whole.

"We may as well be frank about this," Scanlon said. "At that time, the economy was still making halting efforts to get going, and had great reliance on the housing industry. We were concerned, as many others were, that such a massive attack on the thrift institutions as a $1.6 billion issue by us might make, would reverse that [growth in housing] or thwart it. So we shelved it. We still look at it from time to time, and someday we'll find the right combination of interest rates and state of the economy."

Increasingly, the choice narrowed to one of two traditional alternatives. Either an offering of stock to the present shareowners, or a bond offering to the same group. The basic difference between the two is that if more stock or equity is sold, it tends to dilute the value of existing stock. The company's earnings have to be spread thinner when it comes time for dividends to be paid. Furthermore, a critical financial yardstick known as per share earnings suffers, because of the added amounts of stock outstanding. A bond, or debenture, offering, on the other hand, doesn't cause any problems of that nature, but interest charges have to be paid, and someday, because it is in effect a loan, it either has to be repaid or refinanced. So, the choice is difficult and seldom clear-cut.

One other consideration entered the picture, and it came from Washington, D.C., where the Federal Communications Commission had established a special task force to study AT&T. The group occupied cramped offices in a converted brewery located in a shabby corner of the nation's capital.

Asher Ende, a $36,000-a-year civil servant and head of the task force, is a 57-year-old attorney and a veteran of more than two and a half decades with the FCC. His striped tie slightly askew, his eyeglasses held together on the left side with a red rubber band, Ende's appearance contrasted sharply with the immaculately groomed executives from lower Broadway. He pulled out a 202-page document—the findings and conclusions of his staff's investigation into the fees AT&T charges its customers. His task force's conclusion? That AT&T should be forced to reduce its interstate rates by $133 million annually.

"I was there," Ende said, "to act as independent counsel, to ferret out the truth in rate increases. Don't forget, they were asking for $546 million in increased earnings."

At the time when AT&T was considering its alternatives in how to raise $1.6 billion to meet sharply higher 1970 construction needs, Ende and his group were applying pressure for the company to keep its prices down and raise its level of debt. The committee also was sharply critical of AT&T's construction program decisions in the 1960s, citing an "error in judgment made in the middle 1960s," particularly "the drastic fall off in construction expenditure growth in 1966 and 1967, and the scarcely adequate expenditures in 1968."

According to the FCC task force, AT&T's revenue growth of 10.2 percent in 1966 had been followed by a meager increase of only 2.6 percent in the 1967 construction program. "This made service problems inevitable in late 1968, and in turn, triggered the mushrooming construction program in 1969 and 1970, at the height of the inflationary period when interest rates reached the highest levels in this century," the task force observed. In other words, where was AT&T management when its own figures should have warned that Ma Bell was moving into a construction crunch?

Ende reflected about the $1.6 billion offering with warrants—AT&T's answer to its financial problem. "Wall Street had never done it before," he said. "It was touted as an imaginative way a company faced with unprecedented capital demands could raise money. At a time when money was tight, I'd say most investors thought AT&T was offering a good deal. My only question is, should the bond rate have been lower? I don't think there was a major risk, and still don't, that the stock wouldn't hit $52. But I think high company officials have been scaring stockholders off, scaring the bejesus out of everybody by poor-mouthing the company to get higher rates."

By mid 1969, it was too late for second guessing. AT&T needed money, and needed it badly. The question by then was not how much to get, but how to raise it. Robert Baldwin of Morgan Stanley recalls that he had lunch with Scanlon in an AT&T dining room in the spring of 1969, and the subject of warrants came up.

"We were talking about various ways they might handle it, and at that stage I brought up the subject. They had done convertible bonds, that sort of thing, but had they ever thought of warrants? That was in, I guess, April of 1969. Nothing really transpired until either late August or early September, when Mr. Scanlon called me up again and said, 'Why don't a group of you come up, and let's just explore what you were talking about—warrants.'"

A warrant gives its owner the right to buy a share of a company's stock at some future time, for a specific price. If the stock subsequently sells for more than that price, he makes a profit—sometimes a handsome one. But if the stock sells below that price, the warrant is worthless.

The kind of warrant that was being considered by Morgan Stanley at that time was one that would be linked to a bond offering. Baldwin thought there might be some advantage in having warrants and bonds combined, because if the warrants were exercised, AT&T would get an additional $1.6 billion in 1975. Indeed, that was one of the big attractions. Since AT&T was under pressure from the FCC to increase its debt, the company could satisfy the regulatory agency by the massive $1.6 billion bond offering. It could also sweeten the deal for its shareowners by offering them warrants which would enable them to buy more AT&T stock, hopefully at bargain prices, five years hence, assuming that the price of the stock continued to rise. After all, it was then selling for about $53 a share and the warrant offering would give investors a chance to buy similar shares for $52 in 1975, no matter how high their price had risen in the meantime. That would be a good buy, as long as the stock was selling for $55 or $60 a share by then. Of course, if it was below $52, the warrants would have no value.*

The issuance of warrants seemed a sound idea, and Morgan Stanley began to apply more of its resources to the task. Samuel Burton Payne, a senior partner who had been with the firm nearly twenty-five years, joined the discussions, as did Alexander Tomlinson, another senior partner. One of the firm's vice-presidents, Madison Haythe, who provided much of the technical expertise on warrants, also participated. It was a period of intensive research and the firm resurrected some of the previous studies it had gathered on the subject. AT&T asked for a detailed memorandum on the pros and cons of warrant financing, as well as the various alternative methods it might use.

Overshadowing all else was the knowledge that an enormous

---

*In fact, AT&T stock closed May 15, 1975 at $51.87½. Because brokers handling the warrants were allowed a large commission, and could give up some of their margin to customers, about $161.2 million was raised by the telephone company from warrant holders who exercised their right to buy a share of AT&T stock for $52 plus a warrant. Morgan Stanley had hoped the price would be high enough to raise a full $1.6-billion. After the expiration date had passed, the SEC began an investigation to determine whether there had been artificial efforts to raise the price of AT&T stock, but several months later no action had been taken.

amount of money had to be raised. "They were telling us some of the problems they had," Baldwin explained, "and at this stage we started to work very closely with their people on how they foresaw their needs for money. We did two volumes on the subject and a tremendous number of computer runs, making various assumptions on what the return would be, and the mix between securities." Morgan Stanley computerized a simulated debt offering; then a convertible debt offering; then preferred stock. "Then we did it with common stock," Baldwin said, "and then with debt with warrants. We looked at all these alternatives and this took from September until some time in early November. It was during this period that the idea came up that maybe they'd want as much as $1.6 billion in one offering, and I can assure you that this absolutely put us on our back. It took us months of arguing around the firm before we became convinced that we could indeed try to get $1.6 billion. We were talking about something three times as big as anything that had been done in the history of investment banking."

Meanwhile, Scanlon and his staff were going through a parallel set of studies, and concluded that although the use of warrants would be a bold step, it also seemed like a logical one. The overriding advantage was that it would come at a time when the company's earnings were slumping, and it was necessary to develop some sort of unusually appealing package for shareowners if they were to come in. Furthermore, since the company seemed to have reached a new plateau for capital requirements, the added benefit of an additional pool of $1.6 billion, if the shareowners exercised their warrants by 1975, was attractive.

So, on the morning of January 21, 1970, Scanlon; Alexander L. Stott, AT&T's vice-president and controller; and John D. deButts, vice-chairman of the board, presented the plan to the full board of directors. It was approved, and AT&T's course was decided. On the New York Stock Exchange, trading in the company's stock was delayed for the day until the board meeting was over and word of the financial plan could be spread. The company issued a terse press release so that news of the unusual offer could be relayed throughout the financial community and to the shareholders who would be asked to buy.

Then began one of the most intense periods of financial preparation ever seen on Wall Street. The problems remaining were many, and not the least of them was that the New York Stock Exchange had never before considered warrants respectable enough to be included in its list of traded securities. At that time, Lee D. Arning was the Stock Exchange's senior vice-president for operations and a fifteen-year veteran at the Big Board. In addition to the problem of listing the warrants, Arning recalled, serious difficulties were presented by the long period of time between the rights offering and the point at which the securities would actually be issued to the buyers. In other words, values had to be established on a daily basis, and trading would be taking place in both the bonds and the warrants, even though they had not yet physically been issued to the buyers. This would bring a host of problems at a time when the back offices on Wall Street already were staggering under a paperwork avalanche that ultimately would force many of them out of business.

"The issue became effective on a given date," Arning remembered, "but the mailing wasn't done for another two or three weeks, and the subscription period was another month. So, there was a lengthy period, six weeks to two months, in which there was going to be trading, but nobody would be able to physically receive, deliver, or do anything with the security we were trading in."

Baldwin and his Morgan Stanley team spent hours meeting with Stock Exchange officials, discussing the margin requirement operations, the listing requirements for the warrants, and mechanisms to handle the debentures and the warrants before and after they were separated. The difficulty was that three separate trading markets had to be established: one for the bond alone, a second for the warrant alone, and a third for the bond with the warrants attached. A fourth price would also be listed for the rights to the entire offering for a brief period. That was the major complicating factor, Arning said. Three separate markets to conduct in a unique way, where there could be "when-issued" trading for a prolonged period. Altogether, the Stock Exchange had seventy-five or eighty people spending major amounts of time on the AT&T offering over a span of six weeks.

"This was one case," Arning said, "where the Exchange could bring to bear a tremendous amount of talent in a confined period of time, and bring off a winner."

Then came the problem of gearing up for the sale across the country of $1.6 billion in bonds. The primary target was to be AT&T's three million shareowners, who in the past had been a loyal and receptive pool of buyers. But, in addition to the mailing to the shareowners, preparations had to be made to sell the part of the offering that was not subscribed immediately.

Baldwin recalls that he and his partners at Morgan Stanley decided the offering would never work unless the entire U.S. investment community got behind it. To accomplish this, there would have to be "dog and pony shows" in which Morgan Stanley and Ma Bell's representatives would travel around the country to institutions, banks, and security dealers to personally explain what was going on. "You just couldn't leave it to the ordinary mechanisms of the market to take care of," Baldwin said.

The first thing he did was detach one of the firm's members to make a detailed study of arbitrage. Arbitrageurs are specialists in spotting warps and folds within major financial transactions to uncover areas where the day-to-day action of the market has decided that five and five equals eleven. The arbitrageur then trades to profit by such financial differentials. With three separate parts of the AT&T offering (the bond, the warrant, and the bond with warrant) to be traded simultaneously in addition to the rights, there would be times when the separated pieces were selling for more than the unit. Then the arbitrageurs would leap in, buy the package, split it, sell the pieces, and make their profit. They also would be watching for times when the prices seemed to hit unrealistic levels, compared to the market as a whole, and they would then step in to profit by selling short, in effect, betting that the price would decline.

One anonymous arbitrageur, whose firm made more than $1 million buying and selling parts of the AT&T offering at the right time, recalled the hectic days of early 1970.

"There are some basic tricks of the trade," he said. "You know that no matter how attractive any of the pieces of the deal may be, they will have to sell lower just by the sheer weight and size of the offering. The units that they issued—and they were units at that time, which is what made this whole offering unique—were not detachable. They did not want two separate markets and two separate pressures. They wanted just one type of security trading, which to my mind is somewhat unrealistic. So what happened is that there were several arbitrages going on at the same time." He chuckled at the memory of the arbitrageurs moving into the plan that had been so carefully constructed. "One thing we did was to buy rights and sell off units. The other was to split the units apart, and sell the bond. You would deliver your unit and take a due bill for the warrant—that's just a promissary note to pay on receipt. So the first thing we all did was just sit there, and as soon as trading started we just began selling short (in effect, betting the price would later decline) anything we could.

"Now remember, this is an American Telephone Company debt, and as such, it's one of the most senior pieces of paper outside of a government security. But, no matter how attractively priced it is—and they were very attractively priced, by the sheer weight of the overall deal, by that I mean the unbelievable magnitude, the bonds had to come in for sale. Some investors just wanted units so they could end up with warrants. Some wanted just to get the bonds. They traded somewhere around par and the warrants opened at $12. Now that's a good short sale, so we just sat there and offered them short. The warrant is a speculative security, but senior debt of American Telephone sold at distressed levels—well, you just know it's going to be a unique investment opportunity, and that's not hindsight talking, either!"

Baldwin, as well, vividly remembered the period fighting off the arbitrageurs, and the action that was taken to forestall and then combat their incursions.

"We tied the debt and the warrants together so they couldn't be stripped immediately," Baldwin said. "This caused consternation in the Street. Then we had to go around and work very carefully with the New York Stock Exchange, which gave us tremendous support. We talked to a number of firms that said we were going to push the Street right into disaster with the paperwork problem, because there were going to be due bills attached; so we had to understand how that worked. We also had to estimate how many people might try at the beginning, in the interest in getting their warrants, to buy the units and sell the debentures on a when-available basis. This was one of our worries.

"One of the things I will never forget," he continued, "is that the telephone company had said to us 'why should we price these debentures at 8¾ percent when the last ones we sold were 8.65 percent?' The obvious answer was that you had not been selling $1.6 billion before, and did not have to stand there for a period of six or seven weeks while it went on, with something in your gut telling you that there was going to be a lot of short selling. You just had to balance the two out."

Finally, with all due considerations, Morgan Stanley sent a telegram to each of the 4,300 members of the National Association of Securities Dealers urging them to participate in the offering, and a computerized program was set up to handle it. A lay-off system was established so that Morgan Stanley, which was to buy all the unsubscribed bonds and warrants as an agent for AT&T, could resell them. Unlike most public offerings of stocks and bonds, this one was not underwritten. Morgan Stanley was not taking upon itself the risk of absorbing, for its own account, any unsold units. It was, however, taking every possible precaution to assure that it would have the cooperation of all the securities houses in the country to help sell the AT&T offering to investors and institutions. Three separate Morgan Stanley teams traveled to seventeen cities coast to coast, explaining the financing. The firm set up a special room with banks of telephones to facilitate the lay-offs after the offering was made. Some 9,000 brokers, dealers, and analysts, nearly a third of them in New York, were invited to the presentation.

Still, there were instances when the effort almost ground to a halt, such as the time Morgan Stanley held a dry run of the presentation it had developed so laboriously. The Morgan Stanley partners, as well as AT&T officials, were gathered in the Morgan Stanley board room at 140 Broadway. The demonstration had gone no longer than ten minutes when everyone in the room realized it was an absolute disaster. On paper, the warrant presentation made sense to its drafters, who had been so closely connected to it. But as a verbal explanation it sounded much too complicated. That weekend, Morgan Stanley's Baldwin, Tomlinson, Haythe, and David Goodman, got together with representatives of a company specializing in television transparencies, and the pitch was revamped.

Even as Morgan Stanley was preparing for D day, AT&T was equipping its computerized securities center in Edison, New Jersey, for the same event. The total cost of the offering ultimately would add up to nearly $20 million, including the fees to the selling group headed by Morgan Stanley. To supplement its own facilities, AT&T rented an old Lockheed building. It hired over 1,500 temporary employees, while permanent telephone company people were put on as supervisors.

Then, suddenly, it was Monday, April 13. In the financial section of *The New York Times,* the lead headline said "Terms Due Today for AT&T Issue." John H. Allan, the *Times*'s bond reporter, had written the story of the offering that was to hit Wall Street with the force of a spring hurricane. "The directors of the American Telephone and Telegraph Company will meet this morning and set the final terms on the largest corporate financing ever undertaken in this country," the article began.

"They will put the interest rate on $1,569,327,000 of 30-year debentures to be offered to the 3.1 million AT&T stockholders from now until May 18. The directors will also set the price at which warrants attached to the debentures may be exercised.

"When these two figures are announced, it will end a period of intense guessing in Wall Street that caused trading activity to come almost to a standstill last Friday.

"Several veteran traders in Wall Street bond firms speculated that the new issue might be set at 8⅝ or 8¾ percent.

"The company itself and Morgan Stanley & Co., manager of a vast network of dealers helping to handle the historic financing, maintained utmost secrecy about the terms being considered.

"Mr. Romnes [chairman of the board at AT&T] also said in February that the exercise price for the warrants would be 'equal to or moderately above the market price of our shares at the time the terms are set.' AT&T common stock closed at $50.75 a share Friday."

Allan's story turned out to be on target. Baldwin knew it, and John Scanlon knew it, too, because he and his team of AT&T managers had worked all weekend to finish the detailed plan that was to be executed that Monday morning. For two weeks, Scanlon and his staff had been going through dry runs, simulating decisions against the background of changing bond market conditions.

Now, with the terms set, they were ready to make the first mailing of the rights offering to their stockholders—a mailing that would cost $1 million in postage and would involve enough paper to fill twenty railroad box cars, and an army of 4,000 workers to handle the operation. Because of an Internal Revenue Service requirement, some of the prospectuses describing the offering, as well as the rights certificates, had to be mailed the day trading began. Willard Nelson, assistant manager of AT&T's department of Security Issue Procedures in New Jersey, shipped the first mail bag that day to the local post office. The offering was officially launched and within a day or two, the first 3,929 shareowners would tear open their big AT&T envelopes and make a decision on whether or not to buy the bonds. Over the succeeding fifteen days, the rest of the offerings would be bagged, tagged, and mailed to AT&T investors around the world. In the past, they had provided a rich lode of cash for Mother Bell. Scanlon and Baldwin hoped it would be no different this time.

One thought that haunted Morgan Stanley and AT&T, however, was the complexity of the offering. Extraordinary efforts had been taken to explain the deal to the nation's brokers, but Mother Bell's three million shareholders also needed some handholding. For months they had been reading about the impending offering, but suddenly, starting April 14, and continuing for about ten days, the stockholders began receiving their bulky package of instructions from the telephone company. If the deal appeared too abstruse, too complicated, too foreign to anything that had previously been tried by the telephone company, the fear was that investors would take one look at the package of instructions and the thirty-two-page prospectus, sigh wearily, and toss the whole bundle into the trash. If that happened enough times, the millions of dollars in expenses already laid out, would be for nought.

In the package mailed to shareowners, the most important document was the company's official offer of one right to buy debentures for each share of common stock held. It took thirty-five rights to subscribe to one $100 bond. And, each bond carried warrants to buy two shares of AT&T stock at $52 a share from November 15, 1970, until May 15, 1975. The package also included a letter of instruction from the company, telling the investors how to transfer their rights to someone else if they wished, how to sell them, or how to exercise them so they could buy the debenture with the warrants attached. The letter also contained the warning that after May 18, the rights would be worthless. If the debenture was bought, of course, the warrants would be valid until 1975.

It was hoped, of course, that the stockholders would snap up the debentures and warrants for their own accounts. But, if not, if they decided they didn't want them for themselves, the hope was that they would at least sell the rights, which had a value of their own, and were in fact listed separately on the New York Stock Exchange (where they closed the first day at 70 cents). To facilitate this process, the package to shareholders included an envelope preaddressed to the local bank that was acting as rights agent in that area—one of six regional banks that was processing orders —which would send the stockholder a check for his rights at the current market price. And, if the shareowner wanted to go through his local broker, he could simply fill out another form and turn it over to him.

Meanwhile, back on the New York Stock Exchange, the first day's trading had started and was going well. Baldwin watched the figures move across the ticker. The debentures, offered at $100, held firm, picked up strength, and closed the day at $100.75. Baldwin visibly relaxed for the first time in weeks. The price of the debenture had been his most crucial test.

"What we had to do was try to assure the company that the debt could stand on its own." Baldwin said. "In fact, we had to write a letter to the Internal Revenue Service that it would sell at around par [$100]. That probably gave me more nightmares than anything else—that it might sell up or down. It was just a horror."

All Baldwin's figures indicated that the warrants should open around $10 and settle in the $8 or $9 range. This would have put the units up around $123 or $124, which he felt was a very high price.

Surprisingly, although the bonds closed about where expected, the warrants closed the day at a price of just over $12.87, slightly higher than anticipated. The total package of one debenture and two warrants closed at $125.

Since there was demand for them, Baldwin sold—went short—as many units as the market would bear at that time. Then he kept short until the rights started to come out, then slowly diminished the short position.

"I think we were short about $50 million almost continually," he said. "As we went along, the bond and stock market, particularly the bond market, went way off, and for the stock market there were a couple of days when it was off 15 or 20 points on the Dow Jones. You can't imagine a worse atmosphere during this offering period."

In spite of the faltering market, a remarkable thing began to happen.

"As the bond markets got worse, our bonds started down under pressure," Baldwin recalled. "But, for a long while, the warrants held up. Then a lot of people, particularly trust banks who had not been buying bonds, looked at 8¾ percent for AT&T bonds at $95, and said, 'these are just too attractive to turn down,' which proved to be the case. During this period, the warrants were staying up because a lot of speculators wanted to take positions, and, because they were not stripped, it was harder to get hold of a lot of warrants. So, there was a big demand for the warrants during this period."

The action of the telephone company's basic common stock soon affected the pricing of the warrant, however. Since the two are related, as the stock fell on the declining market, so did the value of the warrant. Nevertheless, by then the value of the bonds had begun to rebound. Still, the arbitrageurs were accentuating the market swings, and pushing for their profits.

"We were playing a game of cat and mouse with the arbitrageurs," Baldwin said. "It was a friendly game, but they were doing their business and we were doing ours. They could tell pretty much one day that I purposely bid high, and I'd take them all, and the next day I'd bid low and let them take all they had asked for. This way we kept it off balance, so they could not be sure. The big thing we were trying to do was not let too many units go to the arbitrageurs who were going to immediately strip them and force the debentures down. We were trying to keep them as units as much as possible to put them in the hands of people like the stockholders who were not going to strip them."

Baldwin recalled the hectic pace of the lay-offs at Morgan Stanley. "From a quarter of four, we were fighting the clock because we wanted to tell brokers what their allotments were. Then, they wanted to call their clients before the market opened the next morning. So, we used a whole battery of people, including the partners and everybody else. Of course, we had a permanent group that we brought in during this period, but then we also used partners and staff. It got exciting. You would get on the phone and fan out over the country. We had direct call wires and slips that showed exactly who to call, what the allotment was, and how many this left them on the book. We refused calls up here at the regular Morgan Stanley number because it would have absolutely flooded the switchboard."

At the same time the staff and some of the partners were handling the daily lay-off, other partners were upstairs trying to interest the large institutions in the offering.

Part of Morgan Stanley's and Ma Bell's success came because

they had inhibited the stripping of the bonds and warrants. One reason they prevented such separation was they did not want the bonds competing with other offerings from associated Bell companies.

Scanlon explained: "If the arbitrageurs went in and had immediately separable pieces of paper, they would buy the rights that were sold by the shareowners. Then they'd go to an insurance company and sell the debenture piece, and to someone who is more speculatively minded and sell the warrant piece. The reason we didn't want it was we were looking to the insurance companies to buy the bond issues we were selling to our associated companies. So we made it cumbersome and costly, in a deliberate attempt to inhibit arbitrage."

Although there was no way to prevent the arbitrageurs who bought rights from stripping them on a when-issued basis, and selling off the segments separately, dealers who were formally participating in the distribution were forbidden by Securities and Exchange Commission rules from doing the same thing. Some still tried it, however.

"We had one devil of a time during that period," Baldwin recalled. "Some people thought they were clever doing it. We finally sent telegrams out to them and said we were going to prosecute them and go right to the SEC unless they stopped it dead."

The independent arbitrageurs, of course, couldn't be stopped. Since they were not participants in the formal distribution, they could snap up the rights offerings whenever shareowners decided they didn't want to exercise them for themselves and sold them to rights agents.

Richard G. Rosenthal was handling the arbitrage for Salomon Brothers, one of Wall Street's biggest block-trading houses, during the AT&T offering, and he recalled the period with undisguised glee. "It was the largest single rights offering," he said, "and it was just inconceivable that this much paper—and I'm speaking like an arbitrageur now—could be sold over so brief a period of time. It was incredible."

Various banks across the country were acting as the rights

agents for the telephone company, grouping together those rights mailed in by shareowners, and asking for competitive bids on them.

"What Morgan Stanley would do was either bid for the rights, and then have a lay-off," Rosenthal recalled, "or they just might have a lay-off without buying the rights, creating a short position, allowing them the flexibility of buying rights at a later time against that existing short position. And we, as arbitrageurs, would compete with them to buy these rights. So we were really getting in their hair."

For Rosenthal, one special moment came partway through the offering when, as Baldwin had feared, the bond market took a sharp dip.

"There is a period of time," Rosenthal said, "when the rights hit the public, when they make up their minds whether they're going to exercise or sell. There was a value here. You have to have a value to make it meaningful for the public to make a decision, because the worst thing that can happen is for them to rip them up—then it means there's a final lay-off, a last bidding for the unsubscribed portion. Basically, the hairiest time is when these rights are being mailed into the bank for sale. There are several days of real congestion. That happened when the bonds broke down to $95. And the warrants came in like hell. Everything was for sale. So you say to yourself, 'What happens if they break? What happens if they *really* break that bond because of sheer pressure?' This is not a game like a stock offering, where you are dealing with one isolated security. You are dealing with a keystone to a much larger market—the bond market. There was tension when those bonds broke. One afternoon I bought $10 million in bonds at $95. And I'll tell you, that was a low. Nobody knew it at the time. But you just couldn't believe; I mean you weren't dealing in real quantities any more. You were dealing in jellybeans."

Scanlon also had uncomfortable memories of the sag in the bond market and the delay in shareowners mailing in their rights. He was attending an AT&T conference at the time.

"The thing that concerned me was the fact that we did not get the participation by shareowners to the extent that we had in our earlier stock offerings," he said, "and the people who bought the rights in the street did not want to put up their money until the last day. So, as this offering period developed, I had a growing concern as to where everything was. We could account for the rights that had been sold by the shareowners who had sent the forms back to us and asked us to sell them, or have a rights agent sell them for them. But a substantial number sold them through their brokers, and we did not know if they had been sold and purchased by a potential subscriber, or whether they were just being ignored. It just was not physically possible to match the rights certificates being used with the original issue in the time frame allowed. I must say that for two or three days I was not following the conference very much. I was on the phone all the time."

Baldwin recalled the same period as "just hell!" The Morgan Stanley order book got thinner and thinner and the trading volume increasingly heavy toward the end of April. "There were a couple of nights when I went home and said, 'Good God, if this market keeps going tomorrow, what the hell are we going to do?' Literally, I mean. It was frightful."

From the beginning of the offering, articles had appeared in *The Wall Street Journal, Business Week,* and a host of specialized trade papers and magazines. In addition, stories suddenly blossomed in such general interest magazines as *Time* and *Newsweek.* And the tone was not always pleasant. "Bell Wrings the Market" lamented *Time* in late April. The *Time* article went on to say, "One factor that has kept stock prices down this year is the voracious appetite of U.S. business for new capital at a time when it remains scarce. Instead of moving into existing stocks, investment money has been flowing into new issues of corporate securities. The most vivid demonstration of the trend came last week when American Telephone & Telegraph Co., the world's largest private enterprise, floated a $3.2 billion financing—a size usually associated only with U.S. Treasury offerings. After the issue went on sale, the Dow Jones industrial average dropped nearly ten points in two days as investors switched out of other securities to buy the bluest chip of all."

Time's point was well taken. Not only did the stock market sag, but the bond markets slumped under the impact of the huge offering. Indeed, the day after the opening, the sale of some new issues of bonds were slowed and the prices of most outstanding corporate bonds were depressed. The credit markets had opened with a hopeful atmosphere, expecting that interest rates might be heading downward, which would buoy the prices for existing bonds. But prices fell as traders became concerned about the prospect of the AT&T debentures competing for funds in the bond market. The reason was simply the added supply of securities. It meant that all future borrowers would have to pay higher rates to insure that they could attract funds from investors. And higher rates for new bonds tend to depress the prices for old bonds.

Many analysts were far from enchanted by the magnitude and scope of the AT&T offering. Some thought it a piece of unmitigated hoggishness on the part of Ma Bell. One financial writer sourly commented that an appropriate way of looking at the pressure the offering put on existing prices of stock and bond issues was to imagine what would happen if every auto dealer in the country, through some industry-wide folly of General Motors, Ford, Chrysler, and American Motors, were asked to dispose of from two to three times as many cars in a five-week period as they had to sell a year before. Something would have to give, he went on, and in the case of AT&T, it may have been the bond, debenture, and stock market.

For Morgan Stanley, the AT&T debenture with warrant offering was a new trophy, but hardly the firm's first financial coup. In 1953, the firm engineered what at the time was the largest offering of industrial securities in history—$300 million in bonds for the General Motors Corporation.

Indeed, in the 1950s, it seemed that Morgan Stanley was commandeering one massive offering after another. Less than a year after the G.M. transaction, it headed a syndicate of 245 investment houses in another $300 million offering—this one by the United States Steel Corporation.

Despite its golden reputation, not everything Morgan Stanley touched turned to success. In July 1966, only four years before the big $1.6 billion AT&T offering, a group of seventy investment banking houses, led by Morgan Stanley, was forced to disband after having unsuccessfully offered the public $150 million of top-rated Southwestern Bell Telephone bonds. About 75 percent of the bonds were unsold at the time, and they had dropped from their original offering price of $100 to as low as $97.75. Although bond prices fluctuate, and any profit or loss can be marked only at a specific point in time, the loss to the bankers involved amounted to roughly $1.2 million, even after taking into account the portion that had been sold at par.

Morgan Stanley profited handsomely, as did a number of other firms, from the $1.6 billion AT&T offering of 1970, and indeed, over the years the firm had found Ma Bell to be a faithful client. The fee paid to Morgan Stanley for its financial advisory services on the 1970 transaction was $250,000, and it received an added $100,000 fee in connection with the offering. That was only the tip of the iceberg, however. Altogether, the banking firm collected over $1 million, according to Baldwin, and other estimates ran higher. One competitor said he estimated that Morgan Stanley made nearly $3 million, including commissions for lay-off sales. "It sounds like an awful lot of money," he said, "but I would guess they probably put half or three-quarters of a year into it. It was just an enormous undertaking."

Baldwin and Scanlon later would look back and shake their heads in wonder at the period in which they had chosen to float the biggest offering in corporate history. It was a time of a new seven-year low for the stock market; a financing by the U.S. Treasury that ran into serious trouble; the largest increase in labor costs in fourteen years; student protests erupting at Kent State, resulting in the death of four students; the sending of U.S. troops into Cambodia by President Nixon.

Despite all the problems, however, the two men could still view with satisfaction their landmark deal. They had actually sold nearly 98 percent of the issue during the subscription period, with the unsubscribed portion sold several weeks later. And most crucial of all—AT&T had gotten its $1.6 billion.

Scanlon's major disappointment was that fewer AT&T shareowners than expected took advantage of the debenture with warrants offering. Only about 40 percent of the offering was picked up by shareowners, although both Baldwin and Scanlon had been hoping, even into the final days of the offering, that it would hit 50 percent. The 40 percent compared poorly to the straight stock offerings the company had made in 1961 and 1964, when shareowners took almost two-thirds of the shares offered. Partly it was the depressed condition of the market, and partly the strangeness of the device, Scanlon said unhappily.

Nonetheless, despite the incursions of the arbitrageurs, the vagaries of the stock and bond markets, and the foot-dragging of the AT&T stockholders, it was clear that the mammoth offering had been a success. The task had been staggering and unprecedented. One veteran Wall Streeter considered the feat for a moment and then gave it his equivalent of a Navy "well done."

"They did what they set out to do," he said. For a single offering of $1.6 billion, that was quite a lot.

3 / The Political Storm

The bond markets were in the doldrums in the summer of 1974. Money was tight and interest rates were soaring. Citicorp, New York's largest and most successful bank holding company, needed hundreds of millions of dollars in long-term cash to balance its portfolio. After consulting with investment bankers up and down Wall Street, Citicorp decided on a novel approach. It would fashion a floating note whose rate would rise and fall with the prevailing interest-rate structure. As word of Citicorp's proposed offering leaked out, it dominated the credit markets and held the attention of the investing public for weeks. It was attacked by the nation's thrift institutions and their powerful friends. The Federal Reserve Board questioned it and the Securities and Exchange Com-

mission delayed it. Finally, on a rainy day in July, the precedent-setting offering of $650 million in floating-rate notes was made. Other banks followed, but it quickly became clear that Citicorp had preempted the market. Almost as fast as they had appeared, floating-rate notes disappeared from public view.

It was an extraordinary gathering of investment bankers that took place at 20 Exchange Place. Paul Miller, the pipe-smoking president of The First Boston Corporation, sat beside the door of the conference room. Next to him was Gustave Levy, the aggressive patriarch of Goldman, Sachs & Co. Across the table was Julius Sedlmayr, the round-faced, smiling chief investment banker from Merrill Lynch, Pierce, Fenner & Smith.

"Everybody's here but the customer," murmured Levy, as the three bankers waited for their client. Two minutes later, Edward L. Palmer, chairman of Citicorp's executive committee, strode briskly into the room and sat down. Reaching for the contract on the table in front of him, he scribbled his name, then leaned back and grinned. "How much history does this make?" he asked rhetorically.

Palmer and everyone else in the room knew that the $650 million deal they had just formalized was a precedent-setting financing that would be endlessly debated and dissected in the months and years ahead. In its formative stages, it had triggered fierce opposition in the United States Congress and was attacked by a variety of officials ranging from George Meany of the AFL-CIO to Louis Lefkowitz, the attorney general of New York. Before the almost anticlimactic contract signing at First Boston's headquarters in the midsummer of 1974, it had appeared at times that the scheme would die aborning.

The fact that the offering ever took place was due largely to the power and imagination of Citicorp, parent company of First National City Bank, the nation's second largest commercial bank. In a dramatic exhibition of its growing dominance, Citicorp expropriated the traditional role of the investment banker, and, using its own initiative, fashioned a public offering that raised $650 million at a time when offerings a quarter that size were going begging. In the process, Citicorp brought together an investment banking team of three of the nation's most prestigious houses, after it had determined that none of them alone could satisfy the demands of the deal. In the face of investment banking apathy and misjudgments, Citicorp took the lead, ultimately fighting its own political battles when the offering seemed in danger, and in the end it was Citicorp that reaped the rewards.

Ironically, a misjudgment of the financial markets gave rise to the fantastic $650 million offering of Citicorp notes. As a bank holding company, Citicorp raised money in a variety of ways, ranging from the sale of stock (equities), or borrowing for as little as twenty-five days, through the issuance of commercial paper. In the spring of 1974, Citicorp realized that it was overextended in commercial paper, at times having as much as $1.5 million outstanding, and decided to raise more long-term money so it could retire some of its short-term debt. When a company like Citicorp decides to borrow money by selling bonds, it tracks interest rate trends extremely carefully. The lower the rate, the less it has to pay for borrowed cash. Payments of interest for long-term debt are stretched out over a long period of time, so such money is generally cheaper than short-term cash. As early as the summer of 1973, Citicorp had begun to think in terms of an offering of a quarter-billion dollars or so of long-term debt. So, it began watching interest rates closely, fully expecting they would decline and inflation would cool, bringing interest rates down with it.

By February 1974, Citicorp officials had begun to confer with First Boston, which had been their principal underwriter on two previous issues. Work was started on a prospectus, and First Boston kept Citicorp advised of its view of the bond market. As interest rates drifted lower, both Citicorp and First Boston felt a heightened sense of anticipation. If interest rates dropped to 7 percent, they felt they could fashion the sort of offering that would bring Citicorp the cash it wanted.

Unfortunately for Citicorp, just as it seemed that a deal might be in the offing, long-term interest rates stopped their downward drift. Intermediate-term interest rates were still moving lower, so Citicorp began to think in terms of an offering of $200 million to $250 million in the intermediate range. The rate dropped to 7¼ percent, then to 7⅛. Then, unexpectedly, even the intermediate-term rates began to rise. "We missed the market," said Donald Howard, Citicorp's vice-president for finance. "We just sat there and we watched the damned market move right away from us."

Money began to tighten up swiftly. Market conditions changed drastically and by May, Citicorp had shelved the idea of going into the market with a classic offering of intermediate or long-term bonds. Still, the bank wanted to get away from its heavy reliance on short-term money and to balance its debt structure more effectively. As weeks passed, Citicorp officials became more frustrated. Not only were rates continuing to rise, but the availability of money was clearly shrinking.

For a time, the situation seemed paradoxical. Citicorp's economists were telling them that worldwide inflation was slowing and that a recession was approaching (which in retrospect proved to be accurate). At the same time, First Boston was predicting 12 percent to 15 percent long-term interest rates by year-end. Citicorp recognized that it could probably go into the money markets and raise $100 million by selling 7½ percent notes, but that amount of money was hardly adequate to accomplish its goal, and the rate seemed uncomfortably high to pay for an extended period.

As a result, the company found itself with a portfolio that was heavy on short-term debt, but it still was unwilling to pay the rates required to lengthen the portfolio.

At this point, Citicorp decided to try out an unusual concept on a few Wall Street investment bankers. It was based on the philosophy that an interest rate does not have to be fixed. Just because you offer to pay 7 percent or 8 percent or even 9 percent for borrowed money at the time it is borrowed, is no reason why that same rate must be paid for the entire term of the loan. Why can't the rate float? As interest rates in the market place go up and down, why shouldn't the rates of an issue that has already been sold do the same thing?

Citicorp's top officers already had a good deal of experience with variations of the floating rate. In the early 1960s, when Walter Wriston was head of the bank's overseas operations and before he became chief executive, he had pioneered such a concept. An oil company had asked him to arrange a three-year, $100 million loan in twenty-four hours, and Wriston had come up with the idea of tying it to a rate which was based on the cost of funds for the previous ninety days, plus a spread which would provide the profit for the lender. The loan was not terribly successful for Citicorp, but the bank gained experience from it. First, it learned that the spread was too small. Secondly, it discovered that the concept of basing the interest rate on the cost of funds for the previous period was dangerous. If the previous period was low, and was followed by a period with high rates, losses could be enormous. If the trend went the other way, of course, the bank stood to make a handsome profit. However, it was too risky to gamble on declining rates.

The experience of this first floating-rate loan gave the bank the idea of employing what it called "marginal cost-of-funds pricing" for loans in the Eurodollar markets. Later, following Wriston's promotion to the presidency, he pioneered the concept of a floating rate for commercial loans and then floated the rate on so-called wild card certificates of deposit which the bank sold.

With the money markets in New York rising rapidly, and with the prospect that interest rates would come down in the months ahead, perhaps quite precipitously, Wriston began to think more about floating rates. Why not get the money he needed, admittedly at a high rate, and then pay off at a lower rate as the market softened? The idea seemed appealing, so he decided to try it out on some Wall Street investment bankers.

One of the first firms to hear the Wriston approach was Salomon Brothers, which had the reputation of being one of the more imaginative houses on the Street. Wriston lunched at the Salomon Brothers offices with ten of their top officials, and launched his balloon.

"What do you fellows think of Citicorp selling a floating-rate note?" he asked. The response was negative.

"They had absolutely zero interest in it," Wriston later recalled.

"I wasn't about to sell it. I just floated it, and it didn't float."

Then Wriston discussed his idea with other investment bankers, who were skeptical about the idea. He talked it up at cocktail parties, "wandered around town with it," and finally decided that even if no one else was interested in the idea, he was.

At about the time Wriston was making up his mind to go ahead with some sort of floating-rate note, Gustave Levy dropped by Citicorp to make a pitch for business. He tried to impress upon Howard and Palmer what a good firm Goldman Sachs was, and what he thought it could do for Citicorp. The discussion was persuasive to the Citicorp officials. Finally, Palmer said to Levy, "We've got an idea, why don't you think about this: a floating-rate note."

"That's a hell of an idea," Levy responded. "Let us think about it. We'll be back."

Within a few days, Palmer and Howard were in Goldman Sachs's offices, discussing a specific proposal from the firm on a deal that would raise $350 million by selling floating-rate notes. The approach Goldman Sachs had fashioned was far different from the one that would finally be adopted by Citicorp, but at least the idea was being taken seriously for the first time, and in sufficient scope to accommodate Citicorp's capital needs.

For several weeks, Citicorp and Goldman Sachs representatives discussed variations of the offering. At about that point Robert B. Calhoun, Jr., the First Boston official who handled the Citicorp account, called Howard to bring him up to date on some other financial matters. Howard decided that it was time to let First Boston know what was brewing. "Bob," he said, "here's an idea. Think about it and see what you might be able to do for us." Howard did not tell Calhoun that Goldman Sachs already was working on the project.

Within a few days, First Boston returned to Citicorp with ideas on how such an offering might be structured. Their feel for Citicorp's needs was good, partly because they had been working with the bank for many years. Their technical approach was different, but that didn't bother Citicorp at this point. Later, all the ideas would have to be amalgamated into one master plan, but for the moment the exchange of ideas was an effective way to get the ball rolling.

From the beginning, one of the basic differences in philosophy was the concept of who might buy the floating-rate notes. The investment bankers perceived their potential market as the big institutions, the professional investors. Citicorp, on the other hand, saw a market among the nation's small investors. The bank looked at its experience a year or so earlier, when it had offered floating-rate savings certificates, and had sold over $100 million worth through its branch system in three weeks. The sales had been halted by the Federal Reserve after opposition arose from the savings and loan institutions, but that experience had given Citicorp officials a sense of customer demand for floating-rate securities.

"The two underwriting firms were closer to each other than they were to us," Howard said. "They were looking at a professional buyer, an institutional buyer, and we were looking at the guy in the street. Finally, we decided 'dammit,' there was a market out there for individuals that we should really go after."

So far, all the technical problems involved in a multimillion-dollar offering had been based on the premise that it was to be sold to professionals: the discount basis, how it was to be traded, how quoted, what it was to be tied to as far as the interest rate was concerned. Ultimately, Citicorp came to the conclusion that as professional as Goldman Sachs and First Boston were, their expertise was not in understanding the small investor. Howard went to Wriston one afternoon and said, "Walt, we have to get Merrill Lynch into this."

First Boston and Goldman Sachs still did not know the other firm was involved in the preliminary negotiations. Citicorp called the two investment bankers separately and told them that a meeting was being set up to discuss the offering, at the same time revealing the presence of the other investment banker. Then Citicorp called Merrill Lynch and said, "Would you like to join the party?"

"They gulped a couple of times," Howard recalled, "and said, 'You know, it's kind of short notice, but, hell, we'll be there.'"

The first joint meeting was held, and over the next few weeks, similar sessions took place. Gradually, the investment bankers became convinced that the retail market was the one they wanted. They began to design an instrument that would specifically be attractive to small investors. One early decision was the need for an existing interest rate to serve as an anchor for the note. Even if it was going to float, it had to float with something. The first choice was Citicorp's certificate of deposit rate. That presented a problem, however. The new note would have to be pegged at a lower interest rate than the certificate of deposit. Such a move seemed unwise to the bankers for psychological reasons. It wasn't good business to tell buyers that they were getting less than someone else. It was much better to give them more. Palmer felt that the buyer should be offered a plus if possible, but at least not be given a minus. After a number of alternatives were considered, the group decided that the interest rate should be one percent more than the rate for three-month U.S. Treasury bills.

Now the discussions became more specific. They were primarily concerned with the type of issue that would be most attractive to the public, and on the sort of offering that would bring Citicorp the maximum amount of money at the least cost. The bank assembled a "data base" through which it could evaluate various proposals from its investment bankers. Howard and his team were able to run proposals through their computer in minutes to determine what effect they would have on earnings.

It quickly became apparent that even though the question of what to use as an anchor for the floating rate had been solved, there was an even more pressing matter to contend with. The consumer was concerned with liquidity. He would buy a high-yield note, but he also wanted the opportunity to resell it at face value. Bond markets make it possible for such securities to be bought and sold freely, but just as in stock markets, the values fluctuate, often dropping below face value. Merrill Lynch argued that the consumer had to be guaranteed liquidity. Citicorp must be prepared to buy back the notes whenever the customer wanted to get rid of them.

Until now the discussion had centered around a floating rate with a ten-year maturity, without the option of reselling to the issuer at face value—an option that bankers labeled a "put." Without such a put to sweeten the deal, the investment bankers were pessimistic about their chance for success. They advised Citicorp that perhaps $100 million in notes could be sold without the put, but no more. Citicorp argued that the note would have inherent value and would trade at about par in the aftermarket— that is, at its original price. Merrill Lynch disagreed, saying the value of the note would change as market conditions varied, and it was not likely to trade at par for very long.

After much debate, it was agreed that a put was critical to the deal. Buyers of the notes should be able to resell them to Citicorp after six months if they so desired. Not only would the offering be vastly more attractive to customers, but the investment bankers also became more interested. In effect, the put let them off the hook. In traditional underwritings, investment banking syndicates took the responsibility for selling the entire offering, buying the securities from the issuer, and reselling them from their own inventory.

If the issue did poorly, the investment banker was stuck with the unsold stocks or bonds. In this case, however, with Citicorp offering to buy back any unsold notes at the end of six months, the underwriters had an escape clause. They, too, could sell back any unsold notes, so they were minimizing their own risk. At most, they would have to carry unsold notes for six months, and at the end of that time they could sell them back to Citicorp. Of course, everyone hoped that would not be necessary, but if it was, the option was available.

Even with the put feature, the three investment bankers told Citicorp they believed that a maximum of $200 million of the notes could be sold, an assessment that proved to be woefully inaccurate.

With a little arm-twisting, Citicorp persuaded the underwriters to raise the size of the offering to $250 million, and prepared to register it with the Securities and Exchange Commission. For the first time, the public would have a look at the issue that was to capture the attention of the entire financial community in the weeks ahead.

A few days before Citicorp's June board meeting, Wriston called together as many of the company's directors as he could reach, and explained his plan. The directors gave Wriston their support, and at the board meeting the following week, they officially approved the concept.

With the full weight of Citicorp and the investment banking community behind the offering, a registration statement was filed with the SEC, and the investment bankers began to sound out their customers to determine how many of the notes they might buy. To their astonishment, they discovered that the public was enchanted with the offering. Disillusioned by a dismal stock market, angry over their inability to reap the high interest rates that were being paid for government bonds that sold mostly in large denominations, small investors saw the Citicorp floating-rate note, which guaranteed an initial yield of 9.7 percent, as a chance to jump aboard the high-rate bandwagon, at least for a time.

Howard quickly arranged a meeting with the investment bankers. "It was evident that we were selling the thing like popcorn at a movie," he said. "It was just going like crazy." The meeting was convened, and Paul Miller of First Boston asked Robert Calhoun, his aide, where they stood with the issue at that moment. Calhoun made a phone call, then returned to the meeting. "At the moment, we stand at about $800 million and climbing," he said.

The discussion now shifted from the question of whether the issue could be sold, to a new proposition. How much money did Citicorp want? Howard thought the maximum should be $950 million, because if the offering exceeded $1 billion it would be politically difficult. Citicorp would be accused of draining money from other types of investments, especially from the thrift institutions. Palmer felt the amount really didn't matter as long as it was kept under $950 million.

"Look," he said, "as far as Citicorp is concerned—between $800 million and $950 million—frankly, we are indifferent. We really don't care. Eight-hundred million dollars is enough. We don't want to go over $950 million. You choose a number."

Levy was astonished. "You really know how to hurt a guy," he said. "Do you realize that the range of your indifference is larger than any issue the Street has done this year?"

A decision was made that the presale figure at the end of that day would constitute the stopping point. It turned out to be $850 million, and Citicorp prepared to amend its registration statement to reflect the higher figure.

The outcry from opponents of the controversial issue began to build. Even before Citicorp raised the amount of the offering to $850 million, the National Association of Mutual Savings Banks had issued a broadside calling on the Federal Reserve Board to halt the Citicorp sale on the technical grounds that it circumvented interest-rate controls on time deposits.

Then, on the day Citicorp raised the amount of the offering to $850 million, the Savings Banks Association of New York State joined in the attack. In a letter to Arthur F. Burns, chairman of the Federal Reserve System, the association warned that a proliferation of such offerings could have "dangerous repercussions" not only on thrift institutions but also on commercial banks not offering similar securities.

At the heart of all the arguments was the fact that at $850 million, the offering would be the largest dollar amount of securities, either debt or equity, ever offered publicly by any issuer unconnected with the federal government. Larger sums had been sold by the American Telephone and Telegraph Company, but they had been offered initially to the company's own shareholders. Furthermore, the Citicorp issue was obviously aimed at small investors. Initial purchases could be as small as $5,000, and after that, trades of as little as $1,000 would be acceptable.

More critics jumped into the fray. The Federal Home Loan Bank Board warned that the offering was "fraught with danger" to thrift institutions. The United States League of Savings Associations urged the Federal Reserve Board to dissuade Citicorp from making the offering.

On July 2, the Federal Reserve Board announced that it lacked authority to block such an offering, while expressing its doubts that the offering was in the public interest. In a letter to the SEC, the board cautioned that the result of the offering, and others like it, would be to divert the flow of savings from the residential mortgage market, and "deprive homeowners of needed mortgage finance."

The thrift institutions took their signal from the Federal Reserve Board, and began to concentrate their pleas on the SEC. The National Association of Mutual Savings Banks "urgently requested" that the SEC delay the offering until Congress had a chance to enact legislation that could prohibit such offerings.

Wright Patman, chairman of the House Banking Committee, asked the SEC to stop the issue until Congress had a chance to study its impact. He noted that legislation was pending which would give the Federal Reserve Board "cease and desist" powers over holding company operations.

More fuel was added to the fire when the Chase Manhattan Corporation, New York's second largest bank holding company, said it was going to offer $200 million in floating-rate notes to the public.

Meanwhile, the attack, which previously had sprung mostly from thrift institutions and their associations, broadened. Louis J. Lefkowitz, attorney general of the State of New York, wrote a letter to the SEC. "I am personally concerned that these new forms of investments are addressed to smaller investors, which typically was not the case in prior offerings by such institutions," he said. "For this reason, it would seem that a much more cautious attitude should be taken in reviewing such offering literature."

George Meany, president of the AFL-CIO, blasted Washington officials who had not moved to abort the offering. "The administration's failure to use its authority to halt the First National City Corporation and the Chase Manhattan Corporation from their planned issuance of over $1 billion of special notes with a floating high-interest rate is another in a series of government actions and failures that are clubbing residential construction into a depression," he thundered.

With such furor surrounding its offering, Citicorp was forced to delay. Initially, it had planned to sell the notes to the public during the week of July 8, but instead found itself in a battle to preserve the deal in any form.

Wriston took off for Washington to begin a series of hurried meetings with congressman and senators. He gave them all the same message. It's a consumer issue. The public is entitled to it. If you're poor, you get 5 percent interest on your money. If you're rich, you get 12 percent.

The nation's credit markets, Wriston testified, were a "vicious circle in which the consumer pays a minimum of 18 percent to retailers, certificates of deposit pay up to 12 percent to $100,000-investors, and savings banks pay 5¼ percent to consumers. The consumer is at both extremes of the scale. He pays most to borrow and earns least to save."

Warming to his pitch for higher interest rates for small investors (at least for those who bought Citicorp's floating-rate notes), Wriston said it was curious "in the face of the intense consumerism and concern for the rights of the individual, that the high interest rates charged to and paid by corporations are causing so much public anxiety. In contrast, the much higher interest being charged to small borrowers and the much lower interest being paid to small savers in our consumer society seem to arouse no particular concern."

Wriston also testified that although the savings banks were worried that the Citicorp notes would siphon away money which could be used by the thrift institutions to finance home building, in fact the savings banks in New York were putting half their money in corporate bonds. "When I pointed that out, some of the banks were less than delighted," Wriston said. "There was a fair amount of flak about it."

In addition to talking to congressmen, Wriston called on Treasury Secretary William Simon. "I told him what we were doing, and I explained that while this was an issue of raising money for Citicorp, it was also a consumer issue, and that I believed it was a free market. He said he believed the same thing."

Then, Wriston called on Arthur Burns. Burns said he had a mandate to look at the entire financial structure, and was concerned that there would be disintermediation, a technical term for robbing Peter to pay Paul. Wriston, on the other hand, argued that the floating-rate notes were "just another instrument" and that investors could already put their money in Treasury bills, federal home loan bonds, and all the other methods the U.S. government used to compete with the private sector. "But the political heat on his [Burns's] back was intense," Wriston said.

The banker told Burns that he planned to go ahead with the offering since there was no law against it, but that he would agree to modify it in order to blunt the concern in Washington. Then a period of negotiating, or "reasoning together" as Wriston called it, began. Wriston's initial offer to Burns was formalized in a letter he wrote on July 11. He noted that the major criticism of the offering had centered on the right of purchasers to redeem their notes at full value within six months. He offered to delay that redemption date for a year and a half, even though it would probably hurt the sale of the notes.

The proposal was rejected by the Federal Reserve Board. Burns asked that the period of nonredemption be lengthened to two years. Wriston's back was to the wall. With every day that passed, the offering was losing some of its luster. As Donald Howard put it, it was becoming "shopworn merchandise." Two bills had already been introduced in Congress to stop the issue altogether. Potential buyers were becoming suspicious. "A broker who had a guy on the line with $10,000 and wasn't sure he could sell him our thing was going to try to sell him something else so he could get his commission," Howard said. "So, we had a problem."

It became evident that the underwriting syndicate could no longer guarantee a sale of $850 million. So, once again, the problem shifted. No longer was it a matter of where to cut off the sale. It was a question of whether a satisfactory sale could take place.

"As the negotiations went back and forth with the Federal Reserve Board, we had to assess the impact on the market," Howard said. "Every day it delayed the issue we got in more trouble and people cancelled. It became evident it wasn't an easy deal at all."

Finally an agreement with the Federal Reserve Board was reached. Wriston wrote Burns that he was prepared to delay the first redemption date for twenty-two months and concluded with a plea for quick approval.

The next day, Burns responded in a "dear Walter" letter. In view of the modification, he said, the board felt its concerns were "substantially reduced." Citicorp had met the Federal Reserve Board's basic concern which had given rise to a request for postponement. The letter ended, however, with a painful twist for Wriston. "There may still be serious doubts on the part of Congress and the other regulatory agencies," Burns said, "and you may therefore still want to consider the suggestion for a postponement that I made."

Months later, as he assessed the deal, Wriston would take a philosophical view. "In the real world, the optimum that you can do is what society permits you to do," he said. "You can argue that this wasn't optimum. I can argue that we've got the money. And that's the test of the chef."

At the time, however, he pitched furiously back into the fray. Aligned against him were the savings banks, with their considerable lobbying powers, and through the savings institutions a number of governors and attorneys general. Already the revised terms on redeeming the notes had cost him an estimated $200 million in potential sales. Now, with the Federal Reserve satisfied, he still had Congress and the SEC to worry about.

"There are a large number of congressmen who are affiliated one way or another with savings and loan institutions and savings banks, as shareholders, trustees or something else," Wriston later philosophized. "The toughest lobby in America is the housing lobby. Housing has taken the place of either motherhood or planned parenthood, depending on which side of the fence you're on. If you've said housing you've said the magic word, even though nobody knows quite what it means."

Wriston counterattacked by arguing that Citicorp was making more loans for housing than anyone else. "In the panic days in Washington, people who should know better testified solemnly that floating-rate notes would be sold for $10 billion," he said. "They went to left field and took whatever figure they could to scare hell out of everybody. I told the Congress that I would be surprised if there was $2 billion."

Throughout the increasingly virulent debate, Wall Street kept a close eye on the offering. A report issued by the Argus Research Corporation on July 9, summed up the prevailing Street view. "In the aftermath of Citicorp's announced offer of fifteen-year varia-ble-rate notes, the main question might seem to be whether the supervisory agencies, the courts, and various members of the Con-gress will find a way to block the issue.

"Clearly, the regulators are uncomfortable, as they always are when faced with an innovation that may have far-reaching conse-quences for the institutions they regulate, and hence for them; they probably wish the question had never come up. And they are obviously under great pressure from people who are afraid the new notes will be so popular with small investors that they will pull funds out of savings institutions and reduce the supply of mort-gage money for home-building. Nevertheless, we think the big debate about whether bank holding companies should be allowed to issue variable-rate notes is, at most, a temporary diversion."

Indeed, it did prove to be a temporary diversion, but a painful one. Day after day, the financial press followed the twists and turns of the deal, ferreting out details from sources in Washington and on Wall Street. On July 10, the newspapers noted that the once-delayed offering had been postponed because the SEC had not given its approval. Three days later, they reported that the big offering had been revised, with the put lengthened to nearly two years.

Meanwhile, the syndicate of underwriters was working fever-ishly to hold the deal together. Obviously, a sale of $850 million was out of the question. But how much could be sold? Finally, the decision was made by Wriston, as he, William Spencer, the bank's number two officer, and Edward Palmer sat in front of a Citicorp speakerphone and discussed the offering with the investment bankers. The sale would be sticky at $700 million, the bankers said. There was a pretty good chance of selling out at $675 million, but $650 million dollars was a sure thing.

Citicorp decided not to jeopardize the entire offering by pushing for $675 million, so the deal was structured for a sale of $650 million.

Still, the SEC had to be dealt with. An amended registration statement was filed with the commission, and Citicorp sat back to wait for the agency's response. Five days later, a seven-page letter containing seventy-eight questions was received by Citicorp.

For Citicorp it was a serious blow. "That was the low point of the whole thing, when we got the letter from the SEC with those seventy-eight queries," said Howard. "Having successfully negotiated a deal with the Federal Reserve Board only to be hit with this array of questions in a totally new concept that had never been used before in disclosure. We could have interpreted that as being an attempt to stop us, but it was not."

Citicorp's Washington representatives had telecopied the SEC letter and transmitted it to New York, where a forty-five-man accounting staff was standing by for a weekend of sixteen- to twenty-hour shifts that lasted until Monday morning.

An ironic note was added to the furious, high-finance activity of the weekend. As mealtimes came around, and the accountants sent out to a neighborhood delicatessen for sandwiches, they found that between them they didn't have enough money to cover their food bills.

"We sat there dealing with a $650 million issue and sitting on top of vaults full of millions and millions of dollars," said Howard, "and our major problem was coming up with enough bucks to pay for the food."

By Monday morning, Citicorp was ready to respond to the SEC's questions. The bank presented the SEC with the new draft, which seemed to meet the agency's disclosure requirements. However, the following day, the SEC came back with more questions, so Citicorp was forced to refile on Wednesday.

The bank felt it was urgent that the offering be made as quickly as possible. The previous day, *The New York Times* had led its financial page with a story that the issue had been reduced to $650 million in the face of customer resistance. The newspaper had said that changes in the issue prompted by the Federal Reserve Board, namely delaying for nearly two years the date on which the notes could first be redeemed at par, had reduced its attractiveness.

The Citicorp offering was not the only one in trouble, however. On the same day, the Chase Manhattan Corporation said it was delaying a similar $200 million offering, scheduled to take place later that week, for at least a full week, as it awaited SEC clearance. And, in a final spur to Citicorp, the Crocker National Corporation, parent company of the Crocker National Bank, announced that it was planning to sell $75 million in floating-rate notes. One thing Citicorp didn't need was more competition for investors' dollars.

Finally, it was the day of the sale. At 8 A.M. on Wednesday, July 24, representatives from the 166 brokerage firms in the underwriting group began to straggle up from Exchange Place to First Boston's twelfth-floor meeting room so they could sign the contracts that legally obligated them to multimillion-dollar chunks of the offering.

The first brokers to arrive were Francisco P. Sinatra, an assistant vice-president of Halsey, Stuart & Company, who signed for $8.5 million in notes, and David H. Nichols, a vice-president of Abraham & Company, who signed for $1.2 million. Their allocations were tiny compared to the $75.7 million alloted to each of the three leading underwriters, First Boston, Goldman Sachs and Merrill Lynch.

The brokers continued to file in and out of the room, signing their contracts, passing a remark or two, and leaving. When all but a few syndicate members had signed their contracts, First Boston's officials strode to an elevator for their ride to the seventh floor where they would join the other syndicate co-managers. There, after Edward Palmer of Citicorp, Paul Miller of First Boston, Gustave Levy of Goldman Sachs and Julius Sedlmayr of Merrill Lynch had signed the contract, the tension gave way to bantering.

Palmer chuckled as he referred to the $200 million issue scheduled by his competitor, the Chase Manhattan Corporation. "I came in on the train today and the guy next to me tore out the coupon for the Chase offering," he said. "Can you imagine?" Everyone in the room laughed at his sally.

What about the Crocker National Corporation, which was planning to offer $75 million in floating-rate notes? "Like going out in a sailboat behind the *Queen Mary,*" said Palmer, obviously feeling for all the world like the *Queen Mary.*

As the architects of the deal continued their light conversation, aides waited anxiously for the telephone to ring, bringing them formal permission from the SEC to proceed. Finally, at 9:50 A.M., it did.

Now the scene shifted to First Boston's syndicate and bond desks on the thirteenth floor. At the syndicate desk, the firm kept track of all 166 members, giving more notes to those who needed them, and retrieving securities from those who were having trouble selling their allotment. On the bond desk, First Boston was concerned with selling its own $75.7 million allotment.

Not that there was much doubt about the results. The syndicate managers had done their homework well. At 9:58, Richard Du-Busc of the syndicate desk shouted over the noise to his colleagues, "We're not putting out any more bonds." The telephones on the desk jangled, mostly with requests for more notes which First Boston could not fill. Then, at 10:13, one syndicate member said he was sending back $30,000 worth of notes. They were quickly reallocated.

By now there was action on the floor of the New York Stock Exchange. The first trade was a purchase by First Boston on behalf of the syndicate of $290,000 worth of the notes to stabilize the market. A few minutes later, the firm also bought $800,000 of the notes on the over-the-counter market for the same purpose.

At 10:45, a syndicate desk assistant asked how the issue was going. DuBusc sat back and grinned. "What do you think?" he said, "with the market running par to par and a quarter, with requests for more notes still coming in, and with the stabilization effort limited for the moment to just over one million dollars?"

Around 11 A.M., Miller headed back to his office to ponder other deals. "Looks to me like it's in very good balance," he said, smiling to a visitor he passed on the way.

For Citicorp and its underwriters, it was the end of a long and often agonizing road. Before the day was over, Citicorp would have its $650 million, less fees and commissions, and the underwriters would have a handsome profit. One First Boston official calculated that each of the lead underwriters would make over $1 million on the deal in management fees, net underwriting fees, and commissions.

How did Walter Wriston rate the successful sale of the floating-rate notes?

"You do what you have to do in order to meet the conditions at the time," he said. "With certificates of deposit, for example. Demand deposits in the City of New York hadn't been growing for ten years so you didn't have to be too smart to figure out that New York was dead as the financial center unless something was done about it.

"CD's revolutionized—and it's not too strong a term—the American banking system. They put New York back on the map. At the time, that was responsive. The floating-rate note was in response to the fact that the market was terribly tight. There was a financial crunch of large proportions. And the financial community was not tapping what we perceived to be the largest market. So you say to yourself, what do we do? You drop your hose into a reservoir that's full of water when the one you're living in is empty. The answer was the consumer, and the question was what did the consumer want? He wanted a fair rate and he wasn't getting it."

The "proof of the pudding," Wriston went on, was that 82

percent of the floating-rate notes were sold to individuals rather than institutions. "Sixty thousand Americans bought them," he said. "Now they're sitting there getting 9.7 percent in a 5 percent market, which is not a bad deal."

In early 1975, Wriston was defensive about criticism that the buyers might not have gotten a good buy because rates were coming down rapidly and the guaranteed 9.7 rate would last only a few more months.

Obviously the buyers would not be in as good condition by midsummer when their guaranteed rate expired. Even in mid March, with the Treasury bill rate at 5.30 percent, and a widespread feeling that it might go lower still, it seemed likely that some investors would consider selling their notes and buying something that paid a higher yield. It would be another year before they could redeem their notes to Citicorp at the purchase price, although they could certainly trade them in the open bond markets in the meantime.

"Now that rates are drifting lower," Wriston said, "learned scholars in the newspapers are writing that probably it wasn't a good idea [for investors to buy them]. They completely overlook the point that I make to the personal investor that the notes have to sell at par. It's nice to have a 9 percent note in a 5 percent market, but it's not so nice to have a 5 percent note in a 9 percent market selling at 70 [i.e., $70 for $100 par value]. The consumer has an arithmetical certainty over time of always getting his money back in the marketplace at par."

In the aftermath of the Citicorp sale, it soon became evident that floating-rate notes were not going to sweep the country, sucking cash out of thrift institutions and cutting the legs out from under the housing industry.

Only one day after the Citicorp sale, indications already were growing that investor demand for the notes was waning. Brokers were saying that their customers' appetites for the notes were sated, and a number of other institutions that had planned to offer the public similar notes were beginning to have second thoughts.

By the end of August, there was no longer any doubt. Only $1.3

billion of the floating-rate notes had been sold, including the Citicorp issue, substantially less than had been originally announced by the half-dozen institutions offering them. Furthermore, for those deals that were still alive, interest rates had been sweetened considerably. Continental Illinois Corporation, for example, had to offer an initial yield of 10.3 percent, and even so, it was able to sell only $80 million in floating-rate notes. It had hoped to sell $125 million.

The reason for the saturation was two-fold. First the U.S. Treasury, early in August, had offered its own notes that paid 9 percent interest. It had sold the notes in minimum purchases of only $1,000, making them easily available to small investors. The result was that individuals had grabbed off $2.2 billion worth of the notes, making Citicorp's issue look like an also-ran, and putting an ironic face on the government's earlier opposition to the Citicorp issue.

Secondly, as institutional investors had known all along, some prime corporate bond issues were available with five-year maturities paying 9.7 percent or more, with minimum investments of only $1,000 required. In addition, other corporate bonds were available, with longer maturities paying 10 percent. The problem was that most small investors were not familiar with the bond markets and, therefore, tended to gravitate toward a few highly publicized offerings like the Citicorp issue or the big 9 percent Treasury offering.

As always, in a mammoth financial deal, the Citicorp offering had some bizarre aftereffects. The most tragic was the death of Tom Sanders, the Citicorp official who had labored so hard to prepare a prospectus that could pass the scrutiny of the SEC. Sanders was known to his associates at Citicorp as a man with enormous drive and energy, and as one who was demanding of his subordinates and of himself, a perfectionist in an imperfect world.

On Tuesday, January 14, 1975, Sanders's fifteen-year-old son, Gregg, ate dinner with his father and mother. After the meal, he took a two-foot ax and killed his father with several blows to the head, then killed his mother the same way. His father had been working on bank reports in the kitchen when he was struck from behind.

While Tom Sanders's fate was unrelated to the Citicorp note, another member of the financial community had misfortunes which were not nearly as serious, but which sprang directly from the Citicorp issue.

Early in 1975, Joseph Salowitz, a thirty-two-year-old ex-salesman for Merrill Lynch, found himself in hot water with both his firm and the New York Stock Exchange for letting his enthusiasm run away with him over the Citicorp issue.

Salowitz was fired by Merrill Lynch, reportedly for placing privately printed handbills promoting the Citicorp note on the windshields of cars parked in a Garden City, New York lot. The handbills contained Mr. Salowitz's home telephone number.

When Merrill Lynch found out about the self-styled promotion, it fired Salowitz, claiming he had violated company policies. The Big Board held a hearing on the matter. Salowitz, however, claimed that he no longer recognized the Exchange's jurisdiction over him because he had left the securities business.

"I'm not trying to escape any horrendous penalty," Salowitz told *The Wall Street Journal*'s Richard Rustin. "But, neither am I going to lie back and let them roll a steamroller over me. After all, for the kind of offense for which I was fired by Merrill Lynch, the Exchange probably would hand down a penalty like a year's suspension or something like that. But I intend to contest even the mildest censure. I would consider it verbal abuse against my character and good name."

After the curious sidelights were stripped away from the Citicorp transaction, several facts seemed clear. First, the bank had obtained an enormous amount of badly needed money at a time when offerings of notes were difficult at best. It successfully carried off the deal despite incredible opposition from Washington and a dismal market. Second, the notes had given small investors another means of participating in the high-yield markets of late 1974. And, even if those markets did not last very long, at least investors earned their 9.7 percent interest through the summer of

1975 when their yields were cut back to one percent above the Treasury bill rate. Third, the investment bankers once again pulled down their million-dollar fees, though they had not been the primary architects of the deal.

The most surprising aspect of the Citicorp affair was the fact that the investment bankers had so badly misjudged their own market. "The astonishing thing," Wriston said, "was that we knew the individual market better than some of the underwriters."

4 / The Lebanese Adventure

For more than a year, the *Intra Bank of Beirut, Lebanon's largest bank, had been closed, unable to meet withdrawals and without the cash to live up to its obligations. Relations between the United States and the Middle East were at a low. Then, on October 12, 1967, it was announced that a plan to revive the ailing bank had been worked out by Kidder, Peabody & Company, one of America's leading investment banking houses. The complex scheme required the cooperation of private financiers and governments, ranging from the U.S. Commodity Credit Corporation to Qatar, a tiny Persian-Gulf oil principality. Hours before the salvage plan was adopted, it almost foundered over the size of a fee for Kidder. But the end result for the investment banking firm was $2* *million, a lucrative advisory relationship with the restructured bank, and a promising toehold in the Middle East. Eight years later, a rejuvenated Intra would again occupy an important financial position in the Middle East. And, for a time, at the height of the Arab boycott of firms doing business with Israel, the salvaged bank would find itself at the vortex of a swirling controversy that involved several of the world's leading Jewish-dominated ·investment banks.*

George VonPeterffy hesitated for a moment as he stood in the hallway, facing the door of his fifth-floor room in the Phoenicia Hotel in Beirut, Lebanon. Curious, thought the thirty-six-year-old business school professor, that the door was ajar. It had been closed and locked when he left the room earlier.

He pushed into the room, looked quickly around, then stopped in shocked amazement. Sitting on the edge of his bed, leafing through papers in VonPeterffy's briefcase, was an official of the Middle East's largest and, at the moment, most embattled bank.

Only a few hours earlier, the man had been giving his impressions of the bank's problems to VonPeterffy, while a whirring tape recorder preserved the conversation. Now, he rose hastily, and after a few sharp words from VonPeterffy, fled to the hall, leaving only the question of what he had been seeking. The tapes? Private negotiating papers? Or had he simply been indulging his curiosity, as he had claimed, in the course of whiling away a few minutes waiting for VonPeterffy.

It was the fall of 1966, and VonPeterffy, who five years later was to serve as a Deputy Assistant Secretary of State, was on a highly sensitive and secretive mission for the investment banking firm of Kidder, Peabody & Company. That mission was to lead the young professor and his associates, one of them a former student of VonPeterffy's at Harvard named Roger Tamraz, into a morass of international intrigue involving telephone taps, fugitives from justice, and delicate, minuetlike negotiations with Middle Eastern rulers. At the end of a tense, and often frantic fourteen-month period, one of the biggest bank failures in history would be salvaged, and Kidder Peabody would walk away with a fee of more than $2 million, after performing one of the most speculative international investment banking deals of the decade.

The crisis had begun on October 14, 1966, when Intra Bank of Lebanon suddenly closed its doors. As the largest bank in the Middle East, Intra, during the fifteen years of its existence, had become the pillar of the Arab financial world. Like a Roman candle, it had risen from nowhere, performed spectacularly as it accumulated deposits of nearly $250 million and assets of $500 million, and then plummeted earthward, mired in confusion and controversy. The failure of the bank had come close to dragging the entire economy of Lebanon down with it. In the ensuing days, Yusif Bedas, the flamboyant chairman of Intra Bank, had fled to Brazil, leaving behind him a tangled and nearly incomprehensible skein of dealings that would take months, and in some cases years, to unravel.

For Lebanon, which had become a repository for money from oil sheiks and capitalists in nearby Egypt, Syria, Iraq, Kuwait, and Qatar, the situation had been perilous. If Intra Bank failed it would mean a crisis of confidence in the nation's banking institutions, and a mortal blow to the country's emergence as the financial capital of the Arab world. One thing was certain. Fast action was necessary. Intra Bank must be saved. The only question was how to accomplish the rescue.

Roger Tamraz was the first Kidder Peabody employee to arrive in Beirut. Tamraz, a Lebanese national born in Cairo in 1940 of Lebanese parents, spoke fluent Arabic. After graduating from the Harvard Business School, he had briefly held a research fellowship. Then he had joined Kidder as a junior officer in the firm's international department, partly on the recommendation of his former professor, VonPeterffy. With barely time enough to learn the names of his new associates, he had been sent to Beirut to assess the Intra Bank failure.

The scene Tamraz found in the capital was one of almost unparalleled confusion. For three days, every Lebanese-owned bank in the capital had been closed. When they reopened, depositors hurriedly withdrew a total of $35 million, for fear they might lose it permanently. Business dropped off sharply as Lebanese merchants, now without credit, were forced to rely on cash. Restaurants in the city were nearly empty, and the gambling casinos fell idle. The stock exchange closed for three days. The headline in one Beirut newspaper said that an "earthquake" had hit the city.

Investment banks, like nations, prefer to have their own men on the scene to collect and sort information and to advance their interests. Although Kidder Peabody had had no previous involvement with Intra, it recognized the opportunities provided by a $500 million institution in trouble. Tamraz moved quickly around Beirut and made his assessment. There was value in Intra. It needed help. Perhaps Kidder Peabody could provide that assistance and in the process earn a sizeable fee as well as establish an entrée to the Middle East. He cabled his findings to the United States, setting off a chain of events that would lead ultimately to the reorganization of the bank.

Tamraz's report laid a serious problem squarely before Kidder's senior partners. Since he was a newcomer to the firm, and only in his mid-twenties, he could hardly be expected to make a mature judgment based on sketchy experience. Why not have his professor, VonPeterffy, fly to Beirut, meet with Tamraz, and make his own assessment? Then Kidder could decide whether to proceed.

At 4 P.M. on a Saturday afternoon in mid November, as he was preparing for eighteen dinner guests to arrive later that evening, VonPeterffy received a phone call. It was Chris Boland, head of Kidder's international department on the wire. He told VonPeterffy that Tamraz had been sent to Beirut to analyze the Intra Bank situation. Kidder was apprehensive about the wisdom of sending Tamraz, Boland said. If the firm decided not to become involved with Intra, and that fact became known, it might prejudice others against the Lebanese bank. The word would be out that a major American banking house had refused to help in the rescue.

Secondly, Boland told VonPeterffy, Kidder didn't know the first thing about the Middle East. He said that although Tamraz was a bright young man, he was not familiar with Kidder's techniques and requirements. He was inexperienced in international business affairs, and Kidder simply didn't have the confidence that it ought to be involving itself in Intra Bank on the basis of Tamraz's recommendation.

Finally, there was the overriding necessity for speed. If Kidder was to steal a march on its competition it had to move quickly and decisively to make an appraisal.

VonPeterffy was intrigued. As the son of a diplomat closely acquainted with the ruling families in the Middle East, he was aware that as a professor he could poke around Beirut while camouflaging, at least on the surface, the fact that Kidder Peabody was involved.

After talking to Boland, VonPeterffy decided he would like to help with Intra Bank. But there was a problem. He still had classes to teach, and Harvard did not take kindly to professors who left their students without an instructor. The professor talked to his dean, George Baker, and Baker called Secretary of State Dean Rusk. Was the mission critical enough to disrupt the school's routine? Rusk verified the importance of the salvage operation and Baker gave VonPeterffy his blessing.

Without even enough money in his pocket to hire a taxi, VonPeterffy collected $78 from his guests as they arrived for dinner, and a few dollars more from his wife. He sped to Logan Airport and caught a Pan American flight to Beirut, arriving there Sunday evening. Tamraz met him at the airport, and the two men went directly to the home of Najib Salha, a prominent Beirut businessman who had been a director of Intra Bank and had an interest in its ultimate disposition.

Salha, who had been left in charge of Intra Bank's affairs when Bedas fled, told VonPeterffy and Tamraz that he suspected the Central Bank of Lebanon had participated in a campaign to sabotage Intra Bank. One piece of evidence he produced was a leaflet, distributed in Beirut, which predicted that the bank was going to fail. Salha said that by such techniques pressures had been built up which resulted in the Central Bank's withholding funds from Intra at the time of the liquidity crisis.

When Intra had gone to the Central Bank with its negotiable

securities, the Central Bank had given Intra 5 percent and then suddenly cut off any further funds without warning. Therefore, when the run on Intra had begun, the bank found itself without sufficient cash to handle withdrawals.

VonPeterffy found that Salha was enthusiastic about Kidder Peabody coming into the picture, but the sorry state of Intra Bank ledger books available for study dismayed him. Some books were unintelligible, he said, while others were poorly kept. After perusing the few ledgers that were available, and talking with several other officials and employees of Intra Bank, VonPeterffy concluded that Tamraz's initial assessment that the bank was salvageable had been correct.

After his twenty-eight-hour investigation, VonPeterffy decided he knew enough about the situation to return to the United States and make his report. Arriving at the offices of Kidder Peabody in Manhattan, he told Boland and other Kidder officials that he thought they should take a crack at solving the Intra situation. Under cross-examination he defended his recommendation. How, he was asked, could he conclude that the project was feasible, after just twenty-eight hours of study and no thorough analysis of the books? VonPeterffy conceded that the books were all in Arabic, and that a comprehensive study of them would take three or four months. "The reason I'm making this recommendation," he said, "is that the people I've seen out there, the ones Bedas left behind, are reputable people. You don't have a situation that is fraught with crookedness and embezzlement. And you don't have people trying to cover up their crimes. If you had that—unreliable people with split interests and conflicts of interests, people who were trying to save their own skins—then I wouldn't urge this on you. But I do urge it on you in this case because it is fundamentally a simple illiquidity situation."

After receiving the reports from VonPeterffy and Tamraz, the Kidder Peabody brass decided it was time for a more senior official to enter the picture. So Richard F. Coons, a forty-year-old vice-president of Kidder, flew to Beirut. VonPeterffy also was asked to return to Lebanon for the comprehensive study.

Coons was co-manager of Kidder's corporate finance department and a member of its executive committee. In the months ahead, he would make many of the final decisions on Intra Bank, based partly on recommendations from Tamraz and from Von-Peterffy, who would continue to act as a consultant for Kidder.

When Coons arrived in Lebanon, he, too, discovered that little information was available aside from the published annual reports of the bank. Unfortunately, the reports were short on figures and the kind of detailed financial information that bankers need to work with.

Coons surreptitiously began to interview the officials who had been involved with the bank, to try to piece together a picture of what had caused the collapse, and what might be done to put the institution back on its feet.

Kidder's three representatives were extremely cautious about making their presence in Beirut known, and Coons, Tamraz and VonPeterffy all spent a good deal of time dodging the press.

They took elaborate precautions to avoid being seen. They were careful not to carry papers from Kidder Peabody with them—nothing to identify them in any business way. They paid for everything in cash, left no checks and no records. They registered under their real names, but gave no company reference. Clearly, they did not want either their competitors or the authorities in Lebanon to know precisely what had been discovered, or what recommendations they were making to their superiors in New York.

VonPeterffy's recollections of the period are especially vivid. "We checked frequently with New York," he said, "but the communications were unreliable out of Beirut. Other people were listening in."

U.S. Embassy officials gave the Kidder representatives a list of people who were tracking their cables. Two of the unseen monitors were bank officials, and another was from the Lebanese government. "When they told me about the Telex," VonPeterffy said, "they added, 'You've got to be very careful about telephones here, because it's very easy to listen in!' They said every room in the St. George is bugged."

When Coons learned that his Telex messages were being monitored, he flew to Rome to make a sensitive telephone call and VonPeterffy did the same thing on a subsequent trip there.

"What we were afraid of," VonPeterffy said, "was the political opponents of Bedas—I don't mean political in the Democratic-Republican sense—but in terms of the commercial world out there; his competitors in the banking industry, many of whom were also politicians. They might have been able to block us by passing a law or by intriguing against us before we had announced any agreement to step in."

Instrumental to Kidder's involvement was Salha. He was trying to stave off Intra's biggest creditors, and in some cases to get them to deposit more money in Intra so it could stay afloat. One of those creditors was the tiny sheikdom of Kuwait, the bank's largest single depositor, with about $35 million.

Coons held a clandestine meeting with Salha in a VIP lounge in the back of the Beirut airport, on the very day Salha returned from important meetings in Kuwait. In the lounge Coons gave Salha a hasty sales pitch on how he thought Kidder Peabody could help Intra. Salha listened but did not commit himself.

As the Kidder team continued to check out rumors and interview the bank's officials, it began to piece together a number of scenarios of the Intra collapse. One version was that high European interest rates had siphoned off Intra's deposits in the weeks immediately preceding the crisis. Another story was that the Lebanese government had suggested to Intra that it was too heavily invested in European overseas ventures and should put more of its cash into local enterprises. When Intra spurned the suggestion it supposedly triggered political reprisals.

At any rate, the problem had been exacerbated when wealthy Arabs from nearby Saudi Arabia and Kuwait withdrew millions of dollars from Intra. Bedas went abroad frantically looking for new deposits to replace those he had lost. Then, as word of Intra's troubles leaked out, small depositors began a run on the bank and by October 14, a panic had begun. Before the doors could be closed, $70 million had been withdrawn.

Bedas later complained bitterly that he had been victimized by his enemies in Saudi Arabia, and that the Central Bank in Lebanon had not given Intra the support it needed to weather the financial storm.

Having ferreted out these explanations of the Intra collapse, Kidder's next step was to convince the parties controlling the bank that it should be allowed to participate in the salvage. One person who was helpful was Dwight Porter, U.S. ambassador to Lebanon.

VonPeterffy said Porter briefed Lebanese officials on Kidder Peabody, giving the firm a high recommendation. "It was exactly the kind of thing that some ambassadors argue they can't do, because they don't want to favor one American investment bank over another."

While Kidder Peabody had plenty of competitors nosing around Intra Bank, some American financiers stayed on their own side of the Atlantic. Many Wall Street investment bankers had ties with the Jewish community, and were simply not interested in an Arab project. Kidder's WASP orientation, on the other hand, meant the firm could move into the Middle East more easily than some of its competitors. "What did they have to lose?" said one Wall Streeter. "They didn't have to worry about offending Jewish clients and contacts."

There were banks beside Kidder Peabody, of course, that were interested in breathing life into the big Middle East bank, or at least in getting control of some of its assets. Intra had several attractive European investments, most notably in France, where it owned a big shipyard near Marseilles. It also owned one of the biggest single pieces of real estate on the Champs Élysées in Paris, a building on Manhattan's Fifth Avenue, and a variety of other enterprises ranging from movie studios to cement plants.

The plum, though, was Middle East Airlines, controlled by Intra Bank. Stavros Niarchos, the Greek shipping magnate whose archrival, Aristotle Onassis, owned Olympic Airways, eyed the big Lebanese airline hungrily.

One deal that was provisionally worked out would have seen Niarchos participating in a refinancing of Intra along with the government of Kuwait, which was to lend the bank up to $60 million. The plan was aborted, however, as were a number of other preliminary proposals.

Meanwhile, two new developments began to affect the rescue. First, formal audits of Intra were completed and made available. Second, investigators reported that large and sometimes questionable loans had been made to the directors and to big shareholders of the bank.

The major thrust of the reports, however, was a confirmation that Intra's biggest problem had been its inability to liquidate assets at a time when money was volatile and cash was needed to cope with major withdrawals. Intra had value, the reports said, but it lay frozen in real estate and corporate enterprises, whereas it was cash that was needed to handle the withdrawals that had begun early in September and ended abruptly when Intra closed its door on October 14.

With the auditors' reports available, pressure grew for a solution to Intra's problems. Salha, Intra's new chief, began negotiating a $14 million loan agreement with Kuwait, and at the same time Intra started to pay off its small depositors—those with accounts of $1,500 or less—whose funds had been frozen when the bank closed.

Kidder officials also stepped up their activity. Early in December, Coons, who had flown back to New York, returned to Beirut for further discussions. He then spent several days visiting large banks in London and Paris to enlist their aid in his project. Finally, on January 3, 1967, Kidder Peabody in New York received a letter from the Lebanese finance minister stating that he would welcome the firm's help in reviving Intra. The letter was received one day before the courts in Beirut were to have declared Intra bankrupt and rejected the bank's request for a three-year grace period to settle its obligations. Later, a brief grace period would be allowed. The letter was not a commitment, but it was the first official sign that Kidder's efforts were bearing fruit.

Shortly after Kidder received the letter, the Lebanese Parliament went into a special late-night session to debate a law that would give Intra Bank a six-month breathing spell. On January 10 the law passed, sparing Intra from bankruptcy proceedings by setting aside the earlier court decision. Instead, Parliament asked the courts to remove the bank's directors and to appoint a new management committee representing shareholders, depositors, the court itself, and the Central Bank of Lebanon.

In the face of growing political pressure to isolate the blame for the bank's collapse, a number of arrests were being made. A warrant was issued for the arrest of Bedas, the bank's founder, who had fled shortly before Intra closed in mid October. In addition, four auditors of the firm of Saba & Company, who had signed an audit of the bank's books before it closed, were arrested. They were charged with having approved an inaccurate budget. Five days later, two of the bank's assistant general managers and its chief accountant were also arrested.

The major activity, however, revolved around Intra's future rather than its past.

"There were a lot of people working behind the scenes, and a lot of them were working against the United States because they didn't want us, an American group, getting control of Intra Bank," Coons said. "That was a big problem because the Israeli war had just ended, and the sentiment against the United States was very high at this point. So, we had an uphill fight. Eventually, the Embassy decided they would do what they could to help us, but that isn't always helpful, because the more it looks like they're for you, perhaps the more it looks like it's an American national interest as opposed to a private firm. So, we had to be very careful about how much we associated with the Embassy."

Another problem that the Kidder team had to cope with was the number of Lebanese consultants who had the proper connections, asking fees of hundreds of thousands of dollars for their services.

By now, Kidder had decided on the broad outlines of its plan. Its biggest immediate problem was to get the cooperation of the Kuwaitis and the Commodity Credit Corporation (CCC), a U.S. government agency that was a large creditor. The objective was to persuade these big creditors to leave their funds in the bank rather than pressing for a full and immediate refund. Then the bank could be restructured, and the creditors would receive pro-rated shares of whatever resulted.

"The general idea," VonPeterffy said, "was to get the Commodity Credit Corporation to say, 'We won't present our notes for the $22 million on demand for immediate payment because if we, as major creditors, join with the Kuwaitis and the other major creditors in agreeing to reorganization and structuring under Kidder Peabody leadership, we stand to get more out of this deal in the long run than we do by following such a course.' "

In the end, it would be the willingness of the CCC, the Kuwaiti government, and the other major creditors to take notes in return for their deposits that would enable the rescue to succeed.

As Kidder pursued its plan, it stepped up the number of personal visits paid to the principals. One of the most important visits was made by Roger Tamraz to Salem el Sabah, the emir of Kuwait, who had a claim of $25 million on Intra Bank.

Arabic discussions are seldom brief and to the point, and Tamraz spent about an hour and a half with the emir in a typically Middle Eastern negotiating session. He listened to Arabic sayings and fables, talked in Arabic about the weather, politics, the Americans, and the Arabs. Finally, the emir discussed his reaction to the Kidder proposal for Intra Bank, which involved giving the depositors shares of stock instead of the cash they had deposited.

"His reaction," said Tamraz, "was 'I'm a Bedouin from the desert. I prefer to hold a camel's tail and know he's there in my hands, to holding a piece of paper that claims to have so much value behind it.' " It was hyperbole, of course, but Tamraz had to convince the emir that it was to his benefit to hold onto his claim rather than press for immediate liquidation.

In addition to making personal visits to the large creditors, Kidder began receiving more factual information. In January it had asked Cooper Brothers & Company, a London accounting firm, to audit Intra's books. However, Cooper Brothers hedged by saying that when it began its examination on January 3, many of the Intra files were still under the control of the courts. Access was not obtained to most of these until the middle of January. Furthermore, the firm was unable to obtain most of the records from Intra's head office in Ras Beirut until about the same time. In any event, the resulting 142-page report provided Kidder with its first inside look at the bank's turbulent affairs.

There were other difficulties as well. "In the absence of Mr. Y.K. Bedas, the chief accountant of Intra Beirut," the report said, "Mr. Ayoub is the only person who is familiar with the more important transactions of the bank. But he was arrested two days after our arrival. Several of the files which are stated to be under the control of Mr. Ayoub have still not been located."

Bedas, of course, could provide the key to Intra's problems, but he was never to do so. In mid January he was arrested in São Paulo, Brazil, following a request for extradition by the Lebanese government which had tracked him down. Having suffered a heart attack shortly before his arrest, he was released while the extradition request was being processed, only to flee again, this time to Switzerland.

His presence in Switzerland might have gone undetected but for a bizarre incident in Lucerne. Bedas had forgotten to turn off the lights of his car while parked in front of the Lucerne post office, drawing the attention of the local police. At the time, he was traveling with a Brazilian passport, but a Swiss policeman who spoke Portuguese became suspicious when the supposed Brazilian couldn't understand his native tongue.

Bedas was arrested, but again temporarily released for the same reason: He had fallen ill. On November 29, 1968, Bedas died in a private hospital near Lucerne of cancer of the pancreas.

Bedas, who was fifty-three when his bank collapsed, had been one of the most flamboyant and controversial bankers in the Middle East. The son of a Russian-born school administrator, he had been born in Jerusalem and had joined Barclays Bank there at the age of sixteen. By the time he was twenty-one, Bedas had been named manager of the exchange department of the Palestinian Barclays Bank. He was later named general manager of the Arab

Bank, but in May 1948, when the Arab-Israeli war broke out, he fled to Beirut, arriving penniless.

With three friends, he had rented a small two-room apartment and borrowed a few hundred Lebanese pounds from former customers of the Arab Bank. In one room of their apartment, he and his friends opened a tiny exchange office, using the other room as their kitchen and bedroom. Bedas later said that because he had nothing, he had to give a great name to his business, calling it International Traders. In the four succeeding years, he and his friends attracted capital of over a quarter of a million dollars. In 1952 Bedas expanded his foreign exchange operation into a full-fledged commercial bank. He called his new firm Intra Bank, the cable address of the old International Traders.

Working in Bedas's favor was Lebanon's emergence as a banker for the oil sheiks. Some of the money they deposited was invested in Lebanese ventures. Some was funneled abroad, too, so the business expanded to France, Italy, Switzerland, Germany, Great Britain, the United States, Africa, and Brazil. All this, of course, was before the crash, Bedas's flight, and his death.

Even without Bedas, Kidder Peabody continued to make progress on its plan for Intra. Having received the report from Cooper Brothers, Kidder prepared a memorandum on February 8 outlining the steps it had taken and the competition it faced.

The memo revealed that the bank's officers still faced a complex situation. Hard choices had to be made. There were the strictly Lebanese sources of capital that could be sought to refinance the bank. There were a number of broad international proposals which had been tendered. And there were the outsiders who were interested in acquiring only specific assets of the bank. In effect, they wanted to pick the bones.

Kidder's conclusions were predictable: (1) a purely Lebanese recapitalization was not feasible; (2) Kidder Peabody should figure prominently in any of the international plans under study.

Interest by outsiders still centered on Middle East Airlines. It came from the Niarchos group, from Aristotle Onassis, and from two U.S. parties—National Airlines and the Ludwig Shipping interests. In addition, some of the big commercial banks that had cross-deposits with Intra were keeping a close eye on the situation. They included the Chase Manhattan Bank and the Bank of America.

One of the biggest initial stumbling blocks for Kidder was the U.S. government. The CCC had become a major creditor of Intra's when it extended credit to the Lebanese to buy surplus American grain. More than anything else, the CCC wanted its money back. At the same time, the State Department's main objective was to maintain good relations with the Lebanese.

"You'd think the two were compatible, but they weren't really because the CCC had to take a rather hard line," Coons said. "They were businessmen. The State Department was not acting as businessmen but as politicians, so we had problems even within the official U.S. group on how we should approach the problem."

Ultimately that problem was resolved in favor of the Kidder approach, and as the other major creditors began to fall into line, it became evident that the restructuring plan might be adopted. In September 1967, the committee overseeing Intra Bank decided that the Kidder plan was workable and full-scale negotiations began. Within a month an agreement would be signed, but first there were a number of problems to be resolved.

One of the major difficulties concerned the amount of money Kidder should be paid. The firm had worked out a schedule of fees that totaled $3,170,000, and it was holding to its decision despite pressures to lower the fee.

VonPeterffy, still acting as a consultant to Kidder, advised a hard line. "I said, put it to them, and if they don't buy it, turn around and walk out. They had to do something about that bank within the year, or it would have been liquidated by the government. So I said, they'll come back to you if nobody else surfaces. Hold your conditions."

Kidder held fast, and a ten-day siege of intensive negotiations began. Tension rose and so did tempers as the deadline approached. Finally, it was midnight on liquidation day.

"It literally meant stopping the clock," Coons said, "because the bank was being taken over by receivers if something wasn't signed."

Unable to break the impasse, Kidder signed for a $100,000 down payment, with the major fee to be negotiated. For the next six months, valuable time was spent arguing about the fee instead of working on the project.

Finally, the question of the fee was resolved, though not before a last dramatic round of high-level haggling. Kuwait had balked at Kidder's demand for $3.2 million, and at its insistence, the Kidder executives explained their case to an American who served as an independent financial advisor to Kuwait. He was a highly regarded former head of an international financial institution, an experienced financier, who served on the boards of directors of many American companies. Ironically, he was also a good friend of Kidder's senior partner, Albert Gordon.

"I met with him," Coons said, "and went through the history of how we had gotten into it [the Intra Bank salvage], what the problems were, and what manpower we were going to have to devote to it. He said, 'Well, it's an interesting story. I think it's very imaginative work, but your fee is exactly a million dollars too high.' "

Coons realized there would be no court of appeal. "Once he told that to the Kuwaitis, you know, you couldn't get it back. So he cost us a million dollars. I'm still smarting over it."

VonPeterffy, too, was angered by the decision. "That was a real blow in the groin for Roger Tamraz," he said, "because it absolutely riddled his credibility with the Lebanese."

But the attention of most of the financial world was focused not on the matter of Kidder's compensation, but on the form that the newly restructured Intra Bank was to take.

Kidder's basic plan was to turn the bank upside down. In the past, Intra had been more of an investment company than a bank anyway, putting most of its deposits into long-term investments, such as the Champs Élysées property, shipyards, a casino, and hotel facilities.

Kidder decided that Intra should be transformed into an investment company. It should own all its assets as an investor, and one of the investments should be the commercial bank, although sharply scaled down. The plan was to turn the depositors of the old Intra Bank into shareholders. Two institutions would result. One was the bank, to be called Bank al Mashrek. The other was the Intra Investment Company. Later, the commercial bank would be 40 percent owned by Morgan Guaranty of New York, 40 percent owned by the old major shareholders, and 20 percent owned by the public.

The investment company was to be owned by the original depositors and by the public, although in neither case were there to be shares that were traded on the open market. Morgan would run the bank, and Kidder would continue to act as a consultant to the investment company.

One year after Intra Bank crashed, Kidder's plan to salvage it was formally accepted. The new investment company was capitalized at about $75 million. The U.S. government participated through the CCC, to the extent of $22 million, becoming the second largest shareholder in the new company. The largest stockholder was the government of Kuwait, which along with private Kuwaiti investors, had deposits of about $42 million in Intra when it failed. The third largest stockholder was the Lebanese government, to whom Intra owed $17 million.

As for the smaller depositors and creditors, they were to be paid half their claims in cash over a three-year period, with the remaining half paid in stock.

Finally, in late December 1967, Intra Bank reopened the doors to nine of its twelve branches. Depositors crowded into its branches, and at the main office in Beirut, police were called in to control the lines. Initially, each depositor could withdraw 15 percent of his deposits. This was made possible partly because the Bank of Lebanon had authorized a $6.6-million credit for Intra Bank. The loan was covered by guarantees of securities in the newly formed investment company.

By late 1968, Kidder had been involved with Intra Bank for two years. Coons, Tamraz, and VonPeterffy took stock of what they had accomplished. It amounted to a sizeable pile of reports, including portfolio analyses, recommendations for diversification, management studies, a separate analysis of Middle East Airlines, and an organization plan for the new management company.

Despite the initial work, however, it was clear that the job of transforming Intra into a smoothly functioning organization was only beginning. One report submitted by an Intra man in Beirut contained some devastating criticism of the way the revived company was run during its early months. It said the banking section was having little luck attracting new depositors and gave poor management as the reason. Day-to-day decisions were not being made and staff members were getting little or no guidance.

Another source of concern was the reluctance of the financial community to accept Intra Bank. As months passed, it became clear that the crash that had brought down Intra Bank in 1966 would not quickly be forgotten by the big international financial houses, especially in London, Paris, and the United States.

One internal report on the newly opened bank said the attitude toward Intra had been especially cool in the United States. Similarly, the report said, several of the world's leading commercial banks had been cautious. "Barclays, our clearing bankers in London, have behaved as if embarrassed with our account, and the Bank of America and Chase Manhattan are naturally apprehensive in view of our attitude over the settlement of accounts with them. They have both refused to enter into correspondent relationships with us. Local offices of foreign banks have also been antagonized by delays in our repaying their loans, and their head offices have obviously not received favorable reports on Intra from them."

The report concluded that there were eighty foreign banks waiting for settlement of claims totaling less than $112,000 which had been outstanding for more than two years. "Ten months after reopening, we continue to stall off their steady stream of inquiry letters because agreement to pay them has not yet been achieved. This is not the disgrace of the old regime, of which so much criticism is quite rightly made, but of the new regime which is so surprised to find that it does not enjoy the confidence of other banks."

Neither the voluminous reports prepared by Kidder nor the new leadership at the bank had provided for an assessment of the staff and internal corporate practices. Only one staff member had completed examinations given by a professional banking institution, and only one other had wide banking experience. There was no internal training program, and no encouragement was given the staff to study. There was no salary scale, but tremendously wide discrepancies in pay which could not conceivably be justified by differences in efficiency or responsibilities. The branch manager in charge of the Amman office, with a staff of twelve persons, had an income of about $26,000 a year plus a free car. By contrast, the manager of another office employing seven persons received only one-ninth of the Amman manager's pay. The manager in London, who employed ten persons and had forty-five years of banking experience, earned only $10,000, two-fifths of the Amman manager's salary, and had no free car.

Staff members arrived late and left early, with only minimal supervision. "Morale of the staff is very low indeed," a report stated. "The complete absence of any leadership and the uncertainty of the last two years can be expected to have created a bad atmosphere, but one cannot condone the quarreling which goes on, the jockeying for position, etc., which kills any effort to develop a team spirit, and is sickening to live with. Some personnel are in entrenched positions which they are anxious to protect, even to the extent of never taking leave, and some tremendous backlogs of leave have been built up which should never have been allowed.

"Some employees are known to have other jobs, even jobs concerning other banks, and there are known to be persons drawing a salary who do not attend the office (a dozen, it is said). Outside pressures interfere in staff matters. There were cases recently of two girls employed on probation who proved to be unsatisfactory, but could not be discharged at the end of the probationary period because of outside pressures to keep them."

Despite the personnel problems and the difficulties in attracting new depositors and winning back old friends, the bank and the new investment company began to inch back toward profitability. Costs were cut, new programs instituted, and liquidity improved.

In May 1972, Intra was confident enough to grant an interview to *The Wall Street Journal*'s Ray Vicker, who concluded that Intra was staging a sharp turnaround. The biggest contributor to the improved financial picture had been 66 percent Intra-owned Middle East Airlines, which earned $5 million in 1971, while most of the other major holdings of the company had lost money. As for the bank, its deposits at that point totaled $15 million, giving it only a shadow of its former influence. But it was open and doing business. The rescue operation had prevented Intra's assets from being sold off piecemeal to the highest bidder, and it enabled the bank to continue operating as a viable financial institution.

The investment company issued its annual report to a meeting of shareholders in December 1972. Net assets stood at $122 million. The capital position of the company had been strengthened, partly because it had sold off its three prime lots of real estate on the Champs Élysées to the governments of Kuwait, Qatar, and Lebanon, all of them major Intra stockholders.

The original U.S. share of 15 percent in Intra Investment had been pared in half by the sale of Canada House in New York, which formerly had been owned by Intra.

What did the Americans who created Intra Investment think of the hornet's nest they had stepped into? For VonPeterffy the project had been almost melodramatic. He saw the Intra collapse as having set Lebanon's development as a financial capital back twenty-five years. What's more, it had sent shock waves through the entire Middle East.

"It's just as if Chase Manhattan started to get into trouble, went to the Treasury and said 'Please give us the cash so we can stave off a run on the bank.' The Treasury said 'no,' and the Chase Bank declared itself bankrupt. When you think of compensating balances and correspondent relationships with other banks in Lebanon, the whole banking system in Lebanon was called into question. It was sheer idiocy on the part of the financial authorities in

Lebanon and on the part of the government, which could have stepped in, but didn't."

For Coons, the memory of having had to grapple with Middle Eastern politics was strong, as was the feeling that the Intra Bank deal had given Kidder Peabody its first real foothold in the Middle East.

"It was politically very sensitive in Lebanon," he said. "The Kuwaitis and Lebanese were getting pretty mad at each other because the bank had collapsed, and the Kuwaitis blamed the Lebanese for not having a better central banking system. So there were a lot of political undercurrents. It wasn't just an investment banking transaction. It was definitely getting into the realm of international politics—power plays, Middle Eastern politics, which are unique in themselves."

In the mid 1960s, when Kidder first became involved with Intra Bank, it had virtually no expertise in the Middle East. It was considered a reputable, if somewhat cautious investment banking house, one of the top two dozen U.S. firms in terms of capital. One of its strong points was the private placement of securities with institutional investors such as insurance companies and pension funds, as well as with large individual investors.

Founded in 1865, the firm's modern fortunes had been guided by Albert Gordon. He had started his Wall Street career as a statistician with Goldman Sachs, but had joined Kidder in 1931 as a senior partner.

As an underwriting firm, Kidder had its glory days during the late 1800s and early 1900s. It had offered a series of securities issues of the American Telephone and Telegraph Company, and had acted as New England manager for all the negotiated under-written issues of the telephone company and its subsidiaries after about 1899.

The firm fell on hard times in the early thirties, due partly to declining prices of some securities it owned, and partly to the withdrawal of big deposits by the Italian government. However, money to save the firm was raised, and by the mid thirties, it had begun to prosper. By 1955, Kidder had risen again to a major position on Wall Street.

Despite Kidder Peabody's generally good reputation, the firm was not immune from censure. Late in 1972, the Securities and Exchange Commission cited Kidder for failing to properly supervise its salesmen to prevent violations of antifraud laws. The citation, which Kidder did not contest, charged that the firm had allocated stock in new issues to an official from the state of Washington, who had been responsible for the purchase and sale of securities for various state funds. Like most white-collar fraud cases, this one quickly dropped from sight and Kidder went on about its business with only the tiniest dent in its reputation.

In mid 1973, however, the firm was briefly drawn into an abortive transaction that could have mushroomed into a major cause célèbre if it had been successful.

The incident was disclosed as a federal Grand Jury in New York was investigating Robert L. Vesco, a controversial financier charged with violating campaign contribution laws in an attempt to influence the Nixon administration. The Grand Jury was considering evidence that later would result in the indictments of Vesco, and two high Nixon administration officials—John N. Mitchell, who had served as Nixon's attorney general and campaign director, and Maurice Stans, who was Nixon's Secretary of Commerce and chief fund raiser.*

Reports were published that Presidential aide John D. Ehrlichman, who resigned from his White House post in the heat of the Watergate scandal, had promised to help Vesco buy the U.S. government's remaining interest in Intra.

According to one report, in the spring of 1972 Ehrlichman met

---

*Mitchell and Stans were found innocent in a jury trial. Mitchell, however, was convicted in a separate trial of perjury and conspiracy to obstruct justice in the Watergate scandal, and was subsequently disbarred from practicing law in New York State. Stans pleaded guilty in a separate case to violating federal campaign laws in the Nixon reelection campaign and was fined $5,000.

with associates of Vesco. The meeting occurred within weeks of the time that Vesco, who employed a nephew of President Nixon, had given $200,000 in cash for the President's reelection campaign. The meeting also came at a time when Vesco was in serious trouble with the Securities and Exchange Commission. It was later disclosed that the SEC had omitted from a charge against Vesco the fact that he had contributed the $200,000 to the Nixon campaign. That disclosure led to the resignation of G. Bradford Cook, who only a few months earlier had been named head of the SEC.

The purpose of the meeting between Vesco's associates and Ehrlichman reportedly was to persuade the Presidential assistant to give Vesco a good reference in Lebanon, thus aiding him in his purchase of Intra. Ehrlichman was said to have agreed to call an American Embassy official in Lebanon, although he subsequently denied that he had made any calls on Vesco's behalf.

What was not revealed at the time was that Kidder Peabody was also involved, if only briefly, in the Vesco offer. According to VonPeterffy, Vesco had approached Kidder in Beirut about the possibility of buying Intra, and also had contacted Intra directly.

The approach was unsuccessful and Vesco's $20 million offer was turned down, perhaps because he had become so controversial. But the episode had become yet another sidelight in the complex Intra story.

By late 1974, the bank's retrenchment was complete, although as noted, its operations outside Lebanon had been sharply reduced. As for the investment company, the original shareholders' claims had amounted to about $16 for each share they were given. At the close of 1974, those same shares were valued at about $11 a share, though they were not publicly traded.

Who then had profited from the salvage?

One winner was Roger Tamraz. He left Kidder Peabody in mid 1974 to become chairman of The First Arabian Corporation, which was based in Luxembourg and had offices in Saudi Arabia, Egypt, Kuwait, Lebanon, and New York. In his new position he helped fashion one of the most dramatic financial deals to spring from the Middle East in the mid 1970s. It was the Shah of Iran's offer to pay up to $175 million for the reopening of a Lockheed Aircraft Corporation production line, and to buy ten of the company's $55-million military cargo planes.

Another big winner appeared to be Kidder Peabody, with its fee of $2 million and its new foothold in the Middle East. In the months following the Intra venture, Kidder successfully bid on a number of Middle East projects, the largest being construction of a $380 million Suez-Mediterranean oil pipeline. In that deal Kidder acted as financial agent in putting together the required equity and loan capital from Arab oil countries and the United States Export-Import Bank.

Kidder's other new projects included the reorganization of a group of Kuwaiti fishing companies, and the floating of a $50 million bond issue for Egyptair, with Arab money being subscribed to purchase six Boeing 707 airliners.

As 1975 began, the Middle East was a tinder box. An uneasy cease-fire kept the military forces of Israel and its encircling enemies on constant alert. A massive arms build-up was taking place, and American financiers were maintaining a steady shuttle between Wall Street and the capitals of the Middle East as they helped to foster both the weapons build-up and the more general industrial boom.

Especially attractive was the flow of cash pouring out of such countries as Iran and Saudi Arabia into the pockets of industrialists and bankers all over the world. A five-fold increase in the price of oil had given the Persian Gulf States undreamed-of revenue, and as a result, they were buying everything from steel mills to automobile tires.

So powerful was the lure of the petrodollar that a number of major figures from the Nixon administration were drawn to it. John B. Connally, a former Treasury Secretary, who would be acquitted of bribery charges after a dramatic trial in the spring of 1975, represented Roger Tamraz's First Arabian Corporation.

William P. Rogers, an ex-Secretary of State, represented the Shah of Iran's Pahlevi Foundation, which was aggressively buying up real estate in the United States. Former Attorney General Richard G. Kleindienst, who had pleaded guilty to misleading officials in the ITT affair, was working in Washington for Algerian oil inter-ests. And Spiro Agnew, who had been forced to resign from the Vice-Presidency in disgrace, was reported to be soliciting business with Arab countries.

The sudden creation of a vast pool of petrodollars presented both opportunities and problems for American businessmen and financiers. In the past, they had treated Israel as their premier market for American goods in the Middle East. Now they were scrambling to sign multimillion-dollar contracts with the Arab countries and with Iran.

Because such business was being transacted against an emotion-ally charged backdrop of political infighting and international enmity, caution became the watchword. "We're doing business on both sides of the fence," said an executive of one of America's largest manufacturing companies, "so it just isn't something we talk about."

Early in 1975, the vast surge of American business dealings with the Middle East had become apparent. Exports from America had skyrocketed to $4.5 billion during the first eleven months of 1974, up 77 percent in the span of a single year. Exports from the United States to Israel, which in prior years had been America's largest Middle Eastern customer, rose only slightly, from $905 million to $1.1 billion. On the other hand, exports to Iran overtook exports to Israel, climbing to $1.5 billion, more than double the previous year's total. Other Middle Eastern countries showed even more startling rates of increase. Iraq, for example, bought $247 million worth of American goods and services, up sharply from $40 mil-lion the year before. This dramatic increase in Middle Eastern capital provided an eager market for American investment bank-ers.

In January 1975, an article in *Foreign Affairs* magazine coau-thored by Robert V. Roosa, a partner in the investment banking house of Brown Brothers Harriman & Company, and four international financing experts, discussed various methods the petroleum-exporting nations might employ to invest their excess cash. Their lengthy proposal included the following points: (1) There might be several trusts for different objectives such as capital appreciation, income, a balanced fund, and so forth. (2) Depending on the nature of the assets and the degree of liquidity required, anticipated total return might average between 6 and 8 percent. (3) As a guide to diversification, percentage limits within the total of a trust fund might be set for holdings in a single country or currency area. (4) Individual trusts would not be listed on any public exchanges, but could only be traded among the oil-exporting countries.

Notwithstanding the fact that one of the authors of the piece was Khodadad Farmanfarmaian, chairman of Iran's Development Industrial Bank, the reaction from many Persian Gulf officials was precisely the opposite of what Roosa and his coauthors had expected. Unhappily for them, the article was widely perceived both at home and abroad as being a denigrating bit of gratuitous advice.

One U.S. critic was David Lilienthal, former head of the Tennessee Valley Authority and the Atomic Energy Commission, and later an international consultant affiliated first with Lazard Frères and then with the Rockefeller interests. The impression given by the article, Lilienthal said, was that "oil producing countries would have to have the assistance of the investment bankers of America.

"The term 'Papa knows best' applies to that article," Lilienthal said. "The crux of it was that the oil producing countries—this is the way they construed it, and I'm not just guessing—didn't have the capacity to know where to invest their money. Therefore, they needed the American investment banking group to set up a special fund to guide them. That really hurt. If there's anything anyone resents more than being told he doesn't know where to spend his money when he's finally able to get it together, I don't know what it is."

For manufacturers of goods and services, there was no such problem. They simply sent their best salesmen and tried to outdo their competitors. The Raytheon Corporation, for example, sold Hawk missiles to Saudi Arabia, and supplied the same system to Israel. The Pillsbury Company signed a contract to help Saudi Arabia design and build three flour and feed mills at a cost of more than $80 million. The Swindell-Dressler Corporation signed a $50 million contract to build a steel plant in Iran.

Some companies, however, found it was not so easy to tap the new torrent of dollars flowing from the Persian Gulf. Their stumbling block was the Arab Boycott Office. In the twenty-four years of its existence, the ABO had grown from a petty annoyance to become a full-fledged threat to American businessmen and financiers. An estimated three hundred to four hundred U.S. companies were on the blacklist kept by the Arab Boycott Office in Damascus, Syria. For firms to be on the ABO blacklist meant they were not welcome in the Arab world because of their operations in Israel. The Ford Motor Company had been on the blacklist since 1966, when it entered into an agreement with a dealer in Israel to assemble Ford cars and trucks. Also on the list was the RCA Corporation, which had a record-licensing agreement in Israel. RCA was vigorously protesting its position on the list, and had written Secretary of State Henry Kissinger asking that the State Department try to intervene to eliminate the list. Other prominent blacklisted concerns included the Coca-Cola Company and the Xerox Corporation. Coca-Cola was placed on the list in 1966 because of a bottling franchise in Israel, and Xerox was listed the same year because it had sponsored a TV documentary about the creation of the state of Israel.

As 1975 began, the boycott list was being soft-pedaled by both the Arabs and the Israelis, as well as by the U.S. government. Many American companies also preferred to see it kept in the background. Yet, only the Israelis seemed to sense the real dangers of the blacklist. "What if the Arabs suddenly said they would boycott not only those companies doing business directly with Israel, but also any company doing business with another company that is active in Israel?" asked Ze'ev Sher, economic minister of the Israeli Embassy in New York. "The new rich man who tries to dictate his taste is not acceptable."

A few weeks later, his warning would seem prescient.

Early in February, *Business Week* magazine reported that two Arab investment groups had managed to keep several major Jewish-controlled European investment banking houses out of two Eurodollar syndications. It was the first overt attempt to discriminate against Jewish-backed financial institutions since the big wave of petrodollar spending had begun.

The Arab groups involved were the Intra Investment Company and the Kuwait Investment Company. As a result of pressure from those two institutions, the firms of S.G. Warburg & Company of London, the Rothschild houses in Paris and London, and Lazard Frères et Cie of Paris, had been excluded from two French financings.

The method employed by the Arab institutions to exert the necessary pressure was simply to refuse to participate in a financing if any of the other members of the syndicate were blacklisted firms. The first two cases cited above involved a $42.6 million issue to finance a French highway and the raising of $25 million for Air France, the nationalized airline.

Under ordinary circumstances, managers of international financings might have been expected to ignore such pressure from the Arabs, but these were extraordinary times. The flood of Middle Eastern oil capital into world markets had become the dominant force in international money markets. Consequently, almost all Western bankers were eager to avoid antagonizing the Arabs in order to attract their investments.

What began as a relatively minor event in France quickly escalated into an international crisis. Attempts to build a united front against the Arab pressure tactics were mounted, but had only limited success. In London, a leading British financier, Gerald Thompson of Kleinwort, Benson Ltd., a non-Jewish house, told Terry Robards of *The New York Times* that his organization would not resist Arab pressures. The British firm proved its point by yielding to the Arabs and excluding two Jewish houses from participating in a $25 million loan being arranged for Marubeni, a Japanese trading company.

In Paris, embarrassment over the boycott grew, causing the Banque Nationale de Paris to put off indefinitely a planned $40 million to $60 million issue for Electricité de France. The action came after Jean Guyot, the head of the Lazard Frères operation in France, called on Finance Minister Jean-Pierre Fourcade to present a formal complaint for the issues that had already gone forward without his firm's participation.

A close eye was being kept on the New York investment banking community to see whether Arab pressure would cross the Atlantic and strike at the heart of the world's financial network. Attention quickly focused on Merrill Lynch, Pierce, Fenner & Smith, which was preparing to underwrite a $50 million issue of United Mexican States bonds. On its syndicate list was the Kuwait International Investment Company and Lazard Frères & Company, the New York affiliate of Lazard Frères in France.

On February 12, the air of crisis deepened. The Kuwaiti investment firm withdrew from a Mexican bond offering, as well as from another $25 million bond issue by Volvo, the Swedish automobile maker. In both cases, Lazard Frères was on the underwriting roster. "We cannot be co-managers of an issue in which we have to sign a contract with a boycotted firm," the Kuwaiti company said.

In a comparable situation, Kleinwort Benson of London had excluded Jewish firms. Now the world waited to see what Merrill Lynch would do. The decision was not easy. The volume of securities marketed through the three principal Kuwaiti investment firms in 1974 had been close to $1 billion, and about half of that had been managed or co-managed by the Kuwait Investment Company.

Merrill Lynch bit the bullet. The offerings would proceed. Donald T. Regan, chairman of the firm, said, "We're businessmen, not politicians," and held the line. His offerings would continue to include blacklisted firms. As head of the world's largest investment house, with the most powerful retail marketing organization in existence, Regan had added a strong voice to those who would neither favor nor foster the boycott.

Now politicians and academics began to raise their voices. Senator Jacob K. Javits, Republican of New York, and Senator Harrison A. Williams, Jr., Democrat of New Jersey, in a letter to Treasury Secretary William E. Simon and other government officials, asked the Ford administration to determine whether there had been religious discrimination against "Jewish or any other Americans" by Arab interests, and whether any U.S. laws had been violated.

"It is clearly intolerable to permit Arab—or any—investors to attempt to extend such religious discrimination to the United States," the senators said.

In addition to asking for an investigation by the administration, the senators asked Simon to "promulgate, where possible, such regulations as may be necessary to prevent the occurrence of any such religious discrimination" and to "propose new legislation if needed to prevent such discrimination.

"We feel the United States stands ready to welcome foreign investment, including Arab investment, that conforms to the standards of our society and the national security and interest," the senators concluded, "but Arab oil money should not be permitted to enter our country on a basis contrary to our morality and constitutions."

New York State Attorney General Louis Lefkowitz announced an investigation into charges of alleged pressure from Arab sources against New York securities firms. "This is the first instance I know of where our free market in securities has come under possible pressure and coercive tactics based on bigotry and demeanor unbecoming the securities business," he said.

SEC Commissioner Irving Pollack delivered a personal message. The exclusion of Jewish firms from underwritings, he said, was a misuse of economic power reminiscent of the 1930s. "No society," he said, "can long exist if it permits itself to be black-balled or blacklisted by persons asserting economic leverage."

Professor Glen E. Weston, who taught at the National Law Center of George Washington University, raised the specter of violations of antitrust law.

The matter also was discussed on a more philosophical plane. Felix Rohatyn of Lazard Frères in New York argued that the blacklistings were a moral issue. "It's totally against what I take to be the tradition of the United States," he said. "It's un-American and I would feel the same way if it were directed toward Italians, Irishmen, or one-eyed Chinese."

The broader question of what constituted a Jewish firm also was raised on Wall Street. What about Lehman Brothers, traditionally an old-line Jewish firm? It was headed by Peter Peterson, an American of Greek ancestry, and one of its many prominent non-Jewish partners was George Ball, a former Washington luminary.

Arab businessmen and financiers reacted angrily to the furor that had arisen over the boycott. They insisted that it was not directed against Jews or Jewish-owned establishments, but rather at corporations that had helped the Israeli economy. The Arab financiers seemed especially incensed at remarks by President Ford, who had publicly criticized the boycott. They pointed angrily to the U.S. boycott of Cuba, which prevented Cuban products, even cigars, from being sold in America.

Lucien Dahdah, chairman of the Intra Investment Company, observed that a number of Jewish business organizations were thriving in Arab countries. Arab financiers, he said, had refused to participate only with institutions they considered hostile.

Then, gradually, as tempers eased, the boiling pot began to cool. The controversy left the front pages and was more rationally discussed in the offices of the world's financiers. Before it faded entirely from view, however, there would be one more burst of publicity, one more airing of the moral issue.

On February 26, 1975, *Newsday,* an aggressive Long Island, New York, newspaper, published a startling story written by its correspondent in Beirut. The dispatch said that the U.S. government was a partner in an Arab investment company that was boycotting banks that had given economic assistance to Israel. The investment company? Intra.

Suddenly, it appeared, the decision of the U.S. government's Commodity Credit Corporation to participate in the 1967 salvage of the old Intra Bank had come back to haunt it.

Although the CCC had subsequently tried to sell its remaining interest in Intra Investment, it still held 6.5 percent at the time of the boycott, and the American Embassy's agricultural attaché, Shack Pitcher, sat on Intra's nine-member board of directors. So, like it or not, the U.S. government found itself in the position of fostering a boycott against Jewish investment banking firms.

It was quickly pointed out that the U.S. government was violating its own laws by participating as a partner in Intra. An amendment to the Export Administration Act of 1965, labeled the Arab Boycott Amendment, said: "It is the policy of the United States to oppose restrictive trade practices or boycotts fostered or imposed by foreign countries against countries friendly to the United States."

American officials defended their position by asserting that the United States had been "an unwilling partner" in Intra Investment Company. Theodore J. Becker, controller of the CCC, said his agency had acquired its Intra stock interest only to protect the $10.2 million balance owed on the $22 million loan made almost a decade earlier to Intra Bank. Furthermore, he said, in late 1974, the Lebanese Cabinet had approved a decree to purchase the U.S. stock, but had failed to take action on the purchase.

In addition to the defensive reaction of U.S. officials, the furor over the Intra situation also gave rise to some behind-the-scenes second-guessing. One American diplomat in Beirut grumbled that the United States never should have taken an active interest in Intra. Another diplomat in Washington stressed that the United States was pressing the Lebanese to exercise their option to buy up the American shares of Intra.

Eventually, the dispute about Intra faded, and European investment bankers soon figured out a method of circumventing the Arab boycott regulations. In effect, they had devised an expansion of the two-tier underwriting system in which the issuer sells his securities to an underwriting syndicate which, in turn, resells them to customers. The new scheme called for only a limited number of investment houses to underwrite the issue. They would then sell part of their underwriting to other houses that had not been acceptable to the Arabs. The new procedure worked because the name of an Arab bank did not appear on a contract with a black-listed institution.

One of the first issues offered under this new set of underwriting ground rules was placed by the nationalized coal board of France, Charbonnages de France. The board issued $18.9 million worth of seven-year, 10¼ percent notes, naming six investment houses as underwriters. They were the Banque de l'Union Européenne, Société Générale de Paris, Banque Nationale de Paris, and the Union Bank of Switzerland, as well as two Arab institutions, Intra Investment and the Kuwait Investment Company. European brokers said boycotted investment banks were offered portions of the issue by the syndicate participants.

A problem arose over the compensation offered to the firms that were added to the selling roster after the initial distribution. Ordinarily, underwriting firms were allowed to keep an average of 1½ percent of the gross price of the securities they sold to their customers. Under the new procedure, the second-stage selling group was allowed to keep only 1 percent. To an investment banker, as to an industrialist, a one-third slash in gross income is a painful price to pay for inclusion in a business deal. Clearly, the makeshift solution was an uneasy one.

In the months ahead, the blacklisted financiers would find out whether they would again be accorded full membership in offerings cosponsored by Arab firms. However, the hard feelings spawned by the boycott, and the controversial role of the Intra Investment Company, would not quickly be forgotten.

5 / The Mysterious Client

For Merrill Lynch, Pierce, Fenner & Smith, the world's largest brokerage firm, a $150 million underwriting job is hardly unusual. But when the firm agreed to offer the stock of the Hughes Tool Company to the public in the winter of 1972, it found that dealing with Howard Hughes, the elusive and eccentric billionaire, was far from commonplace. Anxious about speculation that Hughes was in ill health and in a poor mental state, Merrill Lynch's top investment banker, Julius Sedlmayr, embarked on an adventure that would carry him to the Central American outpost of Managua, Nicaragua. The floating of the Hughes Tool stock issue was a simple job technically, but it provided a challenge for Sedlmayr that would call on all the knowledge and nerve he could muster to bring the deal to a successful and profitable conclusion.

In 1972, Julius H. Sedlmayr of Merrill Lynch, Pierce, Fenner & Smith, was chatting with his friend and client, Raymond Holliday, who had called from Texas. Finally, Holliday got to the point. "Howard wants to sell the tool company," he said. "Could you come down to Houston?"

Sedlmayr didn't need a translation. He realized immediately that Holliday was talking about Howard Hughes, the reclusive billionaire whose distaste for publicity and whose lack of personal contact with anyone outside a small personal staff had made him an almost legendary figure.

What Sedlmayr could not foresee, however, was that the conversation with Holliday was to set in motion one of the most extraordinary and profitable adventures of his twenty-six-year career as an investment banker. Once again, Sedlmayr would find himself drawn into the orbit of the mysterious Howard Hughes.

Howard Hughes was an enigma. Since the 1950s, Hughes, whose personal fortune was estimated at more than $2 billion, had lived a bizarre life, shunning outsiders, communicating largely through aides, moving from state to state and finally from country to country, partly in an attempt to avoid the embarrassment of testifying at lawsuits pending against him and his enterprises. It was generally accepted that Hughes, along with J. Paul Getty, the oil magnate, was one of two of the richest men in the United States.

The bulwark of the Hughes empire, as Sedlmayr knew, was the Houston-based Hughes Tool Company, which included a large number of divisions and off-shoots. In addition, Hughes also owned five Nevada hotels and seven casinos which brought in over $75 million annually, about 13 percent of the state's total gambling income.

Hughes also owned Air West, a regional airline which he bought for $90 million, and for a time, he was a major stockholder in Trans World Airways, selling his 6.6 million shares in 1966 for nearly $550 million. Through the Howard Hughes Medical Institute, which conducted medical research in university hospitals around the country, and employed doctors and research teams on a salaried basis, Hughes controlled the Hughes Aircraft Company.

Another major part of the Hughes fortune was invested in real estate—in the Bahamas, California, and Nevada. His desert holdings outside Las Vegas were valued at an estimated $100 million. In the early 1970s Hughes was responsible for the employment of over 60,000 people.

At the time of Holliday's call to Sedlmayr, Howard Hughes was under attack from many quarters. The most serious financial threat to his empire was a long-running suit in a federal court in New York, being pressed by Trans World Airlines. That action stood to cost Hughes the staggering sum of $180 million, and appeared to be an important consideration in his decision to sell the tool company.

The suit had been filed in 1961 as a result of Hughes's ownership of nearly 80 percent of TWA. The suit alleged that the tool company had delayed and diverted delivery of sixty-three new jet planes, thereby damaging TWA's ability to compete. The broad premise of the case was the allegation that Hughes had violated the antitrust laws by monopolizing the company he controlled (TWA) and by using it as a captive market to further his own trade in aircraft.

Using the tool company as his vehicle, Hughes had first begun buying TWA stock in 1939, when the airline was ailing. By 1942, he had 42 percent of the stock, and in 1947, he saved TWA from bankruptcy when he loaned it $10 million and increased his stock holdings to about 80 percent.

It was clear from the outset of the case that Hughes's testimony would be required, and the chief lawyer for TWA explained that three-fourth's of the plaintiff's evidence would have to come from Hughes and no one else. Instead of appearing, Hughes decided to go into hiding, an act which led to the first court decision. In 1963, TWA was granted damages of $135 million and a countersuit filed by the tool company was dismissed because Hughes had defaulted by refusing to appear. The decision was appealed, and for the next ten years, the amount of money that Hughes owed TWA grew steadily with inflation. In opinions handed down by the district courts in 1969 and 1970, the amount awarded to TWA was set at

$138 million plus TWA costs, which included attorney's fees of $7.8 million. Interest at the rate of 6 percent was also levied. By 1971, the case had moved through the United States Court of Appeals, and the judgment of the district court was affirmed. Moreover, the interest rate was raised to 7½ percent.

In November of 1971, however, the United States Supreme Court ordered that the execution of the district court order be stayed. Subsequently, on February 22, 1972, the Supreme Court agreed to hear the case and arguments were presented in October, but ironically, the final decision would be announced thirty-four days after Hughes sold the tool company.

Although Hughes himself, and for that matter, Sedlmayr, never disclosed why Hughes wanted to sell the tool company, it was widely speculated that it was to provide for the possible expense of an adverse Supreme Court decision. Hughes already had been required to post an appeal bond of $75 million with the court, and had done so by obtaining a five-year letter of credit for that amount from the Bank of America National Trust and Savings Association. He had provided the bank with $35 million in securities as collateral for the letter of credit.

On January 10, 1973, a bombshell struck. By a vote of 6 to 2, the Supreme Court overturned the lower court decisions and gave Hughes a stunning victory. Hughes, who had never made a personal appearance in the case, had won. A judgment that had grown to $180 million, more money than most men dream about, was back in the hands of Howard Hughes. The Supreme Court said it had decided in Hughes's favor primarily because the Civil Aeronautics Board had overseen the relationship between the tool company and TWA, and thereby had given transactions between the two companies a sort of statutory immunity from antitrust actions.

For TWA, it was a bitter disappointment. Not only was $180 million in damages lost, but also more than $7 million that the big airline had spent in attorney's fees during the lengthy proceedings. Wall Street gave its judgment. On the day of the decision, TWA's stock on the Big Board was one of the six most active issues of the day and fell by $2.50 a share to $35.50. Earlier in the trading session, it had dipped to a 1972–73 low before recovering slightly at the closing bell.

A second lawsuit that had a major impact on Howard Hughes in the early 1970s was filed by Robert A. Maheu, his former top aide in Nevada. Maheu had been fired from his job in 1970, and as a result, late that year he had sued a number of the top officers of Hughes's company in an attempt to prevent them from removing him as manager of the Las Vegas casinos and other properties. Until then, Maheu had been the $520,000-a-year chief Nevada executive of the Hughes empire. He had held that job almost from the time Hughes had moved to Las Vegas in 1966. Maheu also had been a close adviser to Hughes and often had acted as an official spokesman for him. While Hughes remained secluded in the penthouse of the Desert Inn, Maheu had lived in a $640,000 mansion built for him on the Desert Inn golf course by the tool company.

Maheu's dismissal in 1970 was typically mysterious. Hughes simply vanished from the Desert Inn without notifying Maheu, and soon thereafter, Chester Davis, a New York lawyer, and Frank W. Gay, a vice-president of the tool company, suddenly appeared in Las Vegas and sent word to Maheu that he had been fired. Maheu fought back, saying that only Hughes could fire him, and filed a $50 million damage suit in Nevada.

The quarrel between Maheu and the Hughes forces heated up thirteen months later when Hughes denounced Maheu during a telephone press conference from the Bahamas. Under questioning from seven reporters, Hughes said Maheu was dishonest and that he "stole me blind." Maheu countered by filing a new lawsuit for $17.5 million in Los Angeles.

In his press conference, Hughes's bitterness against Maheu was evident. He confirmed that he had indeed ordered the firing of Maheu and complained about "the devastating, horrifying program of harassment that Maheu and his associates have launched against me." Asked why he had not appeared personally in court to answer the charges, he responded: "How many hours do you think I would have to sit in the Nevada courtroom to do what you have just described, just to come out and tell all the story and straighten it out? How many hours of testimony do you think Maheu and his resourceful lawyers would sweat out of me to do the thing you have described? How many years do you think I would be involved? Look, I have been in the TWA lawsuit a lot of years. They have more than $100 million of my money locked up right now. Now, how long do you think I'm going to be paying up, tangled up in this Maheu litigation if I did the thing you describe?"

As a result of the denunciation, Maheu filed suit against Hughes's company. In December 1974, after a five-month trial and six days of deliberating, a jury of six persons announced their verdict. Maheu had indeed been defamed, they decided, and was entitled to $2.8 million in damages. The award was based on the jury's finding that Maheu had suffered a decreased earning capacity plus humiliation and mental anguish from being labeled a thief by Hughes.

The idea of spinning off the tool company, which was part of Hughes's privately owned empire, had been proposed a number of times over the years, sometimes by Merrill Lynch and sometimes by others. Noah Dietrich, who was Hughes's chief executive officer for thirty-two years before he broke with him, and who later wrote *Howard—The Amazing Mr. Hughes,* said that he had tried several times to convince Hughes to sell the tool company. He recalled one offer made in 1955 would have brought Hughes about $400 million.

Sedlmayr said a discussion of the possible sale of the tool company was an exercise that Hughes often went through, but as far as he could see, the billionaire had no real intent to sell it in those early years. However, it was impossible to second-guess Hughes.

There was some indication in the early and mid 1960s that Hughes might pull out of TWA entirely, and Sedlmayr was regularly put to the test, asked about market conditions, or sounded out about such a deal. But the more he went through such exercises, the less likely he thought it was that a sale would ever take place. "Basically, you never really thought that Hughes was going to sell anything," he said.

Then, in 1966, Sedlmayr received a call from one of Hughes's lawyers, who said Hughes wanted to talk to him. "We had heard that a million times but nothing ever happened," Sedlmayr said. This time, though, it did happen. "I was sitting home playing bridge with the neighbors on Sunday morning before lunch and suddenly the call from Hughes came through. We talked for an hour on the phone."

Hughes told Sedlmayr that he was desperate to sell all his TWA holdings. He apologized for disturbing Sedlmayr on a Sunday morning at home, and asked if it would be more convenient for him to call back at another time. Meanwhile he was sketching out what was to become one of the largest public stock offerings in history.

"No one had ever seen such an offer in all the securities business," Sedlmayr said. "I'd have crawled out to California on my hands and knees to do it."

.Subsequently, the sale of $546.5 million in TWA stock was managed by Merrill Lynch, and it was the last big deal the firm handled for Hughes until the tool company was sold in 1972.

The public sale of the Hughes Tool Company could not have been an easy decision for Hughes. It was, after all, his major link with the past, and had been the spawning ground for the massive Hughes fortune. Founded in 1908 by Howard Hughes, Sr., its initial business was the development, manufacture, and distribution of a rock drilling bit that the senior Hughes had patented in 1909. The bit, a complex piece of machinery rather than the simple bit that fits on a carpenter's drill, was used for rotary drilling through rock formations. It played a significant role in the development of the oil and gas well drilling industries, and although major improvements were made in later years, virtually all rotary drilling bits today employ the principle of the 1909 Hughes bit.

The patent on the bit made Hughes Tool Company the largest manufacturer of oil and gas well drilling bits in the United States, and one of the largest in the world. At one time, the company manufactured more than 75 percent of all the drilling bits used on rigs around the world, although by the time of the sale of the company, its market share had dropped to about 50 percent.

Although the bit was the major product at the tool company, over the years other products for use in well drilling also had become important to the concern. It manufactured tool joints for joining sections of drill pipe, drilling bits for the placement of explosive charges in mining, and diggers and impactors used in the construction industry. It also produced precision gears and manufactured helicopters. Of the company's $82.2 million in sales in 1971, however, almost $62 million came from the sale of drilling bits, which cost customers as much as $4,300 each, and ranged up to twenty-six inches in diameter. Foreign sales had become an important part of the company's operation as well. In 1971, about $36.5 million in sales were to foreigners.

The sale by Hughes of the tool company involved a confused shifting around of corporate names. He actually was selling the Oil Tool Division of the Hughes Tool Company. The Hughes Tool Company, which provided an umbrella for a number of Hughes's enterprises, was to be renamed the Summa Corporation (from the Latin word meaning "the best"). Meanwhile, the Oil Tool Division would assume the name that had been used by the parent company. All the common stock of the Summa Corporation would continue to be held by Hughes, so he would be disposing of only the Oil Tool Division. Five million shares of stock in the new Hughes Tool Company would be issued, with the proceeds accruing to Hughes. Summa Corporation would not have any financial interest in the new tool company, which initially would be headed by Raymond Holliday, who had been chief operating officer of the old Hughes Tool Company.

The announcement in mid October 1972, that Hughes was going to sell the tool company set off an immediate wave of speculation on Wall Street about the reasons for the sale. In addition to the presumption that Hughes needed cash because of the TWA law suit and other legal actions pending against him, other rationales were also offered. Norman Pearlstine of *The Wall Street Journal* pointed out that Hughes had an expensive lifestyle and was said to have little access to ready cash when he needed it in a hurry. In addition, Pearlstine said, money might be needed to finance other operations. For example, Hughes's hotel-casino operations in Nevada had posted deficits of $10 million in 1970, and $6 million in 1971. Hughes Air West had lost $11.8 million in 1970, and $2.9 million the following year. It was also known that Hughes had held secret negotiations with the Lockheed Aircraft Corporation over the possibility of buying $1 billion worth of wide-bodied planes for the rumored creation of a worldwide air cargo operation out of Nicaragua.

Whatever his reasons, Hughes clearly wanted a large amount of cash, and the sale of the tool company was the method he had chosen to get it. When the prospectus for the sale was issued, it revealed for the first time some of the financial details of Hughes's operations. As a privately owned company, Hughes Tool had never been required to issue financial statements of the type that are routinely made public by large, publicly held companies. The prospectus disclosed that Oil Tool Division sales had grown from $71 million in 1967, to a peak of $82 million in 1971. However, net income had remained relatively steady at $4.2 million to $5.5 million during the same years.

One thing the prospectus specified was that the risk of adverse court decisions in suits against Hughes or the tool company would be transferred to Summa, and would not be a concern of the new tool company. In addition to the TWA suit and the Maheu suit, Noah Dietrich, who had been Hughes's closest financial adviser until 1957, was suing for $51 million on charges of defamation of character.

The decision by Hughes to sell the tool company led to some extraordinary moments for Sedlmayr. Dealing with Hughes had always been unusual, but this transaction would turn out to be the most bizarre of all. "It's absolutely number one whenever you're talking about his [Hughes's] deals," Sedlmayr said, "because they're always fantastically large." They also tend to generate disbelief in the investment community, he said, but the saving grace was that they were extremely profitable for Merrill Lynch.

After the telephone call from Holliday with the news that Hughes wanted to sell the tool company, Sedlmayr flew to Houston to review the situation. He had been through this sort of drill before, and was skeptical. He considered Holliday to be a good friend, but knew that he was above all a loyal Hughes employee who would tell his investment bankers only as much as was absolutely necessary. He also knew that Holliday would treat every exploration, no matter how tentative, as a sure-fire deal. For him, it was always the real thing and if it didn't work out, well, that's business. In earlier years, Sedlmayr could remember "spinning his wheels" in California for months on end, on various transactions that never came to fruition. "We were always waiting for that magic phone call," he said, "and it never came."

Once before, Sedlmayr had wasted so much time that he had taken the unusual step of telling the Hughes representatives that he was going to charge them $25,000 a month, plus legal fees, for looking at a deal. Surprisingly, they had agreed.

When Sedlmayr arrived in Houston, he was asked by Holliday whether a fee schedule should be set up. "I know your partners are going to worry about this," Holliday said. "Do you want to make some arrangement?"

"No," Sedlmayr said, "we've gotten two fantastic deals. You get a free bite this time. We'll go along."

There was a problem, however, which had nothing to do with compensation but everything to do with Howard Hughes. A few months before Holliday broached the sale of the tool company, the world had been startled and amused by the spectacle of Clifford Irving attempting to pass off as authentic a spurious autobiography of Hughes which he had pieced together from the published work and research of others. Irving had a signature that purported to be Hughes's, and his documentation was good enough to fool the McGraw-Hill executives who were planning to publish the book.

Irving's bubble had been pricked by Hughes himself when he

held a telephone press conference to denounce the autobiography as a fraud. However, Sedlmayr saw the entire sequence of events as a distinct threat to Merrill Lynch. For years, he had been doing business with Hughes on the basis of third-party assurances, signed documents, and, in one instance, a telephone call. He had never seen the elusive billionaire and had never felt the need to. But this time, it was different. McGraw-Hill had been embarrassed by an elaborate fraud, and Sedlmayr was determined to protect his company from a similar experience. Furthermore, Holliday, who was acting as Hughes's go-between, was on both sides of the deal, first as chief operating officer of the company that was selling the tool division, and then as chief executive of the newly independent tool company. In addition, there were numerous stories that Hughes was under pressure from members of his staff, that he had been spirited out of Las Vegas against his will, or that he was seriously ill and not in full control of himself. Merrill Lynch had to know for certain, as Sedlmayr said, "that he wasn't under duress, that he wasn't ill, and that he really wanted to do this, and knew what was going on—and proved it."

Sedlmayr conferred with Merrill Lynch's outside attorney, J. Courtney Ivey, and the two men came to an agreement. "We knew this would be a good piece of business, a big one with a lot of money involved," said Sedlmayr. "I came to the conclusion from a business standpoint, and Courtney did at the same time, from the legal standpoint, that we had to see Hughes. We had to see him and make sure. Raymond Holliday was going to be chief executive of the new company and he was Hughes's man. So, much as I liked Raymond, it was almost impossible not to have a conflict of interest."

Sedlmayr discussed the problem with Merrill Lynch's executive committee. He told them it was a million-to-one shot that he could get to see Hughes personally, but he warned that the deal was too risky unless such a meeting were held. "I'm just telling you there's not going to be a deal without seeing him," he said. "It's too much." If the prospectus were filed with government authorities, and the stocks offered to the public without such a meeting, it could blow up in Merrill Lynch's face.

The executive committee supported Sedlmayr, and he informed the Hughes representatives that without a face-to-face meeting the deal was off. "They were 100 percent convinced that since no one had seen him since 1954, they didn't think anyone would see him this time," Sedlmayr said. Holliday specifically said he thought it was "highly unlikely" that Hughes would see the Merrill Lynch officials. He tried to convince Sedlmayr that it would be sufficient for him to go to Managua, Nicaragua, where Hughes was residing and talk to the billionaire without actually seeing him face-to-face.

"What the hell, I can talk to him on the telephone from here," Sedlmayr said. "We finally took the hard line and said 'We're not going to do the deal unless we see him and get him to sign this document in our presence and have it cleared by our own proper legal people.' "

After weeks of deliberating and relaying of messages back and forth, the word came from Nicaragua that Hughes had okayed the meeting. Although Sedlmayr had never seen Hughes in person, he was reassured by the fact that Ivey had. In the mid 1950s, Ivey had visited Hughes in Beverly Hills with two other men, both of them now dead. "They had spent an hour with him up there," Sedlmayr said, "maybe even talking the same deal. That's why I wanted Courtney, because they could have rung in Raymond Massey on me."

Arrangements were made for the meeting with Hughes to take place on Saturday, September 23rd. Sedlmayr and Ivey booked commercial airline reservations on Friday, the 22nd, and began to prepare for the meeting. They accepted an offer to return from Nicaragua to the United States on a Hughes plane. Then the two men received a telephone call from Hughes's assistants. The meeting had to be postponed for twenty-four hours, and would take place instead on Sunday. Did they want to fly to Houston that night, and then travel the rest of the way to Nicaragua on a Hughes aircraft? They declined the offer and instead boarded their commercial flight as scheduled. "Now we're both looking at each other thinking it's the beginning of the old routine," Sedlmayr said.

On the flight to Managua, the two men speculated on what was going to happen when they reached their destination. They hoped the trip would be fruitful, but based on their past experience, there was no assurance that it would be.

At the airport they were met by a Nicaraguan Air Force sergeant who escorted them through customs and drove them to the Hotel Intercontinental, taking a shortcut through the palace grounds of President Luis Anastasio Somoza Debayle. Sedlmayr and Ivey spent much of Saturday polishing up their proposal, organizing the presentation they hoped to make to Hughes. Later that weekend, they took a tour of the city, including a drive around Lake Managua and into the surrounding mountains, but they returned to the hotel depressed by what they had seen.

"There's very little to talk about in Managua," said Sedlmayr. "Lake Managua is polluted and you don't see a boat on it. You don't see any swimming and there are no fish in it. You can't drink it and if you fell in, you'd probably dissolve. It's an awful-looking color. The town is absolutely poverty-stricken."

Sedlmayr and Ivey remarked about the irony of one of the world's richest men living, at least temporarily, in such seedy surroundings. The impression was heightened by the rather ordinary appearance of the hotel where Hughes had several connecting rooms. The stories were true, it seemed, that Hughes had never placed a premium on physical surroundings, but instead spent his time concentrating on as many as forty or fifty major business projects at a time. Sedlmayr and Ivey could only hope that the sale of the tool company happened to be one of the most important of his projects at the moment.

As the two men were reviewing their position on Saturday, they were informed that the Hughes plane which was to return them to the United States had broken down, and replacement parts had to be flown in from Houston. They quickly made return reservations on a commercial flight scheduled to leave Managua at 6:45 Monday morning.

"This was typical of things other people had run into over the years," Sedlmayr said. "For example, Hughes would hold up a TWA flight with 120 people aboard so some executive could be removed from it. Then Hughes would talk to the passenger for an hour on the telephone and ask him not to go home, promising that he would see him within a week. He never did see him in his whole life, and there are 120 delayed passengers, with the airline saying 'Sorry, we've got something mechanically wrong.' "

Sedlmayr and Ivey sensed that the same thing was happening to them. It was the old airport holding routine. Suddenly a plane had a broken part. Their answer was to make the commercial reservation, and then stick to their scheduled departure time, come what may. Later, they would be glad they had made such a decision.

Even with the word that their return aircraft had run into problems, the two men still had no reason to believe that their face-to-face session with Hughes had been cancelled altogether. It was now rescheduled for eleven o'clock Sunday morning. On Sunday morning, however, matters took a turn for the worse. They were informed that their meeting had again been delayed and would not take place until two o'clock in the afternoon. They hired a driver to take them for a ride in the countryside, and when they returned to the hotel, were told that the meeting had been put off again, this time until after dinner.

Now Sedlmayr began to have a sense of foreboding. "We were getting more and more down in the dumps," he said. " 'After dinner' rolls around. I'm being very good—haven't had a drink—then we get word that it's going to be 11 P.M."

The Sunday night vigil seemed endless. Sedlmayr, Ivey, Raymond Holliday, and other Hughes aides waited for the summons. The appointed hour came and went. Then it was midnight. Finally, at one o'clock in the morning, Sedlmayr had had enough. He turned to Holliday and said, "Raymond, I'm going to be on the 6:45 plane come hell or high water, with or without the signature and that's going to be the end of it."

Sedlmayr asked if Hughes knew they were booked on a flight that was departing in less than six hours. Holliday said he did. At 4:30 A.M., Sedlmayr returned to his room to shower, shave, and pack. He was weary from the long wait, frustrated by the series of delays, and angry at the inconsiderate treatment. Suddenly his phone rang. It was Hughes's suite. Could he and Ivey come right up?

After waiting for almost two days, and with only two hours remaining before their plane was scheduled to depart, the two men were ushered into Hughes's suite. They were surprised at how ordinary it seemed, hardly befitting the financial status of the occupant. For that matter, the security at the door was not up to the usual rigid Hughes standard. In California, to insure privacy, Hughes had sealed off rooms on both sides of his hotel suite, as well as keeping vacant one floor above and one floor below his own. But here in Nicaragua there was only minimal security. A plainclothes guard was posted outside the door of the suite, and a closed-circuit television camera followed the movements of any-one getting off the elevator. Clearly, no one could get in to see Hughes without an appointment. But it would certainly have been possible for an outsider to get as far as his door unannounced.

Sedlmayr and Ivey were ushered into the suite, which was set up as a sort of sitting room, and found the shades drawn. They had been told that sunlight never entered the room. Hughes pre-ferred to sleep when he was tired, and to transact business when he was not. The hour of the day meant little to him, and he had aides on duty around the clock. The fact that it was nearly 5:00 A.M. was unimportant. To Hughes it mattered not at all whether the sun was setting or rising.

With rumors of Hughes's bizarre appearance buzzing through his mind, Sedlmayr looked eagerly toward the lounge chair where the billionaire was sitting, and where he remained during the entire session. Sedlmayr had been warned that because of an extreme sensitivity to germs, Hughes would probably avoid shaking hands with him, so he was not surprised when he did not offer his hand. Sedlmayr's immediate impression was that stories of Hughes's appearance had been grossly exaggerated. The billionaire did indeed have a beard, but it was a short Van Dyke, complemented by a mustache. His hair was moderately long, curling down to the base of his neck.

After the introductions were completed, Hughes engaged the two men in conversation, reminiscing occasionally about the origins of the tool company and its operations in earlier days, and about the death of his father. He also talked about his problems in Las Vegas. During the conversation, Hughes fiddled with a hearing aid, and remarked that he hoped one of his companies would come up with a more effective model. The one he had was the best on the market at the moment, he said, but was hardly satisfactory. During the conversation, two of Hughes's personal aides stayed with him. After chatting for awhile, Hughes apologized for keeping the two men waiting so long and suggested that one of his jets fly down to pick them up. Sedlmayr responded that he preferred to take the commercial flight at 6:45 A.M.

Finally, the talk turned to the sale of the tool company. Hughes said he wanted to make sure that the company's employees would be taken care of because he had a sentimental attachment for them. There was a discussion of the price which would be charged for the company, and at one point, Hughes quipped that if Sedlmayr were smart he would underprice the stock "and have a million happy clients and one angry customer." Forty minutes after the meeting had begun, Hughes read the document that Sedlmayr and Ivey had brought and signed it.

"We watched him sign," Sedlmayr said, "and Courtney was standing there making sure there was no signature on it in advance or anything like that. We raced out of the place and a guy took us to the airport at about one hundred miles an hour."

After dashing aboard the plane for New York, Sedlmayr and Ivey relaxed for the first time in three days. So frenetic had been the conclusion of their visit that they could scarcely believe they had seen Hughes. Sedlmayr would later comment that if he had agreed to wait for a Hughes plane rather than insisting upon the 6:45 commercial flight, he would still be in Nicaragua, talking about a deal rather than concluding one.

In the days ahead, Merrill Lynch would have reason to be grateful that Sedlmayr and Ivey had seen Hughes in person. One shareholder at Merrill Lynch's annual meeting challenged the company, asking how it could possibly have participated in the tool company deal when everyone knew that Howard Hughes was dead. A more serious version of the same objection arose when the Securities and Exchange Commission asked Merrill Lynch what it had done to make sure Hughes was alive and had personally approved the sale of the tool company. In its letter of comment to Merrill Lynch, the SEC also asked what steps the securities firm had taken to make sure that the signature on the "offering" documents was authentic.

"If Mr. Hughes had been buried for five years and they [the SEC] had approved registration papers, or if he was under duress, it would have been kind of embarrassing," Sedlmayr said.

The document bearing Hughes's signature was kept in Ivey's safe and hand-carried to Washington, where the SEC authenticated it. "They checked the document and gave assurances in a few minutes that it was his signature," Sedlmayr said. "We'd have looked pretty goofy with the SEC if we hadn't gone to the trouble [of seeing Hughes]."

With the documents signed, Merrill Lynch was ready to proceed with the sale. Although the investment bankers were convinced that the company had value for shareholders, there were several problems to overcome. First, was the widespread feeling on Wall Street that Hughes had a special genius for extricating himself from investments at the proper time. It was pointed out that he had sold his interest in TWA for $86 a share and the stock had later plummeted to $13. Next, it was generally believed that it was the personal touch of Howard Hughes which had made the tool company profitable. As a practical matter, Hughes had not set foot in a tool company plant since 1938, and the company was run with great autonomy by his hired managers.

"When we were pricing it, there was doubt around the Street whether a group of people who had never been absolutely charged with running a company before could handle it," Sedlmayr said.

Another reason for skepticism was that the tool company's profits had been relatively static, and it had been losing market share since its patent on a basic fuse detonator had expired. In addition, drilling activity in the world's oil fields had been lagging, and therefore, the need for drill bits had been sluggish. Later, of course, when the so-called energy crisis struck, drilling activity would spurt and so would the demand for drill bits.

Debate over a selling price for the tool company was to cause Sedlmayr a good deal of trouble before the deal was finally set. The Hughes interests were eager to net as large a sum as possible from the sale. Merrill Lynch was eager to accommodate them, but wanted above all to structure the sale so that it would succeed.

In the beginning, Merrill Lynch had proposed a price of $28 a share on five million shares, which would have brought in $140 million. Hughes, on the other hand, wanted a price of $32 a share.

The haggling involved not only the price of the stock to the public, but also the size of the underwriting discount—that is, the amount of money paid to the underwriters and their salesmen for marketing the stock. The selling price finally agreed upon was $30 a share, which would give the entire offering a value of $150 million. The underwriting discount was set at $1.50 a share, but not before some eleventh-hour histrionics. Discussions about the "spread" were still underway at three o'clock in the morning on December 7, the day of the offering. Sedlmayr had returned home from a Christmas party at the "21" Club in Manhattan, and was negotiating on the telephone. Finally, he gave up on the last fifteen cents of the "spread" that he had hoped for. That single telephone call gained Hughes three-quarters of a million dollars, and cost the underwriters the same amount.

Then, on the morning of December 7, the issue went on sale. Merrill Lynch was alloted over one million shares, nearly double the amount to be sold by the other major participants in the syndicate. Among the other leading firms participating—each signing up for 60,000 shares—were Goldman Sachs, Kidder Peabody, Lazard Frères, Salomon Brothers, Kuhn Loeb, First Boston, Dillon Read, Blyth Eastman Dillon, Paine Webber, White Weld, and Shearson Hammill. All together, twenty-three of the top firms on Wall Street were responsible for huge chunks of the offering, and another 163 firms were allocated smaller blocks of stock to sell.

After all the ballyhoo about the tool company and Howard

Hughes, interest in the tool company was keen, and as a result, the entire $150 million offering was quickly snapped up at $30 a share. By the end of the day, there were bids of as much as $32.25 for shares of the stock. The next day, it was trading at $36, and the price would later climb as high as $86 a share. It became obvious as the months passed that if Hughes had waited, his take could have been as much as $280 million higher.

"If he had waited a year, he'd have made another $150 million on the sale," Sedlmayr said. "From everything I've heard about him, I don't think he ever second-guesses 'trade' events. He says, 'Okay, that's where it was? That's where it was!' On the other hand, I haven't heard from him since, so I don't know."

As the sale of the stock boomed, Merrill Lynch reaped huge benefits. The firm pocketed a management fee of about $1.5 million, and collected another million dollars or more in commissions on its own sales of the stock. Purchasers of the stock, at least those who held on to it, would see their investment more than double in a short time. For the lucky investors who got in on the ground floor, there was a quick paper profit of more than $250 million.

What about Julius Sedlmayr? He had added a unique feather to his investment banking cap. In a world where six-figure incomes are commonplace and multimillion-dollar deals scarcely cause a ripple, he had accomplished something that no other investment banker on Wall Street could match. He had seen the legendary Howard Hughes, and had come home to Manhattan bearing one of the world's most exclusive autographs. To his reputation as one of Wall Street's canniest and most powerful investment bankers, Sedlmayr had added that final fillip that investment bankers so cherish. He, when all else was said, had been financier to Howard Hughes.

Editor's note: Howard Hughes died on April 5, 1976, subsequent to this writing.

6 / The Brink of Default

The nation's financial community will remember 1975 as the year of New York City's fiscal crisis. With the city's finances in a state of chaos, investors who customarily bought billions of dollars worth of New York's municipal notes and bonds decided they had risked enough. Its source of ready cash choked off, the city neared the brink of default. It was finally rescued by an intricate plan fashioned in City Hall, Albany, the White House, and Wall Street. Before the incredible episode had run its course, the financiers had mustered worldwide support in their successful attempt to preserve their assets. Ultimately, they forced the President of the United States to reverse his decision and take the necessary actions to save New York City. In so doing, nearly $2 billion in New York securities held by the city's leading banks was also salvaged.

At Rockefeller Center, the huge Christmas tree was lit. New York City department stores were ablaze with brightly colored lights, and the window of F.A.O. Schwarz, the world's most famous toy store, had been transformed into a children's fantasy.

The city's Christmas trappings were hardly noticed, however, by nine of New York's leading financiers as they sped through the swelling rush-hour traffic toward Gracie Mansion, Mayor Abraham Beame's residence on Manhattan's East Side.

One by one they arrived at the unpublicized meeting the morning of December 17, 1974. Present were Wallace Turner of Merrill Lynch, Pierce, Fenner & Smith, an outspoken, disillusioned municipal bond specialist; Frank Smeal of Morgan Guaranty Trust Company, a Phi Beta Kappa graduate of Penn State with an MBA from Harvard and a law degree from NYU; Tom Labrecque, a talented thirty-six-year-old who had just been promoted to an executive vice-presidency of the Chase Manhattan Bank; Richard Kezer, the recently named head of First National City Bank's money market division; Richard Nye of First Security Company, Gedale Horowitz of Salomon Brothers, and others. Collectively, the investment bankers who were sitting down for breakfast with Mayor Beame probably knew more about the municipal bond and note markets than any other group in the United States. Equally important, the banks and investment houses they represented held over $1 billion worth of New York City securities, an investment that would become increasingly perilous in the months ahead as New York inched closer to default.

The bankers laid the problem in Mayor Beame's lap. The nation's bond market, they said, was a "disaster." In October, they had lost $50 million in the course of selling $475 million worth of bonds for the city. Furthermore, a scheduled bond sale in January was highly unlikely to ever get off the ground. There was no one in the investment community who wanted New York bonds.

Beame countered that he was "outraged" by the interest rate of 9.5 percent that had been charged on the sale of city notes just four days earlier. The city was being milked, he felt, and he threatened to use its five pension systems as a method of competing with the banks and securities houses for the purchase of city securities. In effect, the city would be borrowing from its employees' pension funds, hopefully at a lower rate of interest than the banks would charge.

The financiers fired back. Frank Smeal pointed out that the use of the pension funds would be at best a temporary solution. The basic problem, he said, was that the city was simply borrowing too much. Its capital needs had reached $550 million a month, a staggering amount of money to be raised in the credit markets. Why, he asked, had the level soared so high? Smeal and Sellers told the mayor bluntly that borrowing to finance budget deficits was no longer a "viable procedure."

The mayor defended his position. He could not commit himself to reducing the city's borrowing level, he said. He was already taking tough steps to economize, and would look for additional financial aid in Albany and Washington. But the borrowing must continue.

The discussion grew more heated. Smeal repeated that the city could not be run on borrowed money. Beame argued that the borrowing was against "firm receivables." It was the financial community and the financial markets, he said, that were not carrying out their responsibilities. Smeal reminded the mayor that the bond market had just suffered the greatest losses in its history because of its support of the city's debt. Nye took the argument one step farther, and warned that the "whole system could come tumbling down."

Beame said he was fully aware of what was happening. The basic question, he said, was this: Will the banking system "sell" the city? Would it, in effect, act as the city's press agent and get behind it at a moment of need?

The discussion then turned to public opinion and its impact on the securities markets. What was needed, said Nye, was public recognition that the city of New York had "socio-economic" problems. The public and the unions must be made to understand that the city's resources were not infinite. Horowitz added that the newspapers weren't helping the situation any with their talk of deficit financing. Was there any way, he asked, for the city's leaders to persuade the financial writers and the financial community in general that New York's budget problems were not so bleak? Mayor Beame said he had tried repeatedly to do precisely that. Smeal suggested that the mayor and City Controller Harrison Goldin do some joint reassuring. When the mayor said that approach had been tried, Nye argued that it had been "unconvincing."

When the meeting finally broke up, nothing had been resolved. The financiers remained convinced that only massive reform of the city's profligate spending habits could pull it out of the increasingly dangerous debt spiral it had entered. Yet Mayor Beame seemed unwilling to admit that the situation was grave. He had, after all, faced budget deficits before, first as city controller and now as mayor. He didn't need a bunch of bankers telling him how to run his city.

Months later, as the city's financial crisis was nearing its climax, one of the financiers who had participated in the Gracie Mansion breakfast meeting of December 17 sat in his Wall Street office and railed against Mayor Beame. "Except for the sheer incompetence of Abraham Beame, this never would have happened," he said. "He's engaged in a farce. He's doing nothing. I just can't believe he's that stupid."

In less trying times, the commercial and investment bankers of New York City were accustomed to playing an inconspicuous, almost anonymous role in the city's fund-raising processes. When cities occasionally have to borrow money to meet payrolls and to finance expensive projects, they sometimes borrow on a short-term basis, perhaps for a year, in anticipation of tax revenues or government allotments. At other times, they may borrow for ten or twenty years to build new roads and hospitals, or to construct subways and port facilities. Such borrowing is accomplished by selling notes and bonds to the public.

To help a city borrow, banks and brokerage houses join together in temporary alliances known as underwriting syndicates. The members of such syndicates buy the city's notes and bonds, mark them up so they can make a profit, and resell them to the public. Customarily, it is a risk-free undertaking which almost always results in a profit. When the value of the notes or bonds becomes shaky, however, the underwriters have to assume a greater risk. Also, certain questions arise. Will they be able to unload millions of dollars in securities to the public? If not, will they be stuck with them? What kind of assurance can they receive that the city will stand behind its notes and bonds and pay them off when they reach maturity?

As far as Mayor Beame was concerned, questions of this type were both impertinent and unnecessary. New York City had always paid its debts in the past, and it most certainly would in the future. Beame believed that what was needed now was not a lot of hand-wringing by bankers and brokers, but a good hard-sell.

Mayor Beame did not know it then, but this time the financiers were not crying wolf. By the end of 1975, the largest city in the United States would be telling holders of $400 million of its notes which had fallen due that it could not pay them off. And no matter how the city fathers tried to sugar-coat it, the action amounted to a default.

As the city's fiscal problems grew more grave in 1975, the investment community began to play an increasingly important role in the rescue attempt. It participated at two levels, one public, the other private. Publicly, the most prominent financier was Felix G. Rohatyn, a partner at Lazard Frères & Co., who had figured prominently several years earlier in the International Telephone and Telegraph Corporation's acquisition program and in its controversial takeover of the giant Hartford Fire Insurance Company (see Chapter 9). Rohatyn was one of the most political of Wall Street's investment bankers. He had become involved in the city's bailout after giving his assessment of New York's situation to Robert Strauss, national chairman of the Democratic party, an old friend.

Through the intervention of Strauss, Rohatyn met with Governor Hugh Carey of New York. Out of their meetings came the idea for a "Municipal Assistance Corporation" that would help bail out New York City. As the drive to save New York gained momentum, Rohatyn's picture appeared almost daily in the major New York newspapers and on television screens as he fashioned new approaches to the city's problems and explained them to the public.

However, even as Rohatyn was taking a highly publicized role in fashioning New York's redemption, there was another group of financiers working long hours behind the scenes to get the city out of the red. Among this group of bankers were David Rockefeller, chairman of the Chase Manhattan Bank; William T. Spencer, president of First National City Bank; and Ellmore C. Patterson, chairman of the Morgan Guaranty Trust Company. These three financiers were instrumental in developing the New York banking community's attitude toward the city's fiscal crisis. They were portrayed by the press, by government officials, and by labor leaders as villains one day and heroes the next. But they spent much of 1975 working with city and state officials and caucusing among themselves, arguing first for creation of an advisory group, then for sharp cutbacks in city spending, and ultimately for the personal involvement of Governor Carey and of the White House.

Early in the process, the bankers agreed never to get into shouting matches with the politicians and union leaders who were accusing them of abandoning their responsibilities to the city by refusing to buy its bonds. Consequently, while their role in the New York crisis was often attacked, it was seldom defended.

Most intimately involved in the day-to-day mechanics of New York's rescue was a trio of financiers, labeled the "Jersey Mafia" by their peers because all commuted to Manhattan from suburban New Jersey. Although they bore a variety of titles, all three were the chief bond experts for their banks: Tom Labrecque, the young Chase Manhattan executive vice-president; Dick Kezer, the senior vice-president from Citibank; and Frank Smeal, an executive vice-president of Morgan Guaranty. In the background, helping call the shots, were Rockefeller, Spencer, and Patterson, as well as three other senior bankers: Walter B. Wriston, chairman of First National City (and by most assessments the city's most powerful banker); Edward L. Palmer, chairman of the executive committee of Citibank; and Willard C. Butcher, president of the Chase Manhattan Bank.

However, it was David Rockefeller who perhaps played the most influential role in New York City's salvage attempts. Through his persuasion, his brother, Nelson, Vice-President of the United States, publicly came out in favor of federal assistance for the floundering metropolis. The Vice-President's position conflicted sharply with President Ford's hands-off approach, and was believed to be one of the contributing factors in the President's decision not to keep Rockefeller as his running mate in the 1976 national elections.

In January 1974, David Rockefeller had been asked by Mayor Beame to head a committee of bankers to study financial reforms for the city, but he declined in favor of Ellmore Patterson of Morgan Guaranty. Later, however, Rockefeller helped fashion a panel called the Financial Community Liaison Group, which in turn spawned the Municipal Assistance Corporation, the body that ultimately kept the city from going bankrupt.

Rockefeller and the other bankers were confronted with municipal financial problems that generally arose in two areas. The city for years had been spending more than it had been taking in from taxes and from the federal and state governments. The recession that beset the nation in 1974 and the early part of 1975 compounded the situation. It meant that expenses for social services were rising and tax revenues were declining.

Overriding all this was the jumble of outmoded bookkeeping procedures that made it virtually impossible to judge whether the city's budget was in order. Furthermore, it had been customary for city officials to proclaim that a budget crisis was approaching in order to get more money from the state.

By the fall of 1974, Mayor Beame was saying that the city's budget for 1974–75 was running $430 million in the red. To make matters worse, a few months later he said that the next budget, covering 1975–76, would run an even bigger deficit of $1.6 billion. Still, the mayor said, that gap could be closed by a combination of raising taxes, increasing state and federal aid, and cutting costs.

The second part of the city's financial crisis involved the so-called cash flow problem. By the spring of 1975, the city was having difficulty finding lenders willing to come up with the more than half-billion dollars a month it needed to pay its bills. Quite simply, the cash wasn't there because lenders did not trust the city's shaky financial condition.

One of the difficulties encountered by analysts of the city's monetary troubles was the many gimmicks New York employed in attempting to balance on paper what was actually an unbalanced budget. The city, for example, paid day-to-day expense items from its capital budget, which was financed entirely by long-term borrowing—a serious departure from prudent accounting practice. It also counted as current income revenues from state and federal aid and from taxes, money that would not come in until the following year. Mayor Beame himself had been the originator of some of these ruses. However, as Edward Hamilton, the chief financial aide to former Mayor John Lindsay, pointed out, the reward system in City Hall in the late 1960s and early 1970s was geared toward ingenious short-term solutions to sticky long-term fiscal problems. With costs rising 15 percent a year and revenues rising only 5 percent, gimmicks had to be employed if huge tax increases were to be avoided.

As early as January 1971, Citibank had called attention to some of the dangers inherent in New York City's methods of fiscal management. In the bank's monthly economic letter, which was widely distributed in the financial and business community, an article entitled "Why New York Lives with Budget Crises" pointed out that "once again, in what has become almost an annual ritual, the cities are proclaiming budgetary crises."

Noting that Mayor Lindsay faced a potential shortage of $200 million to $300 million, the bank said the "popular 'solutions' to the fiscal squeeze on state and local governments are temporary respites at best." Governments, it continued, "must live with the fundamental economic propositions faced by private industry and consumers: Wants exceed resources and difficult decisions must be made on priorities." It wasn't until the middle of 1975 that the basic truth of that statement hit home.

Throughout the early months of 1975, the city's financial affairs continued to deteriorate and the public market for New York notes and bonds dried up. By spring, the "Jersey Mafia" was convening almost daily, with Rockefeller, Patterson, and Spencer frequently sitting in on the group's sessions. As conditions became more serious, the meetings grew more intense.

By late spring 1975, the crisis had reached the boiling point. Mayor Beame had announced a succession of budget cuts and lay-offs, but the numbers seemed to vary from day to day. Confidence in the mayor's ability to handle the situation was eroding rapidly. President Ford had ruled out the possibility of federal assistance, and Warren Anderson, the state senate majority leader, had rejected aid for the city.

Finally, on Memorial Day, a panel of businessmen and financiers named by Governor Carey met at the home of Richard Shinn, president of the Metropolitan Life Insurance Company. On that day, the foundation for the Municipal Assistance Corporation, or "Big MAC," as it was soon to become known, was laid. The following month, the state legislature officially created Big MAC, and authorized it to raise $3 billion through the sale of its own bonds—enough revenue to keep New York City afloat through the months of July, August, and September.

For the bankers involved, the decisions to be made in the days ahead were, according to Frank Smeal, "probably the most important in many, many years." Together, the big New York banks held over $1.2 billion in New York City securities, and the precariousness of the city's financial structure posed a threat to their profits. The banks were being asked to pump increasing amounts of cash into the city to keep it afloat, and it became necessary to weigh very carefully the advisability of such a risky investment.

By midsummer the banks found themselves at the center of a heated controversy over both their activities and their motives. Mayor Beame was flaying them as the villains who had guided the city down the primrose path of financial irresponsibility and then had deserted at a moment of crisis. The bankers defended their actions with claims of self-sacrifice. The truth appeared to lie in the middle. Clearly, the role of the banks was a combination of self-interest and concern for the survival of their host city. There was little question that they had a great deal at stake. They relied on a healthy local economy for much of their profits. But more importantly, the banks stood to lose about $180 million immediately if the city defaulted on a single note issue worth $741 million that was scheduled to fall due on August 22. (Happily for the banks the city came up with the money.)

Meanwhile, hard questions about the role of the bankers were being asked around the city. Was Big MAC, formed to raise money to redeem city notes, primarily a vehicle to extricate the banks from their precarious bind? Had the banks earned massive profits for years by buying and selling city securities, only to give the city the cold shoulder when the going got tough? Had the city's crisis worsened because investors across the country spurned New York City securities, or was it because the city's banks—the middlemen in such transactions—suddenly hesitated to buy New York's securities?

Much of the backroom talk on Wall Street took on a critical tone. "Big MAC was a bailout for the banks," said an official of one of the country's largest brokerage houses in a private conversation. "They exchanged a piece of paper [city notes] that could end up in default for one [MAC bonds] that had an A rating and plenty of backing."

Indeed, the backing of the MAC bonds was later to become a point of considerable controversy. The new bonds were guaranteed by city taxes and administered by the state. The theory was that investors might be willing to buy bonds that had a guaranteed source of income and were administered by state officials rather than city officials. That money, in turn, could be handed over to the city to help pay some current expenses and to redeem previously issued bonds and notes as they fell due. Investors in such earlier city securities, however, became more and more disillusioned as they saw city tax revenues earmarked for new securities rather than for old ones.

As for making money on the sale of city securities, the big New York banks in 1974 had bought for themselves or for resale to their customers about $5.4 billion worth of the city's short-term notes. Commissions on such underwritten sales ran as high as $3 for each $1,000 note. The banks had made millions of dollars in profits before they went sour.

The bankers defended both their commissions and their growing reluctance to handle city paper. The rising commissions, they said, were necessary because increasingly they had to reach out to smaller investors as more sophisticated institutions like insurance companies grew wary of buying New York City notes. Such a sales effort, they said, was expensive. Furthermore, the banks began to worry that if, by some chance, New York City did go broke and the bonds and notes became valueless, customers would sue the banks for selling them worthless New York securities.

Although there was no question about the past profitability of selling city securities, some bankers said that the profits on some such sales had disappeared in recent months. Citibank, for example, distributed an internal memorandum, in the spring of 1975, indicating that while it had participated in syndicates that had purchased $2.2 billion in New York City bonds over the past five years, it had actually suffered a net loss of $32,000 in its sales of New York City bonds in the previous two years. It also recited its problems in selling city notes.

"In March [1975], Citibank was the manager of an underwriting syndicate which bid for and purchased some $375 million of New York City notes," the memorandum said. "However, because the interest rate incorporated in the bid was not sufficient to attract investors, almost half of the issue could not be resold by the syndicate. The city, of course, was paid for the whole issue by the syndicate. As you can see, underwriting securities for the city is in no event a 'sure thing.'"

One Wall Streeter commented that the Citibank memo illustrated a "fundamental conflict" between the banks and the city. "It is the banks who have the customers with the money to buy the financial products, whatever they may be," he said. The "unspoken message" in the memo, he added, was that "the banks will do what they can to help out the city, but they have no sacred obligation to service the municipal bond market.

"The banks are not necessarily any more right or wrong than the city in the rhetorical pecking that's been going back and forth. In an emergency, everyone does whatever he can." Translation: In a pinch, especially when billions of dollars are at stake, it's every man for himself.

When the criticism of the bankers was at its peak, Frank Smeal, chief of Morgan Guaranty's money market division spoke out. Smeal said the banks had harbored growing reservations about the city's financial health for months, but had not felt they could do anything about it. "The banks were just not in a position to tell the city to reform," he said. "There's a difference between public and private credit. In the private sector, you can get audits, you can do things with management. You just can't do this with a public borrower. You can't impose a crisis on a city that has pledged its credit."

As for Mayor Beame's attempts to alleviate some of the city's financial pressures, he ordered the dismissal of 19,000 city workers from agencies controlled by his own office and another 21,000 workers from other agencies. The layoffs and threatened dismissals triggered a number of short-lived but effective strikes and job actions in New York. Garbage collectors staged a wildcat strike. Police blocked the Brooklyn Bridge. Fires raged in the South Bronx while firemen staged a job action.

During this time, a verbal battle between Mayor Beame and City Controller Harrison Goldin, a fast-talking, ambitious politician with a thirst to run New York himself, accelerated. Goldin pointed out that the investment community was bewildered by Beame's actions concerning job cuts followed by restorations when a sudden influx of cash became available.

The MAC board was also having its troubles. It had mounted an expensive nationwide promotion campaign to convince investors that MAC bonds were worth buying. To its distress, MAC discovered that anything even faintly resembling a New York City security was considered tainted merchandise. And the further from New York the MAC representatives traveled, the greater was the animosity they encountered toward the city. "You cannot underestimate the hostility toward New York City elsewhere in the country," said one broker after returning from the road.

As June ended, the MAC bond sale was concluded. Ultimately, because of investor resistance, the big New York banks had been forced to buy almost half of the $1 billion in bonds themselves. What's more, the interest rate averaged a staggering 9.19 percent, one of the highest ever placed on a tax-exempt bond. For New York City residents, the high interest rate meant that more of their tax dollars would have to go to retire the debt and less money would be available to pay the cost of running the city.

The bankers, feeling more financially vulnerable than ever because of their large holdings of increasingly questionable city and MAC securities, applied pressure to municipal and MAC leaders. David Rockefeller told the MAC officials that if immediate steps were not taken to put the city's affairs in order and balance its budget, the next scheduled sale of $1 billion in MAC bonds would find itself without any buyers.

Rockefeller suggested a wage freeze, accompanied by a dramatic and credible program of cost cutting. In addition, he said he wanted an immediate effort by MAC to monitor the city's accounting procedures.

"We went on record," a Rockefeller aide later said, "as saying that if it wasn't done, we couldn't sell any more bonds. Sure, we sold the first MAC issue, but that was just passing the city's debt from our left hand to our right hand."

Rockefeller was correct in his assumption that unless Beame began to take some stiff new actions, the city would go under. As it turned out, MAC would not again be able to make a public sale of bonds. The public had quickly become disenchanted with the MAC bonds, and as a result, their prices fell in public trading. The banks declared that they would never again expose themselves to such a risk.

"Bear in mind that the total exposure of the banks was now about $1.8 billion, including MAC bonds," said an official of one of New York's leading banks. "We thought we owned about as much as any bank should."

By this time the impact of New York's financial crisis had spread across the nation. It had affected much of the tax-exempt securities market, and consequently city and town treasuries from Maine to Oregon were paying more interest for their borrowings.

Edward F. Renshaw, a professor of economics at the State University of New York at Albany, estimated that the spillover costs to the rest of the nation, in terms of added interest costs on bond issues, was approximately $2 billion a year. Additional interest costs on notes, he said, brought the total to $3 billion, or $14 for every man, woman and child in the United States.

The higher interest costs were already being passed along to taxpayers and customers of utilities and such services as water and sewage disposal, and would later be reflected in higher property, income, and sales taxes.

The problem, Renshaw said, was that although interest rates on securities in general had been rising during 1975, the rates on state and local government bonds had been rising faster, reflecting New York's problems and investor uncertainty.

At about the same time that Professor Renshaw was citing the growing financial burden on government bodies around the country, the Securities Industry Association in Manhattan was issuing a chilling analysis of the potential direct impact of a New York City default on commercial banks.

The SIA reported that twenty-nine of the nation's banks held massive quantities of New York City securities equal to more than 50 percent of their capital funds. It also estimated that nine banks faced probable insolvency if New York defaulted, another eighteen banks would have their capital severely impaired, and twenty-two more would survive only with difficulty.

Even as the banks were hoping for some sort of last-minute bailout for New York, they also were showing signs of concern over the increasing instability of their holdings of MAC bonds and their even larger holdings of real estate investment trusts (REIT).

One analysis of the total holdings of a number of the largest

New York banks in city securities, MAC bonds, and REITs indicated that, although they would surely survive, their exposure in some instances amounted to $1 billion or more. Especially vulnerable were the three giants, Citibank, Chase Manhattan, and Chemical.

In August, Governor Carey searched for an acceptable way to raise another $1 billion for the city. The intricate plan finally fashioned by the governor involved a pledge by the state of New York to buy the MAC bonds, with the bankers acting, in effect, as investors of last resort if the state were unable to resell the bonds to other investors at the end of a year.

Carey announced the plan as a virtually accomplished fact, but the bankers quickly made it clear that they had not agreed to any such terms. The next day headlines proclaimed that the banks had caused the latest rescue attempt to founder. As a result, Citibank, Chase Manhattan, and Morgan Guaranty issued a joint statement: "We were not raising new objections when we told officials of the Municipal Assistance Corporation this morning that it would be impossible for the banks to guarantee to the state the repayment within one year of $1 billion to be advanced by the state to MAC. Bank representatives had informed state officials on Tuesday afternoon [before the announcement] that such a guarantee was impossible."

Beneath the formal bankers' language was a message for Governor Carey. They were mad. They felt they had been put in an unconscionable position, and they made it clear that they would not accept any such strong-arm tactics. Asked about the incident weeks afterward, Edward Palmer, the executive vice-president from Citibank, replied, "They made the statement that it was an honest mistake. We said, 'while it's hard to accept that, we really think you mean it. No hard feelings.' "

As it turned out, the bankers were willing to commit themselves to another piece of New York City's salvage, but hardly the $1 billion MAC officials had hoped for. Meeting in Kezer's office at Citibank, the bankers agreed to subscribe to $100 million in additional MAC bonds as their final gesture.

"There was a great deal of discussion on the amount," said one of the participants at the meeting. "We recognized that we were pumping the bottom of the well and beginning to see cloudy water."

The participation of the bankers was only one element in the jerry-built scheme to keep New York City afloat. As finally enacted by the state legislature, the plan called for a balanced budget within three years, and more loans from the banks, as well as from pension funds and other institutions. But most important, a committee of businessmen and financiers was established to enforce spending limits on the city.

In effect, the power to determine the city's spending levels was taken away from Mayor Beame and put in the hands of a seven-man panel called the Emergency Financial Control Board. Sitting on the board were Beame, City Controller Goldin, Governor Carey, State Controller Arthur Levitt, and three nationally known businessmen: William M. Ellinghaus, $225,000-a-year president of the New York Telephone Company who was moving over from the chairmanship of Big MAC; Albert V. Casey, $200,000-a-year chairman of American Airlines; and David I. Margolis, $364,000-a-year president of Colt Industries.

Other businessmen who emerged as strong forces in the new city financial structure included Richard Shinn of Metropolitan Life, who continued as head of Beame's Management Advisory Board, and Kenneth S. Axelson, a senior vice president of the J.C. Penney Company, who was sworn in as deputy mayor for finance. Felix Rohatyn was elevated to the chairmanship of Big MAC, and continued as a close personal advisor to Governor Carey.

With the new legislation and a general mood of accomodation by the unions, the banks, and the state legislature, it appeared that the city could survive until November. However, with the bond markets still closed to the city, and neither the city nor MAC able to raise any money from private or institutional investors, it became increasingly apparent that only a federal loan or guarantee would save New York. Governor Carey and Mayor Beame made repeated trips to Washington to entreat the administration to provide some sort of guarantee for New York securities. Time and again they were rebuffed by Treasury Secretary William Simon, himself a former bond trader from Wall Street, and by President Ford. The President was particularly scornful in his rejection of aid for New York, and briefly transformed the matter into a campaign issue as he prepared to face the voters a year later in a national election. After one rejection by President Ford, the New York *Daily News* ran a headline that said: "Ford to City: Drop Dead."

With little prospect of federal aid, New York City and New York State mounted a massive lobbying effort in Washington. Executives from both private and public sectors rushed to Washington to argue for aid for New York.

A.W. Clausen, president of the BankAmerica Corporation, the nation's largest bank, traveled from California to argue that federal aid for New York was essential. Mayor Moon Landrieu of New Orleans testified that federal aid for New York had the overwhelming support of the United States Conference of Mayors of which he was president, and of the National League of Cities.

In mid October, the big-three bankers, Rockefeller, Wriston, and Patterson, warned a congressional committee that "voices from abroad" were beginning to express "serious worry" about the potential worldwide repercussions of a New York default. Among those "voices from abroad" was that of West German Chancellor Helmut Schmidt, who cautioned of the serious international impact of a New York City default. So did George Ball, a partner of Lehman Brothers and a former State Department diplomat, who warned that the collapse of New York would be viewed by the Communist world as a "crisis of capitalism."

In New York, the controller's office issued a detailed list of vendors across the country who sold their products to New York City. The list contained the amount of money owed to each company, debts that presumably would be difficult to collect if the city went bankrupt. Also conveniently included were the names of the congressmen from the companies' districts.

The issue became hotly political, with Republicans generally lining up with President Ford, and Democrats siding with New York. Ultimately, the President's position began to cause dissension in the ranks of his supporters. In New York, Gustave Levy, senior partner of Goldman Sachs, and a long-time activist for the Republicans, became so angry at the President's position on New York that he told friends he was going to resign as co-chairman of the President's New York fund-raising effort. He later cooled off and decided to remain on the committee, but his anger was one indication of the passions that were aroused.

The city was barely surviving financially. On one bleak day in October it appeared that the efforts of the bankers, the politicians, and the businessmen had been in vain. The fragile plan enacted by the state legislature and held together by Big MAC nearly fell apart when the teachers' pension fund trustees refused to honor an earlier agreement to buy $150 million in MAC bonds. At the last minute, however, they bought the bonds and the city managed to stay solvent, although precariously.

With the crisis now worsening, and a November deadline approaching when the city would run out of money unless the federal government intervened, a new maneuveur was undertaken. The state called for a forced moratorium on payment of principal to holders of $1.6 billion of the city's short-term notes, or for a swap of such notes for MAC bonds. The plan aroused immediate controversy in the investment community but was viewed favorably by the White House. Suddenly it appeared that the Ford administration might be willing to step in and help New York.

President Ford had long argued that he would not help New York until it had defaulted. Now the White House took the position that a forced moratorium amounted to a default, so perhaps it could provide some help after all.

After additional skirmishes between New York City, Albany, and Washington, President Ford officially relented. On the eve of Thanksgiving he announced that he was dropping his opposition to federal aid for the city, and proposed legislation for $2.3 billion in short-term seasonal loans that would enable New York to avert default.

The loans were to be administered by Treasury Secretary Simon, and would extend through June 1978. The city would pay an interest rate of 1 percent more than the federal bill rate (which at the time was 7 percent).

For Beame and Carey it was cause for jubilation. Beame said the President's decision marked "a crucial turning point in our continuing struggle to resolve the city's fiscal crisis." Carey said it represented "a vindication of New York's case, of the merit of our position." As for the President, reminded that he had pledged to veto any legislation whose purpose was to bail out New York, he replied that New York had bailed itself out by taking tough measures.

The bond market made its own assessment of the new turn of events. MAC bonds with a face value of $5,000 jumped $225 in price in a single day, and sold for $4,325—$850 higher than their price only a few weeks earlier when it appeared that the city was in imminent danger of bankruptcy.

The stock market also reacted favorably, even before the ransom was finalized. *The Wall Street Journal* reported that "the industrial average spurted almost five points at the opening, buoyed by the news that the New York State Legislature had approved a tax package designed to rescue the city from default and spur the Federal Government into providing some assistance."

For residents of New York who had been largely observers through the events of the previous nine months, the headlines were reassuring. However, it soon became apparent they would be affected by the belt-tightening that had accompanied the rescue of their city. Felix Rohatyn summed it up when he said, "the pain is just beginning."

During most of 1975, the discomforts suffered by the average New Yorker had been slight. They had begun paying transit fare increases of fifteen cents and higher bridge and tunnel tolls. They had faced a modest contraction of municipal services. For the most part, however, life in the city had gone on as usual. For all the sound and the fury, the scare talk of rioting in the streets and urban anarchy, the headlines and the intemperate debates that had reached into the White House and Congress, the average New Yorker had been only modestly affected.

By the beginning of 1976, all that was changing. The state legislature had voted an average 25 percent increase on personal income taxes for New York City residents. It had also tacked an additional four cents to five cents on each pack of cigarettes sold in New York City, and a 4 percent sales tax on beauty parlors, barbershops, health salons, and so-called massage parlors.

What's more, the city had cut back about $600 million in its capital expenditures for the fiscal year that would begin in July 1976. The squeeze would be felt not only in the lack of new facilities, but in the increased wear and tear on current facilities slated for replacement. Proposed outlays for the city's parks, for example, were cut by 67 percent. Funds for highways were cut by 43 percent, and for schools by 30 percent. One city official remarked that the budget "takes us back to the spending level of eight years ago."

Perhaps the most visible impact was on city payrolls. With 35,000 jobs already eliminated, Mayor Beame said in mid November that he was cutting 8,000 more. Among the jobs cut as 1975 ended were 8,776 positions from the Board of Education, or 11 percent of the total; 7,028 or 15 percent from the city's Hospital Corporation; 4,315 or 12 percent from the Police Department; 2,946 or 11 percent from social services; 2,101 or 15 percent from the Sanitation Department; 1,549 or 11 percent from the Fire Department; and 1,049 or 22 percent from resorts, recreation, and cultural affairs.

Given all these cuts, and more to be announced, few would quarrel with Rohatyn's assessment that in the coming years New York City would have to undergo "the most brutal kind of financial and fiscal exercise any community in the country will ever have to face."

In addition to the municipal cutbacks and layoffs already imposed, experts warned that more than 15,000 jobs—possibly as many as 60,000—would disappear from the private sector as the city's budget-cutting continued. The losses were expected to occur primarily in trade, construction, and services ranging from hotels to computers.

Herbert Bienstock, head of the New York office of the United States Bureau of Labor Statistics, said there would be "an enormous number of secondary effects, beginning with the laid-off man who doesn't buy this year's suit." Some experts warned that cutbacks in private industry would be critical because the city's rate of unemployment was several percentage points higher than the national average. In the past, they said, gaps opened by declining private employment had been filled by increases in city hiring— a factor that was impossible under the new structures of the Emergency Financial Control Board.

Furthermore, the city would have to contend with the fragile financial condition of New York State, normally a major supplier of funds for the city. Indeed, in late December, as the state grappled with its own deficit, it appeared that Governor Carey's proposed spending cuts at the state level would force the city to trim its own budget still further.

Nevertheless, with difficulties and hard times still to come, New York City had managed to escape default. The bankers had preserved the value of hundreds of millions of dollars in city securities that lay in their vaults. In the final throes of negotiations with Albany and Washington, they had been forced to accept lower interest rates on city and MAC securities, but their capital was intact. Even as urbanologists were debating the future of cities in America, the financiers were warily congratulating one another for having walked away from a potential disaster virtually unscathed.

Their victory, however, was not without cost. In conquering the specter of default, the financiers and their allies in government had cast a shadow over the entire fixed-income security market. No longer could investors take comfort from legal promises like the one inscribed on New York City's notes: "The City of New York promises to pay the bearer the sum of $10,000 on the due date specified above in lawful money of the United States of America."

157

The fact was that on December 11, 1975, investors who held almost $400 million of New York City's 9.5 percent notes, and who wanted their money as promised on the note, did not get it. Instead they were given their choice of holding their notes for another three years (and receiving interest), or of swapping them for newly issued MAC bonds. Although some noteholders sued for full repayment of their notes, the courts upheld the city's moratorium.

For New York, escaping the jaws of default may have been a Pyrrhic victory. Some municipal bond analysts said the city would be a long time in regaining access to the credit markets—a position it would eventually need despite the backing of the federal government. What investor could be sure, they asked, that New York would pay off in the future if it hadn't paid off in the past?

For the financiers, however, that battle would be fought another day.

7 / The Penphil Pals

T he collapse of the Penn Central Railroad sent tremors through Wall Street and every other financial capital of the world. Post mortems, recriminations and lawsuits still flourish. Standing squarely in the center of the financial debacle were David C. Bevan, the railroad's chief financial officer, and Charles J. Hodge, an investment banker who served as adviser to the railroad. The two men played key roles in forming a lucrative personal investment club called Penphil, in organizing an airline service called Executive Jet Aviation, and in fashioning an ill-advised diversification program which drained the ailing railroad's financial resources. Taken in toto, the events leading up to the Penn Central's failure present a sordid picture of big business and invest-

ment bankers working together in an attempt to benefit their own self-serving purposes.

It may well have been the most spectacular bankruptcy in history. On June 21, 1970, the Penn Central Transportation Company, the largest privately owned railroad company in the world, collapsed. To millions of Americans the Penn Central, with assets of more than $6 billion, had seemed as solid an institution as the United States Senate or the New York Yankees—a visible symbol of the transportation industry that would surely last forever. But it didn't.

The big railroad's financial affairs in the months following the bankruptcy were subjected to probably the most searching public examination any company had ever faced. Amid the welter of recriminations and charges that followed the collapse, the law suits and the criminal proceedings, one fact became clear. Scarcely anyone connected with the huge and troubled railroad would escape with his reputation unscathed. Some of the nation's largest banks and most prestigious financial institutions would be called to account for their failure to anticipate the financial debacle. The Penn Central's directors, experienced financiers, and businessmen with previously impeccable reputations, would find themselves under attack for their failure to properly assess and guide the affairs of the railroad. And, above all, the role of the investment bankers who helped shape the railroad's disastrous diversification program would be sharply attacked.

The failure of Penn Central would give critics of big business a chance to release their venom and point out the weaknesses and flaws in a system which often worked well, but could sometimes be a disaster. Just as ITT would become a symbol of greed and subterfuge a few years later, so the Penn Central would seem to many Americans to symbolize inept management and a blatant disregard for the individual shareholders who were left holding millions of dollars in worthless securities.

Standing squarely at the center of the financial catastrophe was David C. Bevan, the chief financial officer of the Penn Central, and the principal architect of the railroad's diversification efforts. It was on his head that much of the vitriol would fall after the collapse. Another key figure in the Penn Central diversification program was Charles J. Hodge, an investment adviser to the railroad, and chairman of the executive committee of the investment banking firm of Glore Forgan, Wm. R. Staats, Inc. Between them, Bevan and Hodge would be singled out for particular attention as the corpse of the railroad was examined for clues to its fatal malady.

At the time of its collapse, the Pennsylvania Railroad had been a central part of the Philadelphia scene for more than a century. Organized in 1846, largely with local capital, to protect the commercial interests of the city, it had played an important role in Philadelphia's social establishment. Its presidents were respected and honored not only within the city, but also nationally.

In 1968, the Pennsylvania and the New York Central merged. The stock of the new company, which was called the Penn Central, skyrocketed. It seemed for a short time that financial problems which had plagued the northeast's major railroads had been solved.

"Against this background, it is not surprising that the Penn Central's collapse caught the nation unaware," said the Senate Commerce Committee four years later. "Warning signals of trouble had been supressed or sugar-coated. Its end approached with uncommon speed after the auspicious culmination of the merger."

The final days of the company were agonizing. Money borrowed from banks dried up. An attempt to float a $100 million public debt offering was aborted. In late May, the company's board of directors forced out its chairman, Stuart Saunders, and its chief financial officer, David Bevan. Administration officials in Washington had been prepared to authorize a loan guarantee by the federal government of $200 million, but that, too, was stalled by congressional opposition, and finally abandoned. So, the railroad filed for bankruptcy under a special section of the law designed to keep bankrupt railroads operating while the claims of its creditors were resolved. And, although the end came as a shock to the financial world, the trains continued to run, and the company continued to operate under the supervision of the court.

The questions immediately arose: What had happened? Why had this seemingly powerful railroad collapsed? What lay at the heart of its problems? While definitive answers never emerged, one by one some of the apparent causes of the collapse began to surface. One of those reasons was Penphil.

On July 10, 1962, eight years before the Penn Central collapsed, a tiny investment club called Penphil was incorporated in the state of Pennsylvania. A close look at Penphil demonstrates how some of the railroad's insiders and their investment bankers were able to take advantage of their powerful business connections and their intimate knowledge of corporate affairs to reap a personal profit.

Initially, there were sixteen members of the little group, among them some names well known in investment banking circles—names like Bevan and Hodge. Curiously, some of the first names had a less familiar ring. There was Thomas R. Bevan, for example, who at various times was to serve as president, secretary and treasurer of Penphil. He was David Bevan's brother. There was Mrs. Marie L. Hodge, who, it was learned, was the wife of Charles Hodge. Another member was Mrs. Dorothy H. Warner. She was the wife of Theodore K. Warner, who served as vice president of accounting and taxation at the Penn Central. And, Mrs. Dorothy B. Stevens, wife of a former partner of the investment firm of Hornblower & Weeks-Hemphill, Noyes.

The membership seemed innocuous enough at first glance. Merely a small group of friends, many of them from the same social set in Philadelphia, pooling their cash and expertise to make some money in the stock market. Nothing unusual about that. Such small groups abound in the United States, and provide a ready means for perpetuating wealth. They are a sort of rich man's parallel to the neighborhood investment club, where every member throws in a few dollars a month and hopes the local stockbroker will pay enough attention to execute its order for an odd lot of Xerox or IBM.

"The Penphil Corporation was a small, informal investment company set up by a number of us who were linked by friendship to invest for capital appreciation," David Bevan would say in mid 1970, under oath. "It was a very small affair and run quite informally. I was a stockholder."

Only Penphil was not simply a neighborhood investment group. For one thing, members of a neighborhood investment club don't usually sit on boards of directors and have advance knowledge of events that will change the prices of the stock they hold. For another, they seldom have virtually unlimited access to large amounts of cash which they can borrow to enhance their fortunes.

Government investigators concluded after an exhaustive study of Penphil that it constituted "a classic example of the use of corporate power for personal profit. In effect," they said, "it is the chronicle of how two men, David C. Bevan, the former chief financial officer of the Penn Central, and Charles J. Hodge, the former chief investment advisor of the railroad, manipulated the financial resources, the assets, and the credit of the nation's ninth largest corporation for the benefit of an investment company, Penphil, which they established and directed. The ultimate goal of Bevan and Hodge was to create a large conglomerate operating and holding company while orchestrating Penn Central investments in a way that would serve the interests of Penphil. In an overall sense, the history of Penphil is not only the story of monumental disservice to the Penn Central, the nation's largest transportation system; it is a detailed record of activities which distorts the concept of the democratic free enterprise system."

The investigators decided that one of the key factors that enabled Bevan and Hodge to establish and build Penphil was an unrestricted line of credit from the Chemical Bank New York Trust Company, the bank where the Penn Central maintained huge loan and deposit accounts.

Another factor, they believed, was the manipulation of Penn Central investments by Bevan and Hodge, giving Penphil far greater leverage than it would otherwise have had. This power was enhanced by the fact that some of the members of Penphil were chief officers of corporations whose stock was jointly held by both Penphil and the Penn Central.

So successful was the club, that in less than eight years most of its members were able to claim a profit of $83,500 on a cash investment of only $16,500.

Because Penphil was a classic case involving corporate executives, their investment bankers, and other well-connected associates and acquaintances, banding together for personal profit, it is worth taking a close look at the individuals who participated, and at their corporate responsibilities. The original members of Penphil included:

David Bevan, who served as vice-president in charge of finance of the Pennsylvania Railroad Company, and chairman of the finance committee of both the railroad and its successor, the Penn Central Company. He had overall responsibility for investments in securities, including the pension and compensation plans, of those two companies and of their subsidiaries. He also was a director and member of the executive committee of such Penphil or Penn Central investments as Great Southwest Corporation, Kaneb Pipe Line Company, Arvida Corporation, and Tropical Gas Company, Inc.

Charles J. Hodge, whose Penphil stock was held in his wife's name. With David Bevan, he controlled Penphil's affairs and was a member of its investment committee. He was an officer of the investment banking firm of Glore Forgan and Company, and its successors. While a Penphil stockholder, Hodge also was a director and member of the executive committee of Kaneb Pipe Line Company, Great Southwest Corporation, Tropical Gas Company, Inc., and Arvida Corporation.

Thomas Bevan, brother of David Bevan, who maintained all Penphil's books and records. A partner of the Philadelphia law firm of Duane, Morris and Heckscher, he handled all Penphil's legal work until 1971.

Lawrence Stevens, whose Penphil stock was held in his wife's name. He was a member of Penphil's investment committee until his death in 1969. He also was the managing partner of the Philadelphia office of Hemphill, Noyes & Company, a stock brokerage firm, and its successor, Hornblower & Weeks-Hemphill, Noyes & Co.

Robert Haslett, who was a member of Penphil's investment committee from the time it was formed, and served during one period as its chairman. During his association with Penphil, he held the positions of director of investments of the Pennsylvania Railroad and Penn Central Company, and vice-president in charge of investments of the two bodies. In those railroad positions, he made the investment decisions, under Bevan's supervision, for the railroad's pension and compensation plans.

Other initial Penphil stockholders were equally prominent. They included: Benjamin F. Sawin, president of the Provident National Bank of Philadelphia; Francis A. Cannon, a registered broker-dealer and administrative vice-president of the First Boston Corporation; Warren H. Bodman, a partner of Yarnall, Biddle & Company; William R. Gerstnecker, treasurer of the Pennsylvania Railroad and later corporate vice-president of the Penn Central Company; Paul D. Fox, a vice-president of the Pennsylvania Railroad and later administrative vice-president of the Penn Central Company; and Theodore K. Warner, vice-president of taxation of the railroad.

The original members of Penphil, for the most part, were friends of Bevan who comprised the membership of a fishing club called "The Silverfish." Later, Bevan invited officers and directors of companies in which Penphil invested to become members of the investment group. This put Penphil in the position of having access to information concerning the day-to-day operations of those companies.

In order to understand how a small investment group like Penphil could get massive loans on virtually nothing but a telephone call, it is important to consider the relationship between the Chemical Bank and the Penn Central. The Pennsylvania Railroad had done business with the bank since 1891, and its account with Chemical was one of the railroad's largest, and the bank's oldest. In December 1961, for example, the railroad had more than $22 million in outstanding loans from the bank, and was maintaining a compensating balance of between $4.5 million and $5.8 million.

Furthermore, the relationship between Bevan and William S.

Renchard, chairman of the bank, was one of long standing. They had known each other at least since 1946, and Bevan had maintained a personal line of credit with Chemical at the prime rate since at least 1960. The prime rate is the rate generally charged the most credit-worthy corporations, and is substantially below the rate generally charged individuals. Glore Forgan also had a long and close relationship with Chemical. Since 1961, Hodge, too, had maintained a personal line of credit, which reached a loan balance of nearly $950,000 by November 1968.

The relationship between Penphil and Chemical was revealed in an internal memorandum written by an officer of Chemical in 1962 when Penphil was asking for its initial loan. Better than any testimony or court argument, it demonstrated how powerful financial figures could use their corporate strength to their own personal advantage. The memo said in part:

"David Bevan, financial vice-president of the Pennsylvania Railroad Company, called me on the telephone today and said he and a group of friends, totaling about fifteen, are planning to organize a corporation to purchase a substantial block of common stock of Kaneb Pipe Line Company [Penphil's first investment]. The group will include Charles Hodge of Glore Forgan and Company, Benjamin F. Sawin, president of Provident Tradesmen's Bank and Trust Company, Messrs. Gerstnecker and Haslett of the Pennsylvania Railroad's financial staff, and others.

"Frankly, the rate [prime rate] on the proposed loan is too low, but, in view of the size of the deal and the fact that it has such good friends connected with it, WSR [W. S. Renchard, chairman of Chemical] felt it was preferable not to quibble with Mr. Bevan over the rate. He indicated that George Bartlett of Glore Forgan and Company would probably be the one to negotiate the purchase of the stock, and very likely Charles Hodge would be the one to work out the mechanics of the loan arrangement."

Chemical worked out an open-ended line of credit on the loans, totaling more than $1.8 million, without any prescribed requirements regarding the payment of either interest or principal. Stock purchased with the loans was used as collateral.

Congressional investigators concluded that without the line of credit, it was doubtful whether the members of Penphil would have been willing to put up the liquid assets necessary to carry out their plan. "The $1.8 [million] in Chemical Bank loans was the primary factor that has allowed Penphil investors to realize a 600 percent profit on their initial investment of $16,500 each in less than eight years," they said. "Another very important aspect of the Chemical Bank loan to Penphil should be highlighted. It was, to say the least, a highly concessionary loan agreement: (1) there were no formal loan procedures or payment schedules; (2) the line of credit was at the prime rate, although usually such loans would have been at a minimum of one percentage point above prime; (3) there was no compensating balance asked or required for these loans, although a 20 percent compensating balance would have been normal for a loan from a big New York bank. It is clear, therefore, that the $1.8 million in loans to Penphil were not made by Chemical Bank on the basis of the soundness of the line of credit. They were made on preferential terms, as compared to loans of a similar nature, because of the value to Chemical Bank of Penn Central's loan and deposit business. In effect, it was Penn Central's compensating balances, interest payments, and deposits that were subsidizing the Penphil line of credit for the personal profit of Penphil members."

An examination of Penphil transactions reveals how investment bankers and other investors with inside knowledge can profit to an extent seldom seen by those on the outside. When Penphil made its first purchase in July 1962—$115,925 worth of common stock of the Kaneb Pipe Line Company—Hodge was a director and a member of Kaneb's executive committee. That purchase was made with knowledge of a substantial increase in Kaneb's earnings during the first third of 1962, and certain per share estimates for the year—developments that have a critical impact on the price of a share of stock on the Stock Exchange. Penphil knew about these estimates, but the public did not. Penphil then bought $40,000 more in Kaneb stock during February 1963. By then Hodge had information about Kaneb's ten-year estimates of favorable revenues, earnings, and cash flow.

During 1962 and 1963, the Pennsylvania Railroad and various

Penphil stockholders also purchased Kaneb stock for their own accounts. This happened at a time when each of them had nonpublic information about major pipeline expansion plans and significant increased earnings of the company. By April 1972, Penphil still held its shares of Kaneb, and had a paper profit of $926,000.

Kaneb, of course, was only the first transaction. Subsequent transactions by Penphil revealed a tangled trail of private information and internal dealings that made it clear how the tiny investment club could make such a handsome profit with its borrowed money.

Penphil's next purchase was 10,000 shares of Great Southwest Corporation stock in July 1963. Hodge, of course, was a Great Southwest director and had private information about a dramatic and unexpected improvement in the company's 1963 earnings. Then, in March 1964, David Bevan personally purchased shares of Great Southwest while in possession of information, not publicly available, that the Pennsylvania Railroad was considering acquiring about 80 percent of· Great Southwest's outstanding stock. In fact, Great Southwest later became a key element in the railroad's ill-fated diversification program, and it is discussed in detail later in this chapter.

In November and December 1965, Penphil, Bevan, and Hodge sold for a substantial profit their shares of Great Southwest. But who bought the shares? None other than the Pennsylvania Railroad, the railroad Bevan served as chief financial officer, and Hodge as a financial advisor. Penphil profited by $212,500.

The major point to be made was simply this. As of June 1971, nearly nine years after its founding, Penphil had made an unrealized or paper gain of over $3 million from securities it held, and had earned a profit of nearly $227,000 from securities it had bought and sold. It did not have a loss on a single investment, with the sole exception of a $40,000 note it purchased from a company called Holiday International Tours. How Penphil must have been envied by investors across the country who were struggling to earn a profit, based only on their assessment of publicly available information.

The government, however, far from admiring Penphil, took the opposite position. "The view has been widely held that Penn Central's investment decisions in the last few years made in connection with its diversification program seemed simply to have reflected bad judgment by management," the staff of the House Committee on Banking and Currency said. "However, a detailed examination of the facts . . . indicates that these decisions make a great deal more sense when viewed in the light of the interests and goals of Penphil and some of its members."

In other words, the railroad was making investment decisions that turned out to be bad for its shareholders, but good for the members of Penphil.

Although Penphil provided the most dramatic example of how a corporate official, an investment banker, and their friends could reap personal profits by using inside connections and information on their own behalf, another episode that occurred just before the collapse of the Penn Central also illustrated the cozy relationship between the railroad and its investment bankers.

It revolved around the Penn Central's flirtation with the airline business, through a tiny company called Executive Jet Aviation, Inc. Before it was over, the Executive Jet adventure, largely a creation of Bevan and Hodge, would seriously tarnish the reputations of the individuals involved and the Penn Central. It also would color the Penn Central affair with a hint of sex and draw increased attention to what had previously been a series of rather dry financial episodes at the railroad.

Executive Jet got its start when a retired brigadier general of the Air Force, Olbert F. Lassiter, conceived the idea of operating a fleet of jet planes and pilots that could fly executives of big corporations on short notice to their destinations. In effect, small- and medium-size companies could enjoy their own jet fleet without the expense of buying planes themselves. Through an intermediary, General Lassiter contacted Charles Hodge of Glore Forgan.

Hodge liked the idea, and so did David Bevan. So, in late 1964, a wholly owned subsidiary of the railroad, called the American Contract Company, advanced $275,000 to Executive Jet. It was the first small step in what eventually was to become a torrent of money and a major involvement.

Through August 1966, the Pennsylvania Railroad advanced about $13 million to Executive Jet to buy Lear jets which were to serve as the backbone for the executive contract flying service. The financial agreement specified that both principal and interest payments would be deferred until 1970, with the level of interest payments geared to the earnings of EJA. The security for these advances, initially, was the airplanes themselves, but when financing from outside banks was required later, the railroad agreed to subordinate its own security interest in the airplanes to the later investors.

One major obstacle to the Pennsylvania's involvement with Executive Jet was a rule of the federal government that forbade rail carriers from becoming involved in the operation of air freight services. At first, there appeared to be no problem, and extra care was taken to make the investment in EJA in nonvoting stock. However, in August 1966, the situation changed dramatically when EJA successfully negotiated the purchase of 80 percent of Johnson Flying Service, which had a permanent certificate from the Civil Aeronautics Board as a supplemental airline, which gave it the right to engage in the air charter and cargo business. What followed proved mind-boggling to the investigators in Washington who conducted the post mortem of the Penn Central.

"The project was initiated with the full realization on the part of Bevan that a railroad's control of an air carrier without Civil Aeronautics Board approval was in direct violation of the law," they asserted. "Indeed, awareness of the illegal nature of the project was dramatized by repeated efforts to conceal from the Civil Aeronautics Board the control over Executive Jet Aviation exercised by the Pennsylvania Railroad. This deception included two attempts by the railroad to appear to divest itself of control of Executive Jet, while in fact, its domination of that company remained virtually intact. Some $6 million in unsecured Pennsylvania Railroad investments were made in Executive Jet after the CAB order to the railroad to divest itself of its air carrier interest.

This illegal control of EJA, along with EJA's foreign illegal activities, cost the PRR and EJA a total of $70,000 in fines levied by the CAB, the second largest fine ever levied by the CAB in a single case."

By the summer of 1969, the directors of the railroad were confronted with a direct challenge. It was disclosed at their August 26 meeting that a suit had been brought by a former officer of Executive Jet against a number of defendants, including the railroad, Glore Forgan, Charles Hodge, and David Bevan. Among other things, it charged that the railroad dominated Executive Jet through Bevan and Hodge, and also that Penphil, the private investment club dominated by Bevan and Hodge, had an improper arrangement involving Executive Jet.

The directors of the railroad had been aware for some time that the Civil Aeronautics Board considered Penn Central's involvement with Executive Jet to be illegal, and they also knew by now that sizeable amounts of money had been advanced to Executive Jet, while the railroad had received no return on the money. An executive session of the board was held to consider the matter, and it was decided to authorize an investigation by the board's conflicts committee. However, when Bevan was told what had been decided, he blew up, said he would consider such an investigation to be a vote of no confidence, and threatened to resign. Bevan's blowup did the trick. The directors backed down, and later explained that the reason they did so was because of Bevan's importance in raising cash to keep the railroad afloat, and the lack of a suitable replacement for him.

The SEC later would comment that "an immediate consequence" of the directors' backing down under Bevan's threats was that Bevan could "continue wasting corporate assets in the EJA activities, and could continue to conceal the need to write off Penn Central's entire investment in EJA in light of the effective bankruptcy of the company."

Moreover, in the view of the SEC, the failure to stand up to Bevan went far beyond Executive Jet in its significance. "The consequences of Bevan's successful intimidation of the board, and the board's knowing and willing refusal to examine direct and accurate challenges to his integrity were far more serious than the continuation of the EJA scandal," it said. It also pointed out that Bevan was the sole representative of Penn Central in dealing with lenders, and had responsibility for billions of dollars of financings.

The most titillating aspect of the Executive Jet debacle evolved around the fondness of General Lassiter for pretty girls, and some explosive testimony given by a former Executive Jet employee named J. H. Ricciardi. During the height of the controversy over Executive Jet, a picture of a smiling Lassiter, clad in bathing trunks, and a busty blonde named Linda Vaughn, in a bikini, her hand on Lassiter's thigh, was printed in popular magazines across the country.

But that was only a curtain raiser to the sworn testimony of Ricciardi, who said he was hired by Lassiter to handle public relations, specifically "social engagements." Some excerpts from his testimony:

Q. What else did you do while you were in New York for EJA?

A. I could possibly refer to this as public relations. During the first day I was here in New York, General Lassiter said I could be of great, great service to him if I would help in the social life of General Hodge and Dave Bevan, since he [Lassiter] was under a lot of pressure from them due to the company having financial problems in not getting their supplemental ticket, and to possibly alleviate some of the pressure he was under if I could see to it while they [Hodge and Bevan] were in New York and they wanted some companionship, that I do what I could to assist.

Q. Did you do any of this?

A. Yes. On one occasion General Hodge asked if I knew of any young ladies who would go on a business trip to Europe that he was taking with General Lassiter. . . . I found a young lady that . . . was agreeable to taking a European trip with an amiable group.

Q. Were there any other occasions where you performed those public relations functions?

A. Yes.

Q. This is still in New York?

A. Yes. I would say approximately in August they were acquiring a new Jet Star and they were planning a trip to Las Vegas and Los Angeles, and again General Lassiter asked me if I would find suitable companionship for David Bevan and General Hodge. . . . I found a couple of young ladies that were willing to take the trip. One was called Beth ————. She was with General Hodge —and a young lady called Corrine————.

Q. Any other occasions in New York that you performed these functions?

A. Yes. I once got a date for David Bevan with a young lady called Norma————.

Ricciardi's testimony went on, detailing his services in "public relations" for Executive Jet. House congressional investigators raised the question of whether it might help explain why a man of David Bevan's supposed shrewdness and financial acumen would persist in having the Pennsylvania Railroad make heavy investments in Executive Jet even after the Civil Aeronautics Board had made it clear that the flow of funds should have been drastically curtailed; and why he resisted having Lassiter removed as chief executive officer of Executive Jet despite the repeated advice of reliable management experts.

"Under the circumstances," they concluded, "consideration must be given to the possibility that public revelation of certain personal activities that might have been extremely embarassing to Bevan is inevitably linked to the question of why Bevan acted in the strange way he did throughout the deteriorating EJA catastrophe."

Clearly, one of the keys to understanding the Penn Central's decline and fall was the remarkable relationship between two key figures: David Bevan and Charles Hodge. Hodge was bluff and hearty, well known in investment banking circles, and scarcely ever called anything but Charlie by his close friends, and General by others—a reflection of his rank in the National Guard. He and Bevan had been friends on a social as well as business level for years, and Hodge considered himself an "intimate friend of the family." He and Bevan both belonged to the Silverfish, and at one time, both owned apartments in the same Florida condominium.

Hodge, for his part, helped Bevan in personal matters such as letters of reference. When Bevan was applying for his Florida condominium, Hodge wrote in a letter of reference: "I have known Mr. and Mrs. Bevan for twenty years. I am acquainted with their two sons and consider myself a friend of the family. Socially, I would consider them top flight."

In addition to his friendship with Bevan, Hodge cultivated Stuart Saunders, Bevan's boss at the Penn Central. He gave a lavish dinner in New York in honor of Saunders and Bevan, just after Saunders was named chairman of the Penn Central. Invitations to the dinner were accepted by the cream of the nation's financial institutions, including such executives as William H. Moore, chairman of the Bankers Trust Company; George A. Murphy, chairman of the Irving Trust Company; and Leslie B. Worthington, president of U. S. Steel.

Hodge also helped arrange part of the itinerary of a European tour by Saunders. He was a man who knew the right people and had an instinct for putting them together in the right place at the right time.

On a business basis, Hodge's contact with Bevan clearly worked to his advantage. Glore Forgan acted as the broker for both the railroad's subsidiary, the Pennsylvania Company, and the railroad's Contingent Compensation Fund in their stock purchases in the early 1960s. In addition, Hodge was sent as an emissary of the railroad to Switzerland to convince Swiss banking interests to vote for the Pennsylvania Railroad–New York Central merger that later proved to be so disastrous.

All this activity served Hodge and his firm well. In addition to all the other fees and commissions from brokerage activities, Hodge and his firm received over $1.5 million in advisory fees and stock commissions relating to the four nonrail acquisitions made by the Pennsylvania Railroad in the early to mid 1960s.

Many investment bankers serve clients by helping facilitate the mechanics of a merger. Some also bring merger candidates to their attention. But the staff of the Senate Commerce Committee saw in Hodge's role the possibility of a darker motivation.

In addition to the surface reasons given for Hodge's recommendations, "other reasons may have consciously or subconsciously prompted his urging the railroad to take the action that it did," the staff said in December 1972. Specifically on the acquisition of the Great Southwest Corporation, the staff said: "Not only was there the possibility of a large advisory fee in connection with the GSC transaction, but from his [Hodge's] position as a member of the company's board of directors and investment banking adviser to GSC, he would have known of its expansionary (through acquisition) plans and the greater fee possibilities obtainable here if it were a subsidiary of the PRR whose larger financial backing would permit greater acquisition potential."

In other words, given the railroad's money, and Great Southwest's ambitious acquisition plans, two plus two could add up to five for Hodge and Glore Forgan. An added bonus was the fact that Hodge and other members of his firm also possessed Great Southwest stock interests themselves, which could have been influencing factors in the recommendation to the railroad to purchase the company.

Bevan had the opportunity and absolute responsibility to evaluate Hodge's suggestions, the Senate staff said. However, "his friendship with Hodge and apparent trust in his judgment may well have impaired the objectivity and analysis he would have employed in a normal arms-length transaction."

On January 3, 1972, a year and a half after the collapse of the Penn Central, Congressman Wright Patman, a Texas populist who delighted in locking horns with the nation's financial institutions, wrote a letter to the members of the Banking and Currency Committee which he chaired. After more than a year of detailed investigation, involving dozens of interviews all over the country, analysis of court documents, correspondence, filings with government agencies, bank records, and documents obtained from the Penn Central, its subsidiaries, and other corporations, Patman concluded that his committee had completed one of the most careful and detailed investigations in its history.

One major finding of the study, Patman said, was that the Penn Central's diversification program, initiated seven years before the collapse, and fostered by the railroad's investment bankers, had a "disastrous effect" on the railroad.

"Despite the claims of success by former officials of the Penn Central, this program was an extremely costly drain on the Railroad's financial and managerial resources," Patman said, echoing a theme that was to resound throughout many of the autopsies of the railroad.

In even more colorful terms, Patman's committee staff was to label the Penn Central's diversification program a "road to ruin." For years, the Penn Central had consisted entirely of railroad or railroad-related activities. But starting in 1963, the railroad had embarked on its diversification program, which included for the first time companies that had nothing to do with railroads. During the succeeding few years, the Penn Central made four major acquisitions, and it was these deals that would be so sharply criticized a few years later when analysts were trying to assess the blame for the railroad's failure.

The acquired companies were the Buckeye Pipe Line Company, and three real estate investment and development companies called the Great Southwest Corporation, the Arvida Corporation and the Macco Corporation. Altogether, the Pennsylvania Company, a subsidiary of the railroad, invested about $144 million in cash in the four companies, much of it obtained through bank loans. In addition, the Pennsylvania Company's preferred stock, which was issued in exchange for Buckeye common stock, had a book value of more than $70 million. Therefore, it had to be counted as part of the investment.

The railroad itself desperately needed additional funds while the diversification was going on, and was having trouble getting them. Furthermore, the real estate subsidiaries, in financing their own expansion programs, were in some cases competing with the railroad for the same limited sources of credit, notably at several large Eastern banks.

What was particularly disturbing to many analysts was the inappropriate nature of the investments. Investments in real estate ventures like Great Southwest Corporation, Arvida, and Macco

Realty required external financing from Penn Central because funds were tied up in unsold properties for future development and because of a high rate of receivables, mainly in the form of second trust notes. These absorbed all the funds generated internally, and for the most part, allowed only small dividends.

Bevan, at one point, told investigators that the railroad had earned a return of $146 million on its investments, but after the bookkeeping had been stripped away and such figures as tax allocation, interest and undistributed earnings had been eliminated, it turned out that only $37.8 million in dividends had actually been paid by the four subsidiaries to the railroad. If the dividends paid by the Pennsylvania Company on preferred stock issued in exchange for Buckeye common stock were subtracted, it turned out that the net cash flow upward to the railroad was only $19.9 million.

The Patman staff said it believed that a net cash drain from the railroad of at least $175 million, at a time when the railroad was faced with a critical cash shortage, "significantly contributed to the ultimate collapse of the railroad."

Probably the most illustrative of the railroad's diversification efforts was the Great Southwest Corporation. Its role in the failure of the Penn Central was documented by the Securities and Exchange Commission, one of the federal government's most thorough regulatory agencies. In examining the collapse of the Penn Central, the SEC called nearly 200 witnesses and took 25,000 pages of testimony. Among its witnesses were most of the major officers and directors of the corporation. It also examined the roles of about 150 institutions, either through submission of documents or by taking direct testimony.

The SEC concluded that Great Southwest "played a major role in the affairs of Penn Central, including the efforts of Penn Central management to conceal the railroad debacle.

"The history of Great Southwest illustrates particularly well," the SEC said, "the deceptions practiced by management and the complex relationship among the different elements in Penn Central."

Two of those elements were David Bevan and his investment banker friend, Charles Hodge. Great Southwest had been formed in 1956, to develop the Waggoner Ranch, which lay between Dallas and Fort Worth, into an industrial park. A public offering of Great Southwest stock was underwritten in 1960 by Glore Forgan and Company, and part of the proceeds were used to develop an amusement park within the industrial park. That park, Six Flags Over Texas, was built for the purpose of generating cash to carry Great Southwest's undeveloped land, and to pay development costs. The Pennsylvania Railroad made its first investment, a modest one, in Great Southwest when its pension fund bought an unsold portion of this public offering at the urging of Charles Hodge.

Then, in the mid 1960s, the founder of Great Southwest was forced into personal bankruptcy. He asked Hodge to find a buyer for the company. Hodge made a presentation to the Pennsylvania Railroad, and both Bevan and Stuart Saunders visited the company's properties.

The railroad, through its subsidiary the Pennsylvania Company, bought over 50 percent of Great Southwest's stock. The management of the railroad quickly pressed for further real estate diversification, and the firm of William R. Staats & Co., then being merged into Glore Forgan, brought to Great Southwest the Macco Corporation, which had a number of undeveloped real estate holdings and an established business of single-family dwelling construction.

However, as the SEC discovered in its post mortem of the Penn Central collapse: "The investment in Macco soon proved to be a bane rather than a boon. Macco experienced a serious cash drain, which by 1967 required advances of over $7 million a year from Pennco."

Pressure was applied to increase the profits of Great Southwest as the railroad's performance became more and more dismal and more difficult to conceal.

"Penn Central's interest in the reporting of profits by Great Southwest was more than the simple pursuit of 'performance,' " the SEC said. "Penn sought desperately to conceal the disastrous performance of the railroad. The profit maximization schemes in Macco and Great Southwest were counterparts to concealment efforts being made in other parts of the Penn Central system. Macco and Great Southwest management . . . knew what Penn Central management wanted and it acted to meet those wants. It should be noted that the booming 'earnings' performance of Macco in Great Southwest not only helped conceal the railroad losses in the consolidated financial reports, but it also gave the false impression that the railroad's diversification program was enormously successful in itself."

One director, Robert Odell, became concerned about the situation and wrote to Saunders to warn him of problems that Macco could face. In a letter dated July 3, 1968, he said:

"Dear Stuart: I am apprehensive about the Macco operations and fear there may be some unpleasant surprises later on. Unconfirmed rumors concerning Macco are quite unfavorable. Large investments in undeveloped land are very speculative in any market, and especially under present and foreseeable money conditions. Interest charges and taxes usually double the cost in about five years without development and planning, which is always very costly. I am for whatever is good for Penn Central, Pennsylvania Company, and Stuart Saunders. However, there is so much chance for bad judgment and manipulation in land development projects, I feel they should be most carefully watched."

When Odell later demanded that the board be furnished with information on Great Southwest activities, management refused his demands by informing the other directors that Odell had a conflict of interest because his own firm was involved in West Coast real estate. Eventually, after repeated efforts to get more information on Great Southwest and to get management changes, including the replacement of both Bevan and Saunders, Odell resigned. After he left the board, the directors stopped further inquiry into the matter.

One of the most revealing events in the tangled relationship of the Penn Central and Great Southwest was an abortive attempt to raise cash from the public. Frequently this is done by floating a stock issue. After revealing their intimate financial details to the SEC, public corporations are allowed to offer shares of stock to the public to give them cash for expansion or other purposes.

On May 13, 1969, Bevan told Penn Central shareholders at a meeting in Philadelphia that the company anticipated selling some of the stock in Great Southwest that it held, and that Great Southwest also would sell additional shares directly. Then, at a directors' meeting of Great Southwest early in June, approval was given to the preparation of a draft of a registration statement that spelled out the issuance of a million shares of preferred stock, and an additional offering by "certain shareholders" of common stock, clearly referring to Pennco.

By October, the offering had begun to take shape. It was to include the sale of 700,000 shares of Great Southwest cumulative preferred stock for $35 million, as well as a secondary offering by Pennco of 500,000 shares of stock from its own holdings. A major problem loomed, however. The offering would have to be accompanied by a prospectus which could meet the requirements of the Securities Act of 1933, and would describe not only the details of the offering, but also the tangled financial affairs of the company. Because of the way Great Southwest was being managed, it seemed inevitable that the price of a full and frank disclosure would be great, perhaps more than either the Penn Central or Great Southwest would want to pay. As the SEC would later analyze the situation, it was obvious that such disclosure would almost certainly cause a drop in the market price of Great Southwest stock.

However, the need for fresh cash was great, and as the end of the year approached, the pace began to quicken. Toward the end of September, a draft prospectus was in existence and was being reviewed by Penn Central's counsel. Great Southwest directors were told on September 23 that the company planned to file the registration statement within the next ten days. A draft prospectus carried the proof date of October 13, 1969. But it was the last draft ever printed, because by now the red flag of caution had been raised and the flow of events was beginning to reverse, this time with the investment bankers playing a cautionary role.

John Harned of Glore Forgan, the investment banking firm that was to underwrite the proposed issue, was in Dallas to make the final arrangements, but was becoming increasingly concerned about the kind of disclosure that would have to be made. He knew that most of Great Southwest's earnings had come from selling off their principal saleable assets, and that there was considerable doubt whether this activity could be continued. He was particularly concerned about the impact that disclosure would have on the market price of the stock, and later said that in his judgment "there would be a serious sell-off in the stock of the company." If the price of Great Southwest declined to $15, Pennco would lose $122 million on paper, and if the decline was steeper, say down to $10 a share, Pennco stood to lose a whopping $244 million. All this would occur at a time when Pennco was planning a public financing of its own, and also at a time when all the common stock of Pennco was pledged on a $300 million revolving credit line.

At an evening work session at the Dallas home of Great Southwest's outside counsel, Harned finally made up his mind. The offering, he said, should not be made. After some discussion, he flew to California to tell Great Southwest's officers what he had concluded, and after winning their agreement, he returned to New York. Other Glore Forgan officials agreed with him, and the offering was dropped with no information offered by either Penn Central or Great Southwest as to the reason.

It must have been little comfort to Harned that his gloomy forecast proved to be so accurate. Even without the offering, Great Southwest's stock began to decline as information seeped into the marketplace. By year-end, the price was down to $16. By the end of the following March, it was $14. And, at the end of May, it was $6.

"It is clear," the SEC said, "that the managements of Great Southwest and Penn Central realized that the true nature of Great Southwest's earnings, activities, and prospects were shockingly less than what was being actively represented to the investing public. For management, the registration statement was the moment of truth. The managements avoided that moment, and continued a calculated course of deception."

The cancellation of the proposed public offering increased the pressure on both Great Southwest and Pennco. Great Southwest urgently needed cash, and Pennco just as urgently needed reportable profits. What to do? The first alternative seemed to be a private placement of Great Southwest stock. In other words, there might be some investor, corporate or private, who would buy a large block of the company's stock, without the necessity of going publicly to market and all the embarrassment of a prospectus that would be available for anyone's scrutiny. A number of potential buyers were approached, including the Bethlehem Steel Corporation, the nation's second largest steel company, but none was willing to buy the stock.

The situation worsened. Surely there was some way to convey the impression that Great Southwest stock was desirable. Finally, another alternative occurred. How about a sale to the principal officers of Great Southwest? A plan was concocted in which several of the company's officers would buy one million shares of their own company for about $20 million. A later refinement of the plan called for them to buy an additional million shares as well. However, there was a problem. None of the Great Southwest officers had the resources to make the purchase. One of the officers later said that he couldn't envision himself raising $20 million and he knew that the other two officials involved had no money, so the whole thing seemed like a "rather far-fetched idea."

The SEC later commented that "the push for the completion of this scheme, which was never more than fantasy, reflects the desperation of Penn Central to generate reportable profits and to salvage some demonstration that Great Southwest stock had some value. From a touted 'billion dollar' asset, Great Southwest stock had become something that first could not be sold publicly without making matters worse through disclosure; that later could not be sold privately; and that, in the end, could not be sold to its own management."

Finally, Bevan made one additional try at utilizing Great Southwest's stock in financing. He wanted a $100-million Pennco debenture offer to have warrants attached for the stock of Great Southwest and for the stock of the holding company, Penn Central Company. In other words, a share of Pennco debentures would also include the right to buy shares of both Great Southwest and Penn Central at a fixed price at some future date. Bevan's idea was that Great Southwest stock could be used this way without having to register it with the SEC, since the warrants would not be exercisable for two years.

However, this plan, too, ran into difficulties, some of them springing from the underwriters who would be selling the warrants to the public, and some from George Davis, the outside counsel for Great Southwest.

It was Davis's opinion that issuance of the warrants would indeed require immediate registration. Davis spoke with David Wilson, Penn Central's in-house securities counsel, asking him to intercede with Bevan to explain the problems involved in issuing such warrants. He also was concerned about what the registration would reveal, even two years after the fact.

In subsequent meetings with the underwriters, mainly First Boston Corporation, the requirement for immediate registration still remained unresolved, and at one point Davis said he would seek an injunction to prevent the Pennsylvania Company from issuing the warrants without registration. Gradually the underwriters became concerned about all this, as well as about other disclosure problems, and at one point there was discussion about the possibility of seeking from the SEC a "no action" letter, clearing the decks for the absence of a registration for the warrants. Finally, however, it became understood among the parties involved that such a registration would be required. Faced with the necessity of exposing the inner workings of Great Southwest to the public, the plan for including warrants in the offering was abandoned.

What then is to be concluded about the Penn Central's diversification program? The staff of the House Committee on Banking and Currency summed it up by observing that the program resulted in "significant financial benefits" to Hodge's company, and that the railroad's acquisition of Great Southwest also resulted in financial benefits "accruing directly to Bevan and Hodge."

Another abuse that arose in the course of the bankruptcy of the Penn Central was the way some of the nation's most powerful banks were able to unload their stock in the failing company before the general public could do the same thing. Most small investors realize that large institutions such as banks have the best securities analysts that money can buy, and have all sorts of private pipelines to give them advance warning of events that later appear in the press.

However, federal securities law specifically states that important inside information must be made public before it is acted upon. It is a law that is so widely flaunted that it is almost laughable. Nonetheless, it is nearly impossible for the Securities and Exchange Commission to document instances of insider trading, and the actions the agency brings are usually against only the most flagrant. Clever Wall Streeters know how to circumvent the rules, and they often do so.

One aspect of the Penn Central collapse that interested the SEC was the massive sale of Penn Central stock by the big institutions. There had been enormous purchases of the railroad's stock during the optimistic period both before and shortly after the merger. But, as the Penn Central's troubles became clearer, and as its fortunes declined, most of the same institutions that had gobbled up the stock began to disgorge it. They included some of the country's largest and most prestigious: The Chase Manhattan Bank, the Morgan Guaranty Trust Company, Continental Illinois National Bank and Trust Company, Investors Mutual Fund, and the Alleghany Corporation.

Ultimately, the SEC was frustrated in its attempts to prove the misuse of inside information. "Although at this point serious questions exist about whether sales were made on inside information," it said, "it should be noted that proof of insider trading is always difficult. The difficulty is increased where, as here, there is some public adverse information which might explain the trade. Unless direct testimony or documents can be obtained on the use of inside information, it is difficult to sustain a charge of misuse of information."

In a rather forlorn footnote, the staff added: "Both of the commercial lending departments of Morgan and Continental had inside information at the time the trust department was selling Penn Central stock, but the parties to the decision to sell deny under oath that the trust department had access to the information."

Standing alongside the performance of the banks as one of the more questionable aspects of the Penn Central collapse was the unseemly scrambling for the fire exits by company insiders when it became apparent that the big railroad would go belly-up. Fortunes had been made in Penn Central stock, which had appreciated handsomely in value over the years, but now that the situation had reversed itself, there was a massive and frantic pullout.

Between the formation of the Penn Central Transportation Company in 1968 and the June 1970 bankruptcy, distorted management reports showed great optimism about the railroad's future. But, during the same period, large numbers of executives from the railroad began selling off their stock. This came to the attention of the SEC because its rules prohibit stock transactions based on "material" inside information which has not been disclosed to the other parties in the transaction or to the public in general. By those standards, any Penn Central officer who was aware that the company's prospects were significantly bleaker than the public had been led to believe, would be prohibited from trading his Penn Central shares. The SEC studied the trading of more than eighty of the railroad's officers and directors as it pursued its investigation, taking special notice of the fact that the price of Penn Central stock slid from a high of $86.50 in July 1968, to a low of $10 in June 1970, just before the bankruptcy. The man the agency singled out for particular criticism for selling off stock was Bevan.

"A stunning example of such a bailout," the agency said, "is that conducted by David Bevan, who was at the vortex of Penn Central's machinations, and who sold 15,000 shares of Penn Central stock in the first half of 1969, at prices ranging between $50 and $66, paying off a $650,000 'stock option' loan and managing to keep his personal fortune virtually intact. In contrast to this was the trading, or lack thereof, of Stuart Saunders, who has made no sales since 1967, even though his 45,000-share block of stock represented almost his whole fortune, and large loans he had made to purchase the stock remain outstanding."

In addition to the sale of stock by Penn Central officers and outside institutions closely connected with the railroad, the management of the railroad's enormous pension funds came under close scrutiny by the government. The purpose of a pension fund is to provide income at a maximum rate for the retirement income of those entitled to its benefits. However, government investigators who scrutinized the investments of the Penn Central Fund which were made by Bevan and one of his assistants, raised the question of whether they were being made for the benefit of the beneficiaries of the pension plan, or for the benefit of Bevan and his friends and associates. After analyzing $47 million of the investments, the government concluded that Bevan's investment decisions served a number of purposes including: (1) protection of his own personal investments and those of his friends, (2) facilitating his dream of turning Penphil into a giant conglomerate, (3) solidifying his directorships with other companies, (4) assisting some of the railroad's directors in their relationships with other companies, (5) appeasing and rewarding some of the railroad's largest creditors, (6) assisting and rewarding some of the railroad's largest stockholders.

"In allowing the pension plan to be controlled by David Bevan, the railroad placed itself in a very unfavorable position," the House committee staff said. "Through his control of the plan, Bevan was able to manipulate its investments for personal reasons. In some instances, Bevan's manipulations were for his own benefit and for the benefit of his friends and associates. In other instances, Bevan used the pension plan to facilitate his role as chief financial officer of the railroad. . . . Once again, the central questions arise: Where were the railroad's directors while Bevan was manipulating the pension plan? Why didn't the board's pension committee exercise its control over the managers of pensions and stop Bevan from misusing the pension benefits of 37,000 active and retired employees? This is just another example of where the railroad's directors—whether it was from ignorance, lack of caring, or personal self-interest—failed to do their job."

More than three years after the Penn Central's collapse, David Bevan, the once high-riding chief financial officer of the big railroad, was spending virtually all his time testifying in a host of law suits and investigations and trying to remove the stigma from his role in the bankruptcy. Vigorous and argumentative, his close-cropped black hair greying at the temples, he dwelt heavily on what he considered the injustices he had suffered in the government's analyses of the railroad's collapse. He could quote verbatim passages from old news reports and congressional studies that particularly offended him. And, as he sat in the office of his attorney, Edward G. German, his world seemed to have turned inward. He and his lawyer would complain to friends that after planning for a retirement on the basis of $100,000 a year, he was getting only a $50,000 a year pension from the Penn Central. Bevan would defend his role in Penphil, deny involvement with party girls, and make it clear that he had broken with his old friend Charles Hodge. The bankruptcy of the railroad had been inevitable, and no one could have stopped it, he would say, adding that the diversification program did not cause the collapse, but in fact, helped keep the road alive.

Before his bitter fall, Bevan had been the quintessential Philadelphia executive. Born on the Main Line, he had graduated from both Haverford College and Harvard's Graduate School of Business. He had worked as a Philadelphia banker for more than a decade and later served in the government on the War Production Board. After a stint as treasurer of the New York Life Insurance Company, he had joined the Pennsylvania Railroad as chief financial officer in 1951. By 1969, his salary had risen to $117,600 and his position as a pillar of the financial and social community in Philadelphia had seemed secure. Only after the government concluded its multiple investigations would he be earmarked publicly as one of the major villains in the bankruptcy and face major court challenges.

In May 1974, nearly four years after the Penn Central declared bankruptcy, Bevan and a number of former officers and directors of the railroad were charged by the SEC with civil fraud for alleged false and misleading statements about the company's financial condition.

Then, in September 1974, Bevan and four other men were indicted on federal charges of conspiring to misapply $4.2 million of Penn Central funds. The five also were charged with mail and wire fraud, in a twenty-three-count indictment returned in United States District Court in Philadelphia.

An earlier fraud prosecution against Bevan and Hodge, revolving around the Executive Jet Aviation acquisition, was dropped by District Attorney F. Emmett Fitzpatrick in Philadelphia. The charges had been filed by a former district attorney.

As the legal pace against Bevan and others picked up, it seemed increasingly likely that actions arising out of the Penn Central's collapse would continue for years, and that the controversial dealings of the troubled railroad would serve as a grim restraint on corporate officials and investment bankers alike for decades to come.

8/ The Broad and Wall Brahmins

I n October 1974, a six-man jury found Goldman, Sachs & Company guilty of defrauding its customers of $3 million by selling them Penn Central commercial paper while the railroad was going broke. For Gustave Levy, senior partner of Goldman Sachs, it was a devastating decision. Waiting in the wings were dozens of other customers with claims totaling $30 million. Furthermore, publicity surrounding the jury trial punctured the air of probity that Levy cherished both for himself and for his firm. Since the early 1900s, when it underwrote Sears Roebuck's first public offering of stock, Goldman Sachs had been one of Wall Street's best-known firms. Now its reputation was being challenged. Yet Wall Street's problems were not confined to Goldman Sachs. The financial com-

munity was tottering, and some observers were wondering whether Levy and other pillars of Wall Street had become paper tigers.

Gustave Lehmann Levy, senior partner of Goldman, Sachs & Company, lion of Wall Street and benefactor of a thousand worthy causes, was doing what he enjoyed most—drumming up business. It was mid October 1974, and Levy was presiding at official opening ceremonies at the firm's new international office in Switzerland.

Befitting the occasion, Henry Fowler, former U.S. Secretary of the Treasury and chairman of Goldman Sachs's international operations, was at his boss's side lending prestige to the event. Levy told his audience that Goldman Sachs was one of the leading investment banking firms in the United States—banker to more of the 650 largest American companies than any of its competitors.

He talked glowingly about the first public issue of equities that Goldman Sachs had underwritten for Sears Roebuck at the turn of the century. He told about the firm's origins as a dealer in short-term commercial paper. But one thing Levy did not recount for the gathering in Zurich that day was an incident that had taken place a week earlier in a Manhattan courtroom.

On that gloomy day, after an extraordinary month-long trial, a jury of three women and three men concluded that Goldman Sachs had defrauded three of its customers of $3 million by selling them commercial paper issued by the Penn Central at a time when the giant railroad was having terminal financial difficulties. The crux of the matter, the jury decided, was that Goldman Sachs had known of the railroad's ills, but had done nothing to protect its customers. So Goldman Sachs was ordered to pay back the $3 million, plus an estimated $1 million in interest.

For Levy it was a damaging blow to both his pride and his reputation as one of Wall Street's most astute and powerful figures. Indeed, as the 1970s approached its midpoint—with the stock market reeling, new issue markets faltering, and investment banking and brokerage firms falling into bankruptcies and forced mergers—much of the old guard leadership of the financial community was being called into question. Names that had dominated Wall Street for a generation, respected names like Loeb, Meyer, and Levy, names that had inspired both awe and fear because of the power they commanded, increasingly were being discounted.

For Goldman Sachs the rise to power had begun more than a century earlier when Marcus Goldman emigrated to the United States from Bavaria. At first Goldman had operated a clothing store in Philadelphia. However, he saw other merchants prospering in the New York financial community, so when his wife Bertha began to prod him, he moved to lower Manhattan. In 1869 he started a small business buying and selling the securities known as commercial paper.

In the beginning, Goldman would simply put on his tall black stovepipe hat and make the rounds of the diamond merchants on Maiden Lane and the leather merchants in the "Swamp" area near what today is Beekman Street. Goldman would purchase promissory notes from his customers and tuck them into the inside band of his hat. Then in the afternoon, Goldman would visit the commercial banks—Chemical, the Importers & Traders, and the Park Bank—where he would extract the notes from his hat and sell them for a profit. He was the middleman, the collector, making short-term loans to the small merchants.

The business prospered and in 1882, Goldman took his son-in-law, Samuel Sachs, into the firm. It was the start of a family tradition which, for nearly half a century, would see all the firm's partners belonging to the interrelated Goldman and Sachs families.

Already entrenched on Wall Street at the time were the great WASP firms, some of them founded by New England bankers whose families went back to the Mayflower and whose ties were intimate. The other center of financial power revolved around a closely knit group of German-Jewish immigrants described by Stephen Birmingham in his book *Our Crowd*. There were the Lehmans and Loebs, the Strauses and Guggenheims, and many of them, like Goldman, had started as peddlers or merchants before moving up to investment banking.

Wall Street of that era was a formal, almost austere place to work. Like others in the financial section, the older men at the fledgling Goldman Sachs wore top hats and morning coats to the office. The firm occupied a single floor at 31 Nassau Street and had only about two dozen employees. Although Samuel Sachs had a female secretary, many of the partners had male secretaries. At that stage of the firm's development, most of the partners rode the El to work, although officials from larger brokerage houses often had private carriages.

As the firm grew, Goldman and his son-in-law continued to earn their living buying and selling short-term promissory notes from businessmen who wanted ready cash. Business was good, but limited. So in the early 1900s, at a time when family corporations across the nation were growing and needed more capital for expansion than short-term commercial paper would provide, Goldman Sachs was ready to move up to a bigger league.

The opportunity to expand came in 1907. The nation's investment community was riding the tail of a boom that had stirred widespread public interest in the stocks and bonds that were being offered by fast-growing companies. It was a heady time for brokers and investment bankers. An almost uninterrupted ten-year business advance had more than doubled the assets of the country's financial institutions, from $9 billion to $21 billion. The financial press was spreading the news of investment opportunities to an eager nation.

Small investors, increasingly attracted to Wall Street, were directing their money toward the burgeoning New York Stock Exchange. From 1904 to 1906, the Dow Jones average skyrocketed from 36.4 to 73.5. The financial skies were clear and the barometer rising. Typical of the signs of optimism was a leap of $40 in the stock of Union Pacific Railroad in a single week, after the road had raised its dividend from $6 to $10.

With the big utilities and railroads already taken as customers by Goldman Sachs's better-established competitors, the firm obviously had to come up with some new approach. So the partners decided on a novel idea. Why not persuade some of the country's growing retail establishments to incorporate themselves and offer their securities to the public? The idea seemed sound, but was not without drawbacks. It was one thing to ask the public to buy shares of a giant railroad or heavily capitalized utility. But would it buy shares of a retail store? There was another problem, too. Would public investors be willing to take a chance on a company that had never before issued securities—one with no proven track record?

The Goldman Sachs partners decided it was worth a try, and by a happy accident of fate their first big retail customer dropped into their laps. To see where he came from it is necessary to look back a few years to the time when Samuel Sachs's sister had taken in a boarder from Germany named Julius Rosenwald. She and her husband hadn't cared much for Rosenwald. In fact, they thought he was crude and uncultured. However, he was a relative so they had accepted him.

It was to their benefit that they did because Rosenwald later became very important to the Sachs family. After getting a good look at New York, he had decided that his future lay not on the East Coast but in the booming Middle West. His goal was to get into the mail order business there. Within a few years he had succeeded and the company he built later became the biggest and most successful of its type in the world. Its name is Sears Roebuck.

Meanwhile back in New York, as Goldman Sachs was testing the financial waters, getting ready to venture into the newer currents of underwriting, Rosenwald found that he needed some capital for expansion. Given the Sachs family's early kindnesses to him, who would be a more logical choice to raise the money than his distant relations?

Goldman Sachs struck a deal with Rosenwald, and a $10 million offering of preferred and common stock was fashioned.

Because the amounts of money required for the underwriting were so massive and the risks were so large, Goldman Sachs decided to work with Lehman Brothers, another new Wall Street firm. Henry Goldman, Marcus's son, was a friend of Philip Lehman, and the two often lunched together at the old Delmonico's restaurant. Like Goldman Sachs, Lehman Brothers was also small. It had gotten its start as a cotton brokerage firm. Like Goldman Sachs, it was eager to prospect for bigger stakes.

As a result of the two men's friendship, Goldman Sachs and Lehman Brothers joined forces in the $10 million offering for Sears, which consisted of 90,000 shares of preferred stock and 45,000 shares of common stock.

It took the two firms three months to sell the stock, a staggering amount of time by modern standards. Most of the desirable issues in today's market are sold out the same day they are offered, and many are spoken for even before the prospectus is made public.

Another major change in the way syndicates were handled in 1907, and the methods employed later, was the so-called step-up.

Earlier, a single investment banker customarily would purchase an entire issue. He would then organize a larger group called a purchase syndicate and sell the members of that group portions of the issue for a slightly higher price, or step-up.

The initial house was known as the originating banker or house of issue and Goldman Sachs was one of the first houses to use this highly profitable pricing technique. Other houses quickly adopted the method and it gradually came into widespread use.

Sometimes the purchase syndicate would resell parts of the issue to an even broader group of investment bankers, at another increase in price. This was called the banking syndicate. The syndicate business in those days operated similar to the familiar chain letter scheme. Those who got in first, did best.

Although the step-up system made underwritings enormously profitable for the originating banker, there were often serious problems in selling the securities.

There was no network of dealers spanning the country as there is today. Modern dealers, with their thousands of brokers talking to customers every day, have an unparalleled ability to offer securities to a broad spectrum of Americans. In 1907, there were only five investment banking houses with a national distribution system: Lee Higginson, N.W. Harris, N.W. Halsey, Kidder Peabody, and William Salomon.

Because the national network was so small, many investment bankers offered stocks and bonds mainly to their existing customers, which was one reason why offerings took so long. The three months Goldman Sachs and Lehman Brothers needed to complete the Sears offering was by no means unusual. Some offerings took much longer, and in a few instances, purchase and banking groups organized for such offerings lasted up to five years.

Another complication was caused by the nation's relative standing in international finance. At the turn of the century, the United States was a debtor nation, and consequently many American firms turned to Europe for customers who could afford to buy security issues. European investment banking houses also participated in the offerings.

Despite all these obstacles, the Sears offering succeeded, and put Goldman Sachs on the threshold of a new era. Finally it was an underwriting leader rather than just another also-ran firm on Wall Street. The company continued to prosper, and before long, a young man named Sidney Weinberg began to make his presence felt.

Weinberg joined the firm when it was still possible for unschooled young men to get a tochold on Wall Street and work their way up the investment banking ladder.

He got his job at Goldman Sachs when he entered the firm's building on Exchange Place looking for a job as an office boy. After the elevator operator told him there were no jobs available, Weinberg rode to the top floor and began to work his way down to the street level, asking on each floor for a job. No one wanted him until he reached the second floor, where a Goldman Sachs official hired him as an assistant janitor. Later, the schoolboy from Red Hook, Brooklyn, became one of the Street's best-known figures.

At about the same time, another Goldman Sachs partner also started with the firm. Walter Sachs had a more traditional debut, but it was not without birthing pains. His college grades had been good, and he had served as editor of the *Harvard Crimson,* whose staff included a classmate named Franklin Delano Roosevelt. But his two older brothers had already preceded him into the firm.

Walter's father wanted him to go to law school instead of coming to Wall Street. Two sons in the business were enough, he insisted. So Walter entered Harvard Law, stayed for a year, and then dropped out and went to work the following summer in the Goldman Sachs back office. Being a Sachs, he was named a partner in due course and worked on a variety of projects, including commercial paper and foreign trading.

Although the firm operated smoothly for years, World War I caused some friction in the partnership, particularly for Henry Goldman, the founder's son. For Germans like the Goldmans, the war caused considerable soul-searching. Many Germans who had emigrated to the United States still considered Deutschland to be their home, in spirit if not in fact. So when war was declared, it was a wrenching emotional experience.

Henry was pro-German in his sentiments, whereas most of the other partners were not. The difference of loyalties was tolerated for a time, but it finally came to a head in 1915, when a massive Anglo-French loan was being underwritten by most of Wall Street's investment banking firms.

Goldman Sachs had a rule that if any of the partners objected strenuously to some particular business venture, that business was not done. Therefore, the firm refused to participate in the Anglo-French loan. Sam Sachs, however, went down the street to J.P. Morgan and subscribed personally as an indication of his political sentiments.

Finally the rest of the partners could no longer tolerate Henry, so they forced him to take his capital and leave the firm. After that, nonfamily members were allowed in as partners for the first time, a development that was beginning to occur at other investment banking firms as well.

The character of Goldman Sachs's business also began to change during this period. Between 1919 and 1929, when the Great Depression began, the firm started to win underwriting participations in lucrative rail issues and other profitable types of businesses.

Through most of the 1920s business boomed. But the good fortune was not to last. It was to be ended by the worst disaster in the firm's history—an experience so humiliating that it would take years to overcome it. Not until the 1970s and the Penn Central catastrophe would Goldman Sachs be faced with a similar public airing of its troubles.

In 1928, with the stock market booming, Goldman Sachs decided, somewhat belatedly, that it would form an investment trust —that is, a vehicle which could be publicly traded. If other businessmen could become rich by taking their companies public and holding some of the stock for themselves while the price leaped, why not Goldman Sachs?

So the firm formed a $100 million investment trust called the Goldman Sachs Trading Corporation, sold 90 percent of the shares to the public and kept 10 percent itself. The stock was brought out in December 1928 at $104 a share. The public snapped it up and within two months it had soared to $226 a share. Flushed with success and eager to expand, Goldman Sachs merged the trust with a company called the Industrial Securities Corporation to form an organization with capital of $244 million. Before long, the combined trust controlled companies with resources of more than $1.6 billion, rather promising for a firm that had handled its first major underwriting only two decades earlier.

Then the bubble burst. In 1929 the stock market crashed and in the rubble lay Goldman Sachs's trust. Shares in the trust, which at their height had split 2-for-1, were worth exactly $1.75. Assets had dwindled to $40 million. An outsider came in and bought up the remains. It was a devastating time for Goldman Sachs. Its house lay in ruins. Its eight partners had lost $12 million. The public pressed for compensation.

Eddie Cantor, one of the biggest theatrical stars of the day, had bought heavily into the Goldman Sachs trust. In 1932 he sued for $100 million. To some it appeared that the firm that had been nurtured so carefully, and then had grown so dramatically, was finished. For five years, Goldman Sachs did not head a single corporate underwriting. Not until 1935 did the partners reestablish a retail sales department to participate in securities offerings brought to the Street by other underwriting houses.

Eventually, however, the firm began its comeback. The Cantor suit was settled, leaving only a sour taste in Walter Sachs's mouth when, years later, his children would laugh at the funny man's antics.

By the 1970s, the conditions prevailing at the time of the original $10 million Sears Roebuck offering of 1907 had changed dramatically. Gone was the frantic, unregulated securities market of an earlier era. Gone was the speculative fever that had made it possible for fortunes to be made and lost overnight.

Gone, too, was the intimate relationship between the Sachs family and Julius Rosenwald, as well as the spot on Sears's board of directors. That had ended in the 1950s when Weinberg had left the board. By the 1970s, none of the Goldman Sachs partners were serving as Sears directors.

Furthermore, Goldman Sachs no longer sold Sears's short-term paper. The big mail order house had set up a credit company to sell its own commercial paper directly to customers.

Goldman Sachs did, however, continue to manage public offerings of Sears securities. In October 1970, with Goldman Sachs as managing underwriter, Sears offered $125 million in debentures and another $125 million in notes. The issue was sold by a nationwide syndicate of underwriters, and the debentures and notes were all sold the same day they were offered.

It was a long way from the original $10 million Sears offering of 1907, which had taken months to sell.

Another difference between the 1907 offering and the 1970 offering was the amount of manpower devoted to planning the issue, working on the registration statement, and consulting with Sears on its capital needs.

In the earlier issue, only one or two partners had been involved. In 1970, however, at least eight people at Goldman Sachs were intimately involved with the Sears offering over a period of several months.

The prospectus that described the debentures and notes also illustrated dramatically how disclosure regulations had changed since the turn of the century. Running forty-four pages in length, the prospectus explained, down to the most minute detail, Sears's finances. It also listed the 177 underwriters and the amounts of the offering they had available to sell to their customers.

The two biggest were Goldman Sachs and Halsey Stuart, each with $13.3 million in debentures and $13.3 million in notes. Next in rank were three firms, each with $1.9 million in debentures and $1.9 million in notes. They were The First Boston Corporation; Kuhn, Loeb & Co.; and Morgan, Stanley & Co. There were twenty other firms that received $1.5 million each in both debentures and notes. They included not only the giant Merrill Lynch, but also such major firms as Bache & Co., Eastman Dillon, Hornblower & Weeks, Loeb Rhoades, Paine Webber, Salomon Brothers, and Dean Witter. In all, the underwriting discounts and commissions the firms and their salesmen would receive would amount to over $1 million for the debentures and $750,000 for the notes.

Sears would take in over $247 million from the offering—a massive amount of money, but not inordinately large when weighed against Sears's sales of $8.8 billion the previous year.

Sears had grown over the years and its capital needs had grown along with it. But so had Goldman Sachs flourished. By the mid 1970s, Goldman Sachs had become the eighth ranking firm on Wall Street, with capital of nearly $80 million. It had ten domestic offices, with branches in such major business centers as Boston, Chicago, Dallas, Detroit, Los Angeles, Memphis, and St. Louis, as well as overseas offices in London and Tokyo. The company employed more than 1,400 people, and in 1973 it managed or co-managed seventy-nine equity issues, valued at nearly $5.9 billion. It participated in another 190 public offerings valued at $8.7 billion.

So sound was Goldman's reputation at the time, that many universities and pension funds that wanted to invest some of their surplus capital in corporate paper, set their minds at ease simply by knowing that the paper was being sold by Goldman Sachs.

Yet the company was not without its share of hard knocks. Between November 1969 and June 1970, a series of incidents occurred that created a crisis of confidence that nearly toppled the nation's commercial paper market, and left Goldman Sachs's customers holding $82.5 million worth of Penn Central Transportation Company commercial paper that was worth less than the envelopes it had been mailed in.

For nearly one hundred years Goldman Sachs had dominated the short-term securities market—the buying and selling of short-term unsecured promissory notes of corporations. Such notes are issued by companies that need quick money, and are then sold directly to investors or to middlemen like Goldman Sachs who resell them. The average term for such commercial paper loans is ninety days, and most investors look on them as the safest kind of investment—safer than stocks, bonds or commodities—indeed as safe as U.S. Treasury notes or bank certificates of deposit. Taking a company's short-term paper is tantamount to saying, I trust your financial health and will be knocking at your door in ninety days for my money.

One shocking development that occurred during the critical period when the Penn Central was faltering involved the National Credit Office. The NCO rates commercial paper in much the same way the government inspects beef to make sure housewives can safely buy it.

On February 5, 1970, Allen Rogers, an official of the National Credit Office, became alarmed over the sharply reduced earnings of the Penn Central that had been announced in the newspapers that day. As a result, he called Jack Vogel, an official of Goldman Sachs. During their discussion, Vogel told Rogers that Goldman Sachs was continuing to sell the company's paper despite the railroad's dismal earnings. He said the Penn Central had a number of valuable properties and securities so there was nothing to worry about.

Vogel apparently was persuasive, because the National Credit Office continued to rate the Penn Central Transportation Company as a "prime" name. Vogel subsequently wrote in an internal memo that Rogers had said the National Credit Office would continue its high rating "as a result of my comments."

Customers relied heavily on the credit agency's "prime" rating as an independent opinion of the credit-worthiness of commercial issuers, and Goldman Sachs used the ratings as a selling point to assure customers of the low risk involved in buying commercial paper. However, some analysts concluded that the NCO continued to base its "prime" rating on the fact that Goldman Sachs was still offering the Penn Central paper, and not as the result of any thorough and independent investigation.

Meanwhile, even as it was selling the railroad's paper to its customers, Goldman Sachs was taking action to secure itself against a disaster at the railroad. On the same day it learned of the railroad's huge first quarter losses, it contacted the company and got a commitment from the Penn Central that it would buy back $10 million of its own commercial paper from the Goldman Sachs inventory. What's more, Goldman Sachs insisted that thereafter the company's paper must be sold under a "tap issue" arrangement. That meant that Goldman Sachs would no longer buy the paper from the company, but would ask the company to issue paper only after it had found a customer. Such an arrangement involved no risk for Goldman Sachs, and at the time the Penn Central plunged into bankruptcy, the big investment banking firm did not hold a single dollar's worth of the tainted paper.

Its customers weren't as lucky, however. Nor was the nation's marketplace for commercial paper from other companies. In the thirty days that followed the Penn Central bankruptcy, there was a massive run on commercial paper in general. An estimated $3 billion in such paper was sold as skittish holders scrambled to cash in their notes. Across the country, the huge corporations that had issued the notes had to borrow from banks in order to pay off the frightened holders of their paper. On June 23, in order to avert a crisis, the Federal Reserve altered its regulations to help banks obtain more money so they could handle the staggering demand for cash from corporations.

The beleaguered banks borrowed heavily from the Federal Reserve in the weeks that followed, $1.7 billion in a single week in mid July. All together, more than $2 billion in bank money went to aid corporations in paying off their maturing commercial paper.

Only extremely quick action by the Federal Reserve averted what could have been a major liquidity crisis that would have been triggered by the collapse of the Penn Central, and the lack of confidence that it caused among holders of commercial paper.

As a result of the commercial paper debacle, Goldman Sachs was censured by the Securities and Exchange Commission. The SEC charged Goldman Sachs with violating federal antifraud laws in connection with its sale of the paper, and enjoined the firm from further violations. As is the custom in securities cases, Goldman Sachs was allowed to consent to the SEC action without either admitting or denying the charges.

However, the firm was required to set up additional procedures to protect commercial paper buyers. In the future, the SEC ordered, Goldman Sachs had to obtain and distribute to its customers more detailed information about the issuers of their commercial paper.

Although the penalties by the SEC against Goldman Sachs seemed mild, the commission was given credit for conducting a tough and intensive investigation which paved the way for actions against the firm by private parties. After its investigation, the SEC noted that although Goldman Sachs had learned a good deal of adverse information about the Penn Central, some from public sources and some from nonpublic sources, it "did not communicate this information to its commercial paper customers, nor did it undertake a thorough investigation of the company.

"If Goldman had heeded these warnings and undertaken a reevaluation of the company, it would have learned that its condition was substantially worse than had been publicly reported," the SEC said.

The first civil case to come to trial was enlivened by two pieces of testimony, both by Gustave Levy. The first was a pretrial deposition Levy had made in 1972, but which did not surface until 1974 when the *Washington Post* unearthed it. In the deposition Levy indicated that he personally was familiar with various developments in the Penn Central commercial paper transactions, and had nonpublic knowledge of the railroad's financial difficulties.

Was Levy aware that the Penn Central probably would not be able to get $100 million in standby credit which it had sought? he was asked during the deposition. "The answer is yes," he responded. Was that nonpublic information? "I presume it was," Levy answered. Did he instruct disclosure of that fact? "I did not."

Was he aware that in February 1970, Goldman Sachs had said it would handle the railroad's commercial paper only on a "tap issue" basis, rather than by maintaining its own inventory? "I knew about it." Was he aware that the Penn Central had been asked to buy back $10 million of its commercial paper from the Goldman Sachs inventory? "I presume I was aware of it." Was that nonpublic information? "That was definitely nonpublic information."

Taken in total, the 263-page deposition revealed that Levy was aware that his firm was continuing to sell commercial paper at the same time that it knew the railroad had serious financial problems.

It also revealed that there were two types of memoranda which the firm had used to report on its commercial paper issuers. One was distributed to insiders at Goldman Sachs and contained nonpublic information. The other was sent from time to time to purchasers of the paper and contained less sensitive material.

While Levy defended the propriety of his actions and of his firm's procedures, it became obvious for the first time that he could not remain personally aloof from the commercial paper fiasco.

In addition to the personal implications, however, the Penn Central bankruptcy and the subsequent collapse of the commercial paper market also placed Goldman Sachs in a tight legal bind.

The firm was named in at least forty-five lawsuits and it settled with twenty claimants for an average of twenty cents on the dollar. Some of the nation's largest companies accepted the 20 percent settlements. American Express, for example, took $1 million in payment for the $5 million of commercial paper it was left holding. Norton Simon, Inc. accepted $600,000 for its $3 million in commercial paper. U.S. Steel took $466,000 for its $2.33 million.

Other buyers, however, decided to wait and shoot for the whole pot. Carnegie Mellon University held onto its $1 million in what appeared to be worthless paper. Greenwood Mills, Inc. held onto $1.7 million of the paper. W.R. Grace & Company's retirement plan, with Marine Midland Bank serving as trustee, kept $2 million worth. Pratt Institute kept $1.3 million.

The Manhattan jury decision against Goldman Sachs in the first case to come to trial put a new light on the thirty-five pending recovery cases. For the first time, it appeared that the buyers, with aggregate claims of $30 million, might be able to get more than the twenty cents on the dollar that others had received. Their hopes were raised as they looked at the success of the three plaintiffs in the first trial: Welch Foods, Inc., a grape juice bottler from New York; and two chain store operators, C.R. Anthony Company of Oklahoma City, and Younker Brothers, Inc. of Des Moines. All three had bought their commercial paper between January and April 1970, and all three would get one hundred cents on the dollar if the jury verdict was upheld. And, in fact, the Getty Oil Company in early 1975 settled for $1.4 million, or seventy cents on the dollar. The Franklin Savings Bank did even better, winning its full $500,000 claim.

In addition to the attention focused on the commercial paper, other information elicited during the trial also attracted widespread attention.

Many on Wall Street were titillated by Levy's acknowledgment during the trial that Walter H. Annenberg, the U.S. Ambassador to London, had lost almost $9 million on Penn Central stock, even though Levy was acting as trustee for Annenberg's stock portfolio at the time. Levy told about Annenberg's losses to bolster his contention that he did not think the Penn Central was going to fail. Why would he hold onto Annenberg's stock if he thought the railroad was on the brink of bankruptcy? However, one interpretation of the revelation of the Ambassador's losses was not to vindicate Levy but to raise the question of how effectively the portfolio had been administered.

Annenberg had asked Levy to act as his trustee when he became

Ambassador to the Court of St. James. At the time, there had been more than $10 million worth of Penn Central stock in the portfolio. Levy sold off a small amount of the stock, but held onto most of it. After the railroad went bankrupt the price of the stock dove from about $60 a share to $6 or $7 a share, and Annenberg was out almost $9 million.

"Anyone who reads how Levy lost Annenberg's money on the Penn Central is going to wonder about how good he is," said one well-connected Wall Streeter. As for commercial paper, he said, "people are going to be a lot more careful in dealing with him.

"It's not going to put Goldman Sachs out of business. It's a very cynical crowd down here [on Wall Street] and as long as Levy can do things for them, like moving big blocks of stock, he's going to do all right. But he's not the great knight in shining armor any more."

Indeed, the Levy admissions undoubtedly gave many rich Americans cause to wonder whether their portfolios were getting the care they deserved from some of the nation's most prestigious investment bankers.

In a broad sense, the collapse of the Penn Central and the subsequent scrambling for the fire exits by Wall Streeters also opened a window on the financial community for the rest of the nation. And the country learned a valuable lesson: If millions of dollars are at stake, don't expect to be politely ushered by friendly investment bankers to the front of the line. It's every man for himself.

Although the Penn Central collapse was at the heart of Goldman Sachs's troubles in the mid 1970s, the firm was criticized on other matters as well. For example, eyebrows were raised over an ingenious plan Goldman Sachs fashioned in 1973 for Consolidated Edison, one of the world's largest privately owned utilities.

It had begun when Con Ed wanted to finance the purchase of about $40 million worth of fuel for one of its nuclear plants. Because the utility preferred not to add debt to its balance sheet, it discussed the matter with Goldman Sachs and at the firm's suggestion decided to set up a dummy corporation called Broad

Street Services to borrow the necessary cash in the commercial paper market. The dummy corporation bought the fuel, then in a bit of bookkeeping legerdemain, leased it back to Con Ed.

The plan worked well until the market for commercial paper dried up and Broad Street Services' paper had to go begging for buyers. Goldman Sachs temporarily put the paper in inventory, but finally told Con Ed it would have to find a new source of financing for the dummy corporation.

The only thing Con Ed could do was ask for a loan from its commercial banker, Chemical Bank, which had guaranteed the paper. Then, at least partly, it seemed, because Con Ed had to take $40 million out of its available bank line of credit, it was forced to eliminate the quarterly dividend, which would have required an outlay of about $28 million. Although Con Ed later denied the connection, it seemed to many Wall Streeters that the link was there.

The company's common stock nosedived as a result of the dividend passing and half a billion dollars of stock values were wiped out almost overnight. For Con Ed's 352,000 shareholders it was a traumatic time.

Later, Con Ed would restore the dividend, but not before serious damage had been done not only to its reputation for financial acuity, but also to the public's perception of the profitability of all the nation's utilities.

For Gustave Levy, public criticism of Goldman Sachs's role in the Penn Central and other transactions was both unaccustomed and discomfiting. He was used to having his own way, and much as he might want to flick such matters away like so many pesky gnats, they kept coming back.

Although there were hundreds of men named "Gus" on Wall Street in the 1970s, there was no confusion when a financier or corporate chairman said he would talk to Gus about a pending project. As far as Wall Street was concerned there was only one Gus, and he was the self-made millionaire and one-time chairman of the New York Stock Exchange who ran Goldman Sachs.

Once known for furious outbursts, by the mid 1970s Levy had learned to control his nervous energy, and was more likely to maintain a calm facade even while his mind was racing. But like James J. Hill, a nineteenth-century railroad magnate, Levy had too much nervous energy to keep his hands still. Hill had carried a bag of uncut stones to finger as he talked. Levy preferred a string of "worry" beads, given him by a friend in Greece.

Levy was a complex man, with three almost totally different personalities that emerged as circumstances dictated. To customers of Goldman Sachs he could be sugary, employing his soft New Orleans accent to good effect. To outsiders who meant little to him he could be brusque and businesslike. To subordinates at Goldman Sachs he could be a tireless and voluble taskmaster, flying into towering rages if his standards were not met.

Some described him as moody, mumbling one moment and shouting orders the next. Others said he had spent so many years racing—first to build his reputation as Goldman Sachs's best arbitrageur, then working his way up the firm's hierarchy, and finally, building Goldman Sachs into a preeminent force on Wall Street, that he scarcely knew how to relax. "He can be a monster or very sweet," said one long-time associate, "but he's the hardest-working, toughest guy I've ever met."

Above all, friends said, Levy spent long hours on the job, often to the neglect of his family life. Many evenings were spent attending board meetings of various organizations, or entertaining clients at restaurants like "21."

One associate of Levy's said he had an insatiable desire to win every piece of business that was up for grabs. Another said that like many businessmen and financiers, Levy was not given to pondering the philosophical implications of his profession.

"He's not the most brilliant guy in the world," one friend said, "but then the average genius on Wall Street, when you meet him, usually turns out to be just a clever guy. People aren't stunned by his brilliance, but they feel that Gus will get things done."

As for the Penn Central debacle, some of Levy's friends said that although his reputation had taken a buffeting outside Wall

Street, it was accepted by professionals as one of the risks of doing business. Other financiers, however, were openly delighted to see Levy's name associated with words like fraud and lawsuit.

Levy was not the only well-known investment banker who was feeling the sting of adverse publicity in the mid 1970s. His exposure may have been among the most controversial, but another so-called pillar of Wall Street also found himself in a federal courtroom in mid 1973, facing even more serious charges. He was John Langeloth Loeb, the austere founder and senior partner of Loeb, Rhoades & Co., who later that year, at the age of seventy-one, would be named "Investment Banker of the Year" by *Finance* magazine.

Loeb was the sort of man Wall Street was proud of. A graduate of Harvard, he was a long-time financial angel to his alma mater, which in 1971 awarded him an honorary Doctor of Law degree. His wife, Frances Lehman, was an offspring of the Lehman Brothers family, and served as New York City's Commissioner to the United Nations.

Like Levy, Loeb was a sort of eminence grise of Wall Street, well regarded, respected, nearing the end of a successful career.

It shocked Wall Street, therefore, when the morning newspapers on May 17, 1973, reported that Loeb had been accused by the federal government of having illegally disguised a $48,000 contribution to Senator Hubert H. Humphrey's unsuccessful 1972 campaign for the Presidency. In a clear violation of the law, Loeb had eight employees of his firm sign checks for Senator Humphrey. The money given was his, and he later reimbursed the employees. Loeb pleaded "no contest" to three charges of having disguised campaign contributions, and was fined $3,000. So the affair ended, adding another layer of tarnish on Wall Street.

Yet beyond the occasional illegalities or court suits that captured Wall Street's attention in the mid 1970s, the matter of national leadership of the financial community had been raised. Wall Street was hemorrhaging. The stock market had plunged to the lowest levels in a decade. One firm after another was going out of business. New issues and hot issues were almost a thing of the past. Millions of investors were buying antiques, or works of art, or real estate—anything but stocks. Brokers were selling insurance, or automobiles, or fire prevention systems.

The nation's confidence in the financial community was at a low ebb. And throughout the nation, financiers were wondering what had happened to the titans of the Street. Where was Gustave Levy now that he was needed? Where was John Loeb? Where was Andre Meyer of Lazard Frères? Where were the giants of Wall Street whose names and faces had graced the pages of the nation's financial publications; who had sat on the daises of a thousand conventions and fund-raising banquets?

Their fortunes secure, their careers nearing an end, their glory days behind them . . . had they become the paper tigers of Wall Street?

9/ The Hartford Merger

The *$1.5-billion merger of International Telephone and Telegraph Corporation and the Hartford Fire Insurance Company was fashioned by the investment banking firm of Lazard Frères & Company, against a backdrop of political intrigue. Involved in the complex scheme were a secret IRS tax ruling that was subsequently overturned, a controversial decision by the U.S. Justice Department, and arcane dealings between ITT's representatives and an Italian bank called Mediobanca. At center stage was Felix Rohatyn, a Lazard Frères partner and protégé of Andre Meyer, one of Wall Street's wiliest inhabitants. Despite government and private attempts to scuttle the merger, including a series of law suits by Ralph Nader, Hartford Fire remains a vital and profitable part of the ITT empire.*

Harold Geneen scowled at the clutch of photographers and reporters who were juggling their cameras and tape recorders as they pursued him down a corridor outside the ornate Senate hearing room in Washington, D.C., where he had just finished testifying under oath about the tangled affairs of his huge conglomerate, International Telephone and Telegraph Corporation.

The vein on his left temple pulsed and he brushed a hand over it as he strode away from the impromptu press conference he had abruptly terminated. A few minutes earlier, when the reporters' questioning about his company's relationship with the Republican party had turned hostile, Geneen had bristled and walked away from the session. It was an unusual performance because he seldom showed his testy side in public, preferring to reserve such behavior for his subordinates in private encounters.

But these were unusual days for Harold Geneen. It was the spring of 1972, and ITT, the mammoth corporate empire he ruled with absolute authority, was under seige, charged with trying to influence the Republicans in order to get favorable treatment in its massive merger program. Although the charges were never proven, they left ITT with a cloud over its head, and gave the public a new three-letter symbol for corporate power, cunning, and subterfuge.

Of the hundreds of corporate chief executives in the United States in early 1972, few were as powerful as Geneen, or as highly paid. In the previous two of his ten hectic years at the helm of ITT, he had earned more than $3 million in salary, bonuses, and stock options. He had exercised nearly total control over more than three hundred companies that fell under his giant conglomerate's umbrella. And he had paid five of his key headquarters executives a salary higher than that earned by the President of the United States. The sixty-two-year-old chairman, president, and absolute monarch of ITT operated in a secretive, overprotected world of power and money that was seldom penetrated. Just as heads of state used vast fleets of airplanes and arsenals of atomic weapons as their battlements, Geneen used money—staggering amounts of it—enough to buy him the nation's best attorneys, accountants, and tax advisers. He had his own fleet of jet aircraft and his own security force, which was occasionally put to work shredding sensitive documents.

Despite all this power and influence, Geneen had grave problems in the early months of 1972, which were brought to public attention by newspaper columnist Jack Anderson. Anderson told of an internal ITT memorandum that he claimed was written by the company's tough-talking Washington lobbyist Dita Beard. The memo had mentioned a link between the U.S. government's settlement of several antitrust suits against ITT and a $400,000 contribution toward the upcoming Republican National Convention in San Diego, California. A public furor had ensued and before the burgeoning scandal had faded from view, it was to precipitate a clutch of investigations, hearings, and law suits, and involve the United States Justice Department; John Mitchell, the former U.S. Attorney General who headed President Nixon's campaign for reelection; and indeed, the White House itself. Up till then, it was the biggest scandal to hit the three-and-a-half-year-old Nixon administration, and it would deeply affect Geneen, a man totally unknown to most Americans, but one whose name was to make headlines in the weeks that followed.

The scandal also would shake ITT, the company that Geneen had almost single-handedly moulded in his own image. The structure that he had so carefully built would come under attack from all sides, and although it would survive, the company's reputation and the image that Geneen had hoped to achieve as a master corporation builder and super-executive would be badly tarnished. In the wake of the Senate hearings, three directors would be temporarily barred from serving on the ITT board. Two of the company's officers would be rebuked by the Securities and Exchange Commission for illegally trading their own stock on the basis of inside information. And law suits by Ralph Nader and others would seek to overturn some of ITT's corporate actions.

How could all this happen to one of the most inventive and hard-working executives in the country? For one thing, there was Geneen's ambitious merger program, in which he swallowed up one company after another, exchanging ITT stock for shares of the smaller companies' stock. For another, there was Geneen's practice of setting difficult goals for his corporate managers, and his unwillingness to tolerate failure to reach those goals. Indeed, there were many reasons for Geneen's difficulties in 1972, but probably the most important factor leading to his plight was his single-minded pursuit of the Hartford Fire Insurance Company, a mammoth moneymaker that Geneen had acquired only three years earlier, following a complex chain of maneuverings that tested even his considerable ingenuity. It was Hartford Fire, more than any other acquisition, that would lead ITT into the private suites of government officials as it fought to preserve the historic merger in the face of Justice Department opposition.

Many of ITT's maneuverings were accomplished with the aid of the investment banking firm of Lazard Frères & Company, a New York firm that was so influential in Geneen's merger program, and profited so magnificently from it, that some critics wondered aloud whether the mergers were not performed more for the benefit of the bankers than for ITT.

Investment banking firms can be useful to conglomerators like Geneen in many ways. They can find partners for mergers— companies that need more capital than they can raise by themselves for expansion, or firms with officers who want bigger salaries than they can earn as a big fish in a small pond. The financiers, with their powerful connections, also can be persuasive in arranging the mergers, and they have the intimate knowledge of financial markets required to judge the price that should be offered for the acquired company, and the form the offer should take. Should the appeal be made directly to shareholders? Should the stock be bought on the open market, or through privately held blocks? Should there be an exchange of ITT shares for the smaller company's stock? If so, how many shares should be offered, and should they be common or preferred? There are a thousand such questions, and a sophisticated firm like Lazard Frères can provide ready answers.

At the time of the Washington hearings, the ITT chairman had been busily gobbling up companies for nearly a decade. He had

built up ITT from a modest $811 million foreign-oriented com-
munications company with telephone operations in South America to a giant $6.4 billion conglomerate with hundreds of subsidi-
aries. As a result of Geneen's feverish acquisition program, aided
by Lazard Frères, it was almost impossible for Americans to pass
a day without using or buying some ITT product. They rented its
Avis cars, slept and ate in its Sheraton hotels, bought its Levitt
homes, made sandwiches out of its Wonder Bread and used a host
of other ITT consumer and industrial products.

Still, in the late 1960s, Geneen's ambitions had been unfulfilled.
For him, growth was the magic word, and the acquisition of
Hartford Fire, the big insurance company, would cap a decade of
feverish empire-building for the immigrant accountant, a decade
that had been characterized by one of the most fruitful partnerships between a major corporation and a powerful investment
banking firm—ITT and Lazard Frères.

The Lazard general partner who concentrated on ITT affairs
was Felix G. Rohatyn, a controversial, Austrian-born financier in
his early forties who served on seven corporate boards of directors.
For more than four years he had been the big conglomerate's
primary adviser on mergers and the intricate stock issues that
facilitated them. Indeed, it was largely through Rohatyn's efforts
that ITT had arranged and brought to fruition the $1.5 billion
merger with the Hartford Fire Insurance Company that was to
become such an albatross around Geneen's neck. Rohatyn, more
than any other outsider, knew the intimate details of the ITT
merger program.

Almost from the beginning of his career as an investment
banker, Rohatyn had been at Geneen's side. He had set up a tiny
merger deal between ITT and a company called Jennings Radio
fifteen years earlier, when he was a thirty-one-year-old novice in
Lazard's corporate finance department. It had been his first deal
at Lazard, and Geneen's first at ITT. Later, Rohatyn became a
director of ITT, and his work for the company brought him both
fame and notoriety.

In the late 1960s, Geneen had been looking at insurance companies as a logical extension of his interests in financial services. He already had acquired a finance company and a couple of small insurance companies, and had held preliminary talks with some sizeable life insurance companies. But his idea always had been that ITT should go into life insurance rather than fire and casualty insurance, because life insurance was more predictable. In other words, benefit payments for life insurance were reasonably easy to foresee and followed established patterns, whereas fire and casualty insurance was subject to huge and unpredictable claims. There could be unexpected claims of millions of dollars as the result of fires, or hurricanes, or other disasters, and the atmosphere of unpredictability was foreign to Geneen's philosophy of business.

Nevertheless, this didn't prevent other companies from trying to buy up fire and casualty firms in the 1960s. One of the most prominent attempts to make such an acquisition was Dow Chemical's unsuccessful try at the Hartford Fire Insurance Company. It was soon after that deal was terminated that Lazard Frères received a telephone call from a broker who specialized in insurance companies; a call that was to start a chain of events that would culminate in Geneen's appearance in Washington early in 1972.

The broker had been trying unsuccessfully to interest ITT in a fire and casualty company. Now he pointed out that Hartford was the crown jewel of the insurance business, and a fund on the West Coast called Insurance Securities owned 1.8 million shares of Hartford Fire stock. The broker also warned that several companies were trying to raid Hartford by buying the stock and then running a tender offer, that is, offering to exchange their own stock for the Hartford stock held by the insurance company's shareowners. The broker asked whether ITT might not be interested in purchasing the block for itself.

After studying the insurance business in some detail, Geneen became convinced that contrary to his original assessment, the fire and casualty business could indeed be profitable.

An insurance company basically makes money two ways. First, it is an underwriter. It sells insurance at a premium high enough to cover the expenses of the payouts it must make to the people it insures. Secondly, by virtue of the premiums it collects, it has an enormous pool of cash to invest, and it can make huge profits through those investments, if they are made wisely. In effect, management has an equity fund to invest. ITT reasoned that even in a fire and casualty insurance business, if the underwriting aspect was considered separately from the investment aspect, it was clear that the pool of investment money provided an open-ended, continually growing equity fund. What's more, it avoided some of the built-in handicaps of a similar equity fund held by, say, a mutual fund company. There would be a continuous inflow of money, and unlike mutual funds, there would not be the handicap of redemptions—investors who decided it was time to take their money elsewhere.

What that all meant was a regular growth that could last for ten or fifteen or fifty years, as long as the country provided a basically healthy investment climate. Furthermore, it appeared that underwriting was a business where the superimposition of ITT's management controls might improve the basic profitability of Hartford. Perhaps ITT might ease the huge swings the company was having by use of reinsurance or by limiting the amount of risk assumed in any one area.

Geneen decided that he would like to acquire Hartford if its management was interested. So Andre Meyer, the managing partner of Lazard Frères, called Harry Williams, the Hartford chairman. Hartford had gotten all kinds of calls after it called off its merger with Dow, and was extremely jumpy because of rumors about raids. "We've got a committee that's been set up to handle these things," a Hartford officer said, "but if we have to see you, we'll meet you at the coffee shop at the airport in Hartford." Meyer observed that it was not a very civilized approach, and the insurance officials relented, agreeing to see Geneen, Meyer, and Rohatyn at their Hartford offices.

Geneen told the Hartford executives he was prepared to buy the stock held by Insurance Securities. The executives listened but showed little interest. About ten days later, ITT learned that Insurance Securities was about to make a deal with another buyer who was planning to run a tender on Hartford. Geneen decided to buy the stock himself, and to inform Hartford of his action.

At that point there was considerable discussion on the Hartford board about repelling the ITT bid, and plans were made to bring in a new chief executive to replace Williams.* ITT decided to force the issue, however. The week before Christmas, 1968, while Geneen lay in bed with the flu, Rohatyn and Stanley Luke, an ITT executive who was in charge of mergers, set out for Hartford after working over the weekend on a letter to the insurance company's board. Their plan was to present the letter, and immediately afterward they would issue a press release saying that a merger had been proposed. The situation was critical for ITT, and it decided it had to act before the Hartford board moved to preclude a merger.

Rohatyn and Luke arrived in Hartford and began looking for a place where they could telephone the insurance company and ask for an appointment. Across the street from the company's headquarters, an aging, rundown hotel caught their eye. They entered the lobby, and Rohatyn headed for a telephone booth. Rohatyn got through to the company, but his primary contact, Harry Williams, was not available. Another Hartford official, Herb Schoen, was there, however, and he was willing to accept the letter from Rohatyn and Luke. Then, both Hartford and ITT announced that the big conglomerate had made an offer for the blue-chip insurance company, and the matter was formally made a matter of record. There was no immediate decision, but Hartford

---

*The man sounded out for the job was Robert H.B. Baldwin of Morgan Stanley. One remarkable aspect of investment banking is the frequent involvement of financiers in each others' business affairs. Felix Rohatyn, for example, administered a blind trust for Peter Peterson while Peterson was in Washington (before he returned to head Lehman Brothers). Gustave Levy, whose image was tarnished by the Penn Central commercial paper fiasco, was a key figure in the Citicorp floating-rate note issue, as was Julius Sedlmayr, who earlier had met with Howard Hughes.

agreed to study the proposal, and it appointed a negotiating committee for that purpose. It also hired the firm of Drexel, Harriman, Ripley, Inc. to conduct an independent study of the prospective deal. Most important, the die was cast for ITT, and as it later became evident, for the first time in the Geneen era, ITT had, in effect, forced its attentions on a reluctant partner.

It was a difficult offer for shareholders to turn down. The terms were about 20 percent better than those offered in an earlier negotiation by ITT, when a preferred convertible share was to be offered share for share. The new offer was 1.2 preferred convertible shares for each Hartford share. In dollars, the original offer was worth about $66, and the final offer about $72 or $73. This was for a stock that had been selling in the $45 to $50 range before the ITT merger discussion began.

On the other hand, there was intense criticism of the deal in the city of Hartford, where fears were expressed that ITT was going to bleed the insurance company of its vast store of funds, and perhaps even move it to another city. To counter such criticism, ITT committed itself not to take any capital out of Hartford or to use any of Hartford's funds for anything but internal purposes in the insurance company. It did say, however, that it would take out of Hartford the amount of cash every year that was required to pay the dividends on the stock it had issued to the Hartford shareholders. In other words, the cost of the acquisition would be borne by the acquired company. The Hartford board of directors would remain intact, and there would be three additions from ITT: Geneen, Eugene R. Black, former president of the World Bank, and Charles T. Ireland, an experienced financial executive who would later leave ITT for the presidency of the Columbia Broadcasting System, only to die of a heart attack soon thereafter.

In addition to the internal assurances and incentives, Geneen and his executives made a variety of overtures to the Hartford community where the insurance company was located. They committed ITT to keeping the insurance firm's headquarters where it was, and Geneen traveled to Hartford to talk to the Chamber of Commerce, to the presidents of other insurance companies, and to the community, to try to assuage their fears that ITT was a wild-eyed conglomerate coming in to rape their company and take it out of Hartford.

The merger was subject to approval from two major sources at this point—the Department of Justice, which had been moving against some ITT mergers, and the Insurance Commissioner of Connecticut.

While all this activity was going on, there was a tremendous arbitrage position in the Hartford stock, which already had risen substantially. If the merger went through it would soar in value, and plummet if it didn't. This type of arbitrage is classic when the merger of two publicly held companies is announced. Theoretically, since one security is to be traded for the other at a fixed ratio, the two values should be identical. Often they are not, however, because of a risk that the merger might not work out, and because of abrupt changes in the securities and money markets. Given the mechanics of the arbitrage, the arbitrageur buys the security of the company being acquired and simultaneously sells short the security being offered by the acquiring company. A short sale involves selling shares not then owned, borrowing them to deliver against the sale, and acquiring them later to replace those borrowed. Although it sounds complex, in practice it is simple. It does require a high degree of judgment of markets and merger prospects, however, as well as a strong constitution. The profit on the transaction is the difference between the cost of the shares bought and the price received on the shares sold short, less expenses. If the merger goes through, the profits can be immense, but if it does not, losses often are staggering.

Goldman Sachs, Loeb Rhoades, and other firms had taken huge positions in Hartford stock and were short in ITT stock. "I never, in my life, had as many telephone calls from the same people saying 'How does the merger look? Is it going through?' " Rohatyn said. It was a question of what the Insurance Commissioner was going to do. And, then, whether the U.S. Justice Department would approve it.

Finally, the matter of approval came to a head. It was shortly before Christmas, 1969, one year after Rohatyn and Luke had made their call from the phone booth opposite the Hartford headquarters. Geneen was at his weekend retreat on Cape Cod. Rohatyn was at his country home in Mt. Kisco, New York. At 2 P.M., Rohatyn's telephone rang. It was Howard Aibel, ITT's general counsel, and his first words to Rohatyn were: "You'll never believe this." The Connecticut authorities had ruled against the merger. It was a moment of crisis for Rohatyn and Geneen, with the possibility that the whole merger deal would go up in smoke.

It was a dramatic turn of events, because almost inevitably the price of the Hartford stock was going to go down by twenty points or more. "We had these 1.8 million shares of stock that were going to plummet, but that wasn't the worst of it," Rohatyn said. "My phone almost went off the hook five minutes after I got this call, because all the arbitrage houses who had lawyers up there could see their position just absolutely going to pieces."

The arbitrageurs not only had Hartford stock that was going to decline sharply, but they also would have to cover their ITT short positions. They were desperate.

Geneen, remaining at Cape Cod, took charge. He ordered his lawyers to study the alternatives, because by Monday morning, two days later, an announcement would have to be made as to whether ITT was going to drop the merger or try another approach. Reading the Insurance Commissioner's decision, Geneen saw that he had objected to two main points. First were the stock options granted to Hartford management, a sweetener that had helped overcome their original coolness. And, second, the Commissioner felt the merger was wrong because it would force all Hartford stockholders to go along with the deal, even if some might not want to exchange their shares for ITT. If there were to be such an affiliation, he felt it should be on the basis of a voluntary exchange offer to the stockholders.

The ITT lawyers spent the weekend studying questions of appeal, and the possibility of asking for a reopening of the hearings. On Sunday, the spade work completed, a decision was made that ITT would offer the following proposal: The items the Commissioner objected to would be dropped by the Hartford management; and ITT would change its merger terms to a voluntary exchange offer to the stockholders instead of a mandatory merger.

Now, the decision having been made, the pace quickened. Along with Geneen, Rohatyn, Aibel, and Ireland, were about a dozen supporting officials from ITT's accounting, legal, and public relations staffs who had been summoned to ITT's Manhattan headquarters. The group worked Sunday from 5 P.M. until 11 P.M., then issued a statement asking for a reopening of the hearings on the basis of acceding to the Commissioner's wishes on the form of the offer and on the stock options.

Despite the reassuring statement from ITT, Hartford stock, as expected, plummeted that Monday on the New York Stock Exchange. The reason for its decline was that there was no assurance that the Commissioner would reopen the hearings, nor if he did, that he would approve the merger in its new form. Even then, there was the Justice Department to worry about. What would its position be?

Financial columnists later described the rejection by the Connecticut Insurance Commissioner as a Wall Street blood bath. For arbitrageurs who had considered the merger deal a virtual certainty and bought Hartford Fire stock while selling ITT short, there had been a ten-point spread, and the likelihood of a magnificent profit if the deal went through. Indeed, earlier, Hartford Fire had been selling in the $60s. Then came the Insurance Commissioner's ruling, and the stock dove to the mid $40s. Rumors swept Wall Street that losses on the deal among the major arbitrage houses ranged into many millions of dollars, perhaps as high as $25 million.

A new set of hearings in Hartford was held in the spring, and in May, the Commissioner ruled in favor of an exchange offer, amid highly publicized charges that the entire matter had become politicized.

However, a new and potentially disastrous element entered the picture. Because ITT had switched merger types, it had to dispose of the stock it already owned in Hartford Fire. The reasons were complex, but based on this fact: For an exchange of stock to be workable, it must be tax-exempt. In other words, stockholders in Hartford probably were not going to exchange their shares for ITT stock if they had to pay taxes on profits from the deal. Such tax-free rulings are routinely granted by the Internal Revenue Service, but the deal has to conform to certain ground rules. One of those rules forbids the acquiring company, in this case ITT, from owning stock in the company it is trying to acquire. Furthermore, the sale of any stock it does own must be unconditional—with no strings attached. To complicate matters even more for ITT, the Justice Department said it was going to continue to ask for an injunction to prevent the merger.

ITT decided to dispose of the remaining roadblocks. In a complicated transaction that was later to become the subject of an intensive investigation by the Securities and Exchange Commission and provoke a number of law suits, ITT, through Lazard Frères, sold its Hartford stock to an Italian bank called Mediobanca. It was an unusual arrangement in which ITT protected Mediobanca against losing money on the deal if the price of the stock should decline. Furthermore, Mediobanca, less than two years later, unloaded some of the Hartford stock, which by then had been converted into ITT stock. It sold the stock to the Dreyfus Fund, a massive but beleaguered mutual fund. And almost simultaneously, an affiliate of the Dreyfus Fund was awarded trusteeship of $10 million in ITT's pension fund money. No conspiracy was ever charged, but to some it seemed like a tight little circle designed to get ITT out of a precarious spot, and to preserve the Hartford merger at all costs.

With the Hartford stock disposed of, the Justice Department action remained the major stumbling block. However, in 1970, a federal judge in Hartford ruled that ITT could go ahead with the exchange offer as long as the two companies were kept separate in case divestiture was later required. That meant ITT could now gear up for the exchange itself, and although that would seem to be the simplest part of the entire transaction, it was to provide some frightening moments.

In order to get the accounting benefits it wanted, ITT had to obtain 90 percent of the outstanding Hartford stock. As befitting the biggest such exchange offer in corporate history, ITT set up a "war room" at its Park Avenue headquarters. The room was filled with huge charts and overhanging banks of telephones, with enough staffers from ITT and from the dealer managers to keep track of all the brokerage houses and the stockholders lists. They had to be sure they knew how much stock was coming in to the exchange agent every day, and what percentage of the shareowners had subscribed to the offer. Geneen was certain they would get the required number. After all, it was a fantastic deal for the Hartford shareowners. For an over-the-counter stock that had been selling for about $40 with a dividend of $1.40, they were getting a preferred stock traded on the New York Stock Exchange valued at about $70, with a dividend of $2.25.

Despite his confidence, however, Geneen discovered with dismay on the day the offer was to close that he was short of their 90 percent. At one o'clock in the morning, there were reports from the banks that the figure was holding at about 86 percent.

A decision had to be made at ten o'clock as to whether the offer had been effective. ITT could take a chance that there might be 4 or 5 percent in the pipeline to put it over the 90 percent—or find that it didn't have 90 percent, and suddenly have $800 million of goodwill on its balance sheet.

The company officials and investment bankers stayed up until 2:30 A.M., and still the figure didn't change. Geneen had to make a decision, but couldn't bring himself to do it. Finally, the top executives went to bed at three o'clock. At 6 A.M., Rohatyn's office called him to say that the exchange agent had made a mistake and that the stock total was 95 percent.

"I woke Geneen up and told him we were at 95 percent," Rohatyn said. "I don't think anyone had ever awoken Geneen at six o'clock in the morning. We went down to the office where we met at eight o'clock to prepare the press releases and say that the offer was effective."

By this time, of course, a Justice Department antitrust campaign against ITT, involving a number of its subsidiaries, was in full gear. The company began devoting major efforts to working out a solution. The federal attorneys thought Hartford should be part of any divestiture package, but ITT was adamant that it would keep Hartford unless ordered by the Supreme Court to cut it loose.

In March 1971, Geneen asked Rohatyn to play the critical role of presenting the ITT position to high federal officials. Attorney General John Mitchell had disqualified himself from the case because of prior connections with ITT through his old law firm of Nixon, Mudge, Rose, Guthrie, Alexander and Mitchell, so Deputy Attorney General Richard Kleindienst, who later would get the department's top job, was the man to see.

Rohatyn met with Kleindienst early in April, and argued that a divestiture of Hartford would be detrimental to ITT's shareholders. It would impair the company's borrowing ability, he said, and would damage its ability to compete abroad in the telecommunications business. That in turn, Rohatyn said, might hurt ITT's ability to repatriate large amounts of money to the United States, thus damaging the balance of payments, and also might have some stock market effects that would go beyond just one company, since the market was in early stage of recovery from a severe slump. In addition to meeting with Kleindienst, Rohatyn also had sessions with Richard McLaren, who was in charge of antitrust matters, and with other treasury and justice officials.

He also met with Attorney General Mitchell, though he claimed he never discussed ITT with Mitchell, but rather confined his discussions to a broader Wall Street problem he was working on with other financial leaders.

In addition to meeting with Kleindienst, Mitchell, and McLaren, Rohatyn also met with Peter Flanigan, the White House aide who was responsible for dealing with the business and financial community.

While ITT contended that its discussions with administration officials revolved around broad antitrust policy, Flanigan recalled different circumstances in his meeting with Rohatyn.

In a letter which he submitted at the request of the Senate Judiciary Committee, Flanigan said he met with Rohatyn on June 29, 1971 to discuss the problems of Wall Street. Before the two men parted, Flanigan said in his letter, Rohatyn told him that the Justice Department's proposal on ITT's pending antitrust cases was so tough that the company could not accept it, and that ITT would fight the suits in court. A couple of days later, Flanigan said, he passed on Rohatyn's comments to Kleindienst.

Later, as negotiations between ITT and the Justice Department continued, the shape of an agreement began to emerge. The government would be satisfied if ITT gave up companies it considered insurance-related—Avis and Levitt, as well as Canteen and most of Grinnell. In return, it would be allowed to keep Hartford, its crown jewel. Late in the negotiations ITT asked its lawyers to try to retain a part of Grinnell that clearly was not insurance-related. Failing that, it said, the whole matter might as well go to the Supreme Court.

At this point, however, another crisis overtook Geneen and Rohatyn, and caused another hastily-called weekend work session. On a Thursday evening, when Rohatyn was at his Mt. Kisco home and Geneen was in Brussels, ITT learned that a reporter from the St. Louis *Post-Dispatch,* which had led every newspaper in the country in uncovering a variety of questionable tactics ITT employed in its Hartford merger deal, had gotten hold of some Justice Department position papers which outlined the entire divestiture program. The newspaper was preparing to print the story on Sunday and ITT officials were thrown into a tizzy. With the details out, the secretive atmosphere that fosters antitrust settlements would be shattered.

ITT's lawyers quickly scheduled another session with the Department of Justice on Friday, and Geneen hurried back from Europe to meet his attorneys at the airport and get a report on the situation. That evening and the next morning, the lawyers were in Washington negotiating. By Saturday noon, the matter seemed to be wrapped up to the satisfaction of both sides, and Geneen called his directors to tell them about the agreement. The rules of the divestiture were clearly spelled out in simple Justice Department language in a forty-seven-line news release issued that Saturday. It was probably the most important single document ever issued concerning the affairs of ITT, and is worth repeating in its entirety.

Assistant Attorney General Richard W. McLaren announced today that the Department of Justice and International Telephone and Telegraph Corporation (ITT) have reached an agreement in principle on the terms of consent decrees which, if approved by the courts, would terminate the government's antitrust suits challenging ITT's acquisition of Canteen Corp., Grinnell Corp., and Hartford Fire Insurance Company.

Mr. McLaren said that ITT would be required within two years to divest Canteen Corp. and the Fire Protection Division of Grinnell Corp. and, within three years, to divest either (1) Hartford, or (2) Avis Rent-A-Car, ITT-Levitt and Sons, Incorporated and its subsidiaries, ITT Hamilton Life Insurance Company, and ITT Life Insurance Company of New York.

In addition, ITT would be prohibited from acquiring any domestic firm with assets of over $100 million and from acquiring leading firms in concentrated U.S. markets, without the approval of the Department or the court. Under the agreement, a leading firm is defined as one with total annual sales of over $25 million and holding 15% of any market in which total annual sales exceed $100 million. A concentrated market is defined as one in which the top four companies account for over 50% of total sales.

ITT would also be barred from acquiring any substantial interest in any domestic automatic sprinkler company or any domestic insurance company with insurance assets exceeding $10 million.

The agreement would also prohibit the practice of reciprocity—using purchasing power to promote sales—by ITT and all of its subsidiary companies.

Mr. McLaren said that the proposed agreement will assist in stemming the trend toward undue concentration by merger which was alleged in these cases. In addition, he pointed out that most of the companies to be divested are industry leaders which the Department contended would be entrenched in their positions under ITT ownership.

Hartford has annual premiums of about $1 billion. Canteen, the Grinnell Fire Protection Division, Avis, Levitt, and the two life insurance companies have annual sales of approximately $1 billion.

The Canteen suit was filed on April 28, 1969. The other two cases were filed on August 1, 1969.

District Courts have ruled against the Government's contentions in the two cases involving Grinnell and Canteen. The Government has appealed the Grinnell case to the Supreme Court and was considering a similar appeal in the Canteen Case. The trial of the Hartford case had been scheduled to begin in September.

Attorney General John N. Mitchell did not participate in any aspect of these cases because his former law firm represented a subsidiary of ITT.

The verdict was in, and Geneen, Meyer, and Rohatyn could breathe easier. Hartford was theirs. Although they had been forced to give up some important subsidiaries, they had at last managed to get government approval of the biggest corporate merger in history. The months of planning, studying, explaining, and influencing had paid off.

The profits that were to spring from Hartford would gladden the hearts of the ITT and Lazard executives in the months ahead, but there also were darker events that would follow the successful takeover.

One of the most serious came in June 1972, when the Securities and Exchange Commission ended a lengthy investigation into the dealings of the two concerns with the announcement that it was charging two top ITT officials with illegal dealings in the company's stock at a time when they knew, but the public did not, that the antitrust suits against the company were about to be settled.

At the same time, the SEC filed suit against Lazard Frères and Mediobanca, charging that they had violated the securities laws in order to save taxes for ITT. According to the SEC suit and testimony given at a hearing before the Senate Judiciary Committee, the Justice Department had first indicated on June 17, 1971, that it would let ITT acquire Hartford Fire. The next day, the SEC said, Howard Aibel, ITT's general counsel, sold 2,664 shares of his ITT stock for about $163,000, without disclosing that he knew of the suddenly improved prospects for settlement of the antitrust suits. The price of the stock declined by $7 a share on July 31, the day the settlement became known to the public.

Also cited in the suit was John J. Navin, secretary and counsel for corporate affairs of ITT who sold 1,500 shares of ITT stock for approximately $100,000 on July 16. Navin was alleged to have known of the good prospects for settlement of the case, but not to have disclosed them. In both cases, the ITT officers were accused of violating the SEC's rules against corporate insiders failing to disclose material information in connection with the purchase or sale of the stock.

The suit asked a federal court to enjoin the two men from repeating such acts, but made no provision for restitution of any profits they made from the dealings. In its charges against Lazard Frères, the SEC said the transaction which sent shares of Hartford Fire to Mediobanca should have been registered with the SEC but was not. The court was asked to enjoin ITT, Lazard Frères, and Mediobanca from similar acts in the future.

Four days after the charges were filed, ITT, Lazard Frères, and the other defendants agreed to settle the suit on the terms proposed by the SEC. And so to all intents and purposes, the questionable dealings, so laboriously raised to the surface by investigative reporters and government agencies slid gently from public view. No mention was made, and apparently no illegality found in the stock dealings of six other ITT officers and directors who sold shares in the eleven weeks immediately preceding the company's antitrust settlement. Altogether, more than $1.5 million in such sales were made during that period. ITT maintained that in some cases the apparent proximity of the dates to the significant meetings with the government resulted from clerical errors or coincidence.

The following are among the sales not cited by the SEC:

On May 13, one day after Geneen committed ITT to help finance the Republican National Convention in San Diego, William R. Merriam, head of the corporation's Washington office, sold 1,000 of his 3,500 shares of stock. It was his first reported sale since 1967.

Fourteen days later, John Seath, a vice-president of ITT, sold 2,200 shares, his first reported sale since 1967.

On July 6, 7, and 8, Harry Williams, an ITT director and chairman of Hartford Fire, sold 8,500 shares of his preferred stock.

One embarrassment for Lazard was the charge by an associate of Ralph Nader that the investment banking firm had sold hundreds of thousands of shares of ITT stock to the public and to trust and pension funds shortly before the announcement of the antitrust settlement. In a letter to Senator James O. Eastland, chairman of the Senate Judiciary Committee, Reuben B. Robertson III, who worked with Nader, said that "during the weeks immediately preceding the announcement of the settlement, Lazard was perhaps the most active seller in the world of ITT series N preferred stock."

The Nader wrath was not solely confined to insider trading. In April 1972, he called on the Internal Revenue Service for an explanation of why it granted two unusual tax rulings in 1969 to ITT, allowing it to complete its merger with Hartford. Nader questioned the secrecy of one of the rulings and the extraordinary speed of another. Why, he asked, was ITT allowed to purge itself of Hartford stock, in order to engage in another type of merger when there was no precedent for such a ruling? And why was the company allowed to sell its Hartford stock to Mediobanca in an unusual sale that protected the Italian bank against any possible loss on the deal? The questions were obviously pertinent because the IRS would later revoke its controversial ruling.

To many businessmen who observed the ITT affair, and to

investment bankers who had been bested by Lazard in the past and were therefore not altogether unhappy to see the venerable firm do some squirming, ITT's behavior was deplorable for one over-riding reason—it had been caught at some common corporate finagling at a time when the nation was feeling a growing antipathy toward big business. "They made us all look bad," was the prevailing attitude among executives who were willing to talk candidly about the affair.

For ITT, the ultimate humiliation came in mid 1972 when a Temple University law student successfully sought a federal court ruling preventing three ITT directors from running for reelection at the company's annual meeting.

The student, John W. Rafal, charged that ITT had failed to disclose in its proxy statement that three suits were pending against the directors, charging them with trading stock in their personal accounts on the basis of inside information. One of the directors was Harry Williams. The others were Hart Perry, ITT's executive vice-president for finance, and R. Newton Laughlin, chairman of ITT–Continental Baking Company. None of the three men was cited by the SEC when it made its charges against ITT for insider trading.

So intense were the attacks on ITT in the wake of its antitrust problems that in 1973 *New York* magazine chose Geneen to grace its list of the five most powerful businessmen in New York, simply because he had managed to emerge from the year with his skin intact. Joining such executives as Donald Kendall of Pepsico, William Kane of A & P, Walter Wriston of First National City Bank, and Donald Regan of Merrill Lynch, Pierce, Fenner & Smith, all of whom had led their companies to new heights that year, Geneen was cited by the magazine as follows: "The measure of Geneen's power in 1972 was—survival power. After all the scandal and the testimony and the divestiture orders, the man is still there. He continues there, obviously, because profits are good and the stock is doing nicely. Geneen's grip on the assets which generate $8 billion in ITT sales around the world seems as tight as ever. He is not noted for making speeches on good corporate citizenship. He continues to be admired for his devotion to the bottom line. He is the ultimate capitalist."

By late 1974, however, ITT and the officials most closely involved in its affairs were not faring so well. In the spring of that year, as previously mentioned, the IRS revoked the ruling which had allowed the Hartford merger to take place. Mediobanca, it seemed, had come back to haunt ITT. It was expected that the revocation, while not undoing the merger, would result in the payment by ITT of millions of dollars in taxes.*

As for Geneen, he had clearly lost some of his luster. After boasting about a decade of steadily rising profits, his giant conglomerate had begun to slide. Its earnings were declining, and the price of its stock had skidded sharply. Former Attorney General Kleindienst and other government officials who had become enmeshed in the ITT affair also were bruised.

Rohatyn, too, was undergoing considerable scrutiny on Wall Street. On one hand, he was highly regarded as the architect of some imaginative investment banking deals. But, on the other hand, he had to live down his characterization as "Felix the Fixer," given him by Nicholas Von Hoffman of the *Washington Post.*

None of the ITT or Lazard Frères officials who were involved in the Hartford deal could have foreseen at the beginning of their relationship that they would face such turbulence in the ensuing years.

The dealings between Geneen and Lazard had begun almost haphazardly, well before Geneen joined ITT. In fact, Geneen at first had dealt with neither Rohatyn nor Meyer, but with a third Lazard partner named Albert Hettinger.

Geneen was serving as chief financial officer of the Jones &

---

*There was other bad news as well. Late in August 1975, ITT settled three law suits in which stockholders had claimed damages for the alleged misuse of inside information regarding the antitrust settlement. Under the terms of the agreement, ITT had to provide a cash fund of $3.3 million to repay the stockholders for their losses.

Laughlin Steel Corporation in the late 1950s, when he first met Hettinger, who was a partner at Lazard Frères and a director of Jones & Laughlin. A former Harvard professor, Hettinger soon became somewhat of a mentor to Geneen.

When Geneen left the steel company to become an officer of the Raytheon Company, a Massachusetts electronics firm, he remained in touch with Hettinger. So it was a logical step when Geneen moved to ITT in 1959, to ask his old friend "Het" whether Lazard Frères might not help him find some merger candidates for the staid old communications conglomerate.

Lazard was a logical choice for Geneen. It was one of a handful of wealthy financial establishments that dominated the merger field. It was accustomed to moving quietly through the world's stock exchanges and bourses, in and out of corporate board rooms, investing millions of dollars as casually as most men buy a new shirt. It had a financial sophistication that Geneen needed—and was willing to pay handsomely for. In six years Lazard earned fees and commissions of more than $6.6 million from the giant conglomerate, for helping to arrange and consummate the mergers that were the foundation of ITT's growth.

The first of these mergers came just after Geneen took over at ITT and was looking for a company to acquire. Rohatyn had heard about a tiny firm in San Jose, California, called the Jennings Radio Manufacturing Company, that was eager to go public or merge. In other words, it wanted either to issue stock to the public, and take a step up into the world where someone else's money could be used for expansion, or sell itself to a larger company, which could accomplish the same end with its greater resources.

Rohatyn, who had heard of Geneen's desire for mergers, suggested to his partner, Dr. Hettinger, that ITT might like to look at Jennings Radio. Three months after so doing, a deal was struck.

For Geneen, Jennings Radio was the first step in what was to be one of the most dramatic acquisition programs in United States corporate history. More important, it allowed Lazard Frères and Rohatyn to lay claim to their positions in that merger program. Furthermore, Geneen used the acquisition of Jennings Radio as a test case with his own board of directors to see whether they would go along with his expansion program. They questioned him sharply about the merger, but ultimately approved it.

Geneen's philosophy at ITT had been shaped by the expropriation by Fidel Castro of the Cuban Telephone Company, a move that cost ITT $100 million. From then on, Geneen was determined not to be dependent on overseas operations, which had provided about 80 percent of the company's earnings. He also believed that ITT stock would never sell at a high multiple as long as the company was heavily dependent on overseas earnings. So he decided that there must be a better geographic balance in earnings.

After discarding the idea of buying up domestic telephone operating companies, because of a wide disparity in stock prices and multiples, ITT turned to companies in areas that were basically engineering or electric-related. In quick succession it acquired such concerns as Cannon Electric and Gilfillan. At the same time, it began to diversify the activities of its European telephone companies. Because of this foreign expansion, ITT always seemed to be chasing its tail in terms of trying to get a geographic balance. It soon became apparent that larger domestic acquisitions would have to take place. One thing seemed to stick in Geneen's craw: ITT still was relatively unknown to the investing public. So if the new domestic acquisitions were well-known corporate names, so much the better. Before long, a company appeared that seemed to fit the bill perfectly, and once again Lazard Frères was in the middle of the deal. In 1962, Lazard had bought control of the Avis Rent-A-Car Company. In 1965, Eugene Black, who was a director of ITT and a friend of Andre Meyer, asked if Lazard would sell Avis to ITT. Clearly, the main reason for Geneen's interest in Avis was not its modest sales volume of $50 million or so, but the fact that Avis was a household word. Geneen realized that Avis would help make ITT better known in the financial community.

As noted, other companies that Geneen bought during the ensuing few years—acquisitions that enhanced domestic earnings and massaged Geneen's ego because they were well known to the public—were Continental Baking, maker of Wonder Bread; the Sheraton hotel chain, and Levitt & Sons, home builders.

Through all these acquisitions, ITT boasted that it never made an unfriendly merger. Geneen's press agents touted him as a superexecutive who knew more about the acquired company's business than its owners by the time he stepped into a conference room. However, a long line of critics also have pointed out, somewhat less admiringly, that one reason why Geneen was able to consummate so many mergers was because he doled out to the top management of the acquired companies huge salary increases, and in many cases offered the shareholders large increases in their equity. He did exact his pound of flesh, however. "What you have to adapt to," one former company president who decided not to stay under the Geneen umbrella, confided "is a total loss of independence. Everything has to be cleared by his staff—every press release, every man you hire at a salary over $30,000. I just found it was asinine and refused to do it. But, you know, the guy put together forty-eight consecutive quarters [of continuously rising earnings] and when he says 'march' you march."

In the 1960s, ITT was not alone in its merger binge. Throughout the country there was a rash of takeover attempts by fastgrowing conglomerates, some of them friendly, and some decidedly unfriendly. Given this situation, Geneen tried to play the role of the benevolent big brother when an appropriate occasion arose. For example, the O.M. Scott & Sons Co. of Marysville, Ohio, an old, respected grass seed firm, was being pushed hard by other corporate raiders when its chairman approached Rohatyn seeking an amicable merger. Rohatyn brought Geneen into the picture, and the ITT chairman spent an evening with the Scott chairman. That weekend, the deal was made and Scott became part of ITT.

Acquisitions of companies like Scott and Hartford Fire for ITT were far from the only mergers Lazard Frères had facilitated. Among the major deals it had helped engineer in recent years were the acquisition of the Douglas Aircraft Company, Inc. by the McDonnell Company for a fee of $1 million, and the acquisition of the Lorillard Corporation by Loew's Theaters, Inc. for a fee of

$1 million. It also was involved in the merger of Warner Brothers-Seven Arts Ltd., and Kinney National Service, Inc. for a fee of $1.5 million; and in RCA's acquisitions of the Hertz Corporation and Random House, Inc., for $1 million in fees. Additionally, Lazard helped accomplish the difficult merger between Fiat, the Italian auto company where Meyer was a director, and Citroen, the large French auto maker.

By virtue of all this activity, and other more traditional activities such as underwritings, private placement of securities, advice for selective investment accounts, and venture capital activities, Lazard had earned as much as $15 million or $20 million in a single year, which was distributed among its partners.

Although Rohatyn was the primary link between Lazard Frères and ITT, there never was any question on Wall Street about the source of power at Lazard. The man who ran Lazard Frères in almost dictatorial fashion, influencing every deal the firm engineered, was Andre Meyer. Friends and enemies alike said Meyer ran the firm with an extraordinarily tight rein, and was privy to even the most minute details of his partners' dealings.

A seventy-three-year-old French-born, naturalized U.S. citizen, with a personal fortune estimated at $200 million or more, Meyer's holdings included about $4 million in stock of the Newmont Mining Corporation, and $2 million in RCA stock. Furthermore, he had all the world-wide financial connections necessary to practice the complex and controversial art of making mergers and provided the perfect counterpart to the hard-bitten, crusty Geneen. Meyer was an important figure both at home and abroad, and to his apartment in Manhattan's Carlyle Hotel trooped finance ministers and politicians from two continents to converse about financial trends. The walls of the apartment were lined with paintings by Rembrandt, Monet, and Manet. It was true that Meyer was no longer in his physical prime. By early 1972 he was beginning to slow down. His voice, characterized by a slight lisp, was wavering slightly, and he maintained his vigor with a weekly vitamin shot. However, he was mentally sharp, and had wisely surrounded himself with talented younger men. When corporate officials like Harold Geneen wanted to fashion a complex deal, they knew where to go—Andre Meyer's Lazard Frères & Co.

In addition to Meyer and Rohatyn, Lazard's roster of general partners was studded with men whose powerful connections and knowledge of the inner workings of government and finance could go a long way in helping corporate clients like Geneen and ITT.

However, Meyer was the key. "No other partner has any say whatsoever if Andre doesn't want to do something," one former partner said. "He's personally involved with everything that's done in the firm, and God help the guy who does something without informing him. That goes right down to the minutia. He [Meyer] personally decides who is going to get the new issues, the hot issues, rather than the syndicate department. He makes sure they go to the accounts that will do the firm the most good. Andre personally must get a memo on any new account and approve it."

However, the same former partner said he had little regard for the firm's method of operating. "This whole business is just a matter of 'you scratch my back and I'll scratch yours,' " he said. "There's a weekly operating committee where the partners reduce the information they gained to investment decisions. The people are high quality, but the structure is rotten."

Another investment banker, who had for many years been a Lazard-watcher, told of the Meyer technique. Before Lazard bought Avis, he said, Meyer hired an expert on auto leases, and paid him $5,000 to spend twenty-four hours with him at the Carlyle. When they were through, Meyer knew more about car leasing than anyone he was likely to deal with.

Although Lazard Frères was widely believed to be a French firm that had been transplanted to the United States, the movement was precisely the opposite. It began as an imported dry goods store business in New Orleans more than one hundred years earlier, the creation of a trio of French immigrants. Three brothers —Lazare, Alexandre and Simon Lazard—contributed $3,000 each to the firm, which was moved to San Francisco after a fire swept through New Orleans. It was from the American base that Lazard Frères was later expanded to both Paris and London where its sister organization still operated.

Companies like Lazard Frères and ITT were accustomed to having their way. From year to year, they harvested enormous profits, and shaped the public view of their activities by carefully fashioning a slick facade. Occasionally, of course, lightning struck and they found themselves on the front pages of the world's magazines and newspapers, stripped of their pretensions and fighting to preserve their images. It was only then that the true nature of such companies surfaced, and the style they used to perpetuate their power became evident.

Perhaps the character of ITT was most colorfully spelled out by Representative Emmanuel Celler, chairman of the House Antitrust Subcommittee, on the occasion of one of Geneen's sessions before a congressional committee. "Having this great economic concentration in your company," said the Brooklyn Democrat, "you remind me of what somebody said before this committee some years ago: 'Every man for himself, said the elephant as he danced among the chickens.' "

10/ Cleaning House

Scores of investment bankers sit on corporate boards where they can gather inside information and keep an eye on their investments. Occasionally, their roles as directors plunge them into a quagmire of corruption and fraud. When Peter G. Peterson of Lehman Brothers joined the board of the Minnesota Mining and Manufacturing Company in mid 1973, he scarcely dreamed that within months he would be investigating one of the most sordid political financing scandals of the post-Watergate era. What he found, and what the board did about it, adds a new dimension to the increasingly controversial role of the "outside director."

On August 13, 1973, Peter G. Peterson, the new chairman of Lehman Brothers, climbed what is widely considered to be an important rung in the investment banking ladder of success. He was elected to the board of directors of the prestigious Minnesota Mining and Manufacturing Company, one of the nation's most successful industrial concerns.

For Peterson, it was an indication that he was making it in the world of investment banking, which he had recently joined after quick passes through the business world and the Washington political arena.

Then, two months after Peterson joined the 3M board, a collective shudder ran through the company's executive suites following a terse announcement from the office of the Watergate Special Prosecution Force in Washington.

Papers had been filed in a U.S. district court in St. Paul, charging both 3M and Harry Heltzer, its chairman of the board and chief executive officer, with nonwillful violation of federal law Title 18, U.S.C. Section 610—making illegal political campaign contributions. The maximum penalty for Heltzer was one year in prison or a fine of $1,000, or both. For the corporation, it meant a possible fine of $5,000.

Peter Peterson was about to discover that sitting on the 3M board was more than he had bargained for. Far from occupying a secure haven in the heart of corporate America, he would be plunged into an arena of controversy and dissension.

Peterson was no novice at being in sensitive spots. He had spent several hectic years in the Nixon White House as a Presidential envoy, and had later served as Nixon's secretary of commerce. Still, he had been able to escape to Wall Street from a scandal-ridden administration without any of the stigma of Watergate clinging to him. Furthermore, he was a crafty negotiator, and had a reputation for keeping his back to the wall.

The 3M case, however, had taxed even his considerable resources. As a member of the 3M board, he had become familiar, after the fact, with the details of how the company had made massive illegal contributions. He knew who had made them and when. Indeed, he had voted on whether to insist upon reimbursement of the illegally donated funds, and whether to demand the resignations of the officials involved.

Settling back in the limousine that was rushing him to La Guardia Airport, where he would board a plane for St. Paul and a 3M meeting, Peterson weighed each word as he cautiously described the role he had played in one of the most distasteful corporate episodes of the 1970s. He parried questions and, after some verbal sparring, pulled a sheet of stationery from his pocket. "3M Comments," it was labeled, and on it was written: "When a board of directors faces a tough question, reasonable men can disagree. It is true I did not see eye to eye with my fellow directors on this matter. I think it is inappropriate to review the reasons for my decision. You are right, however . . . I did get special counsel which did confirm my views. The issues were fully debated and I believe the directors voted for what they felt was in the best interests of both the shareholders and the employees."

The statement was a classic example of the all but meaningless generalization that investment bankers so often present for public consumption. With it, Peterson shut off further debate over his role. As President Nixon's roving trade envoy he had probably never been more effective.

Like most investment bankers, Peterson lived in a world that consisted of high-level meetings and decisions that could make or break the careers of powerful business executives and the fortunes of giant companies. Furthermore, as a corporate board member, he was playing a part that had become increasingly controversial in recent years. Once considered an attractive listening post for aggressive investment bankers, or a catbird seat from which they could keep a close eye on their investments, a seat on a corporate board in the 1970s had become an increasingly perilous spot. Former board members of the Penn Central still were fighting law suits, years after the huge railroad went bankrupt. In the aftermath of Watergate, a new moral dilemma had arisen. How much responsibility did an outside director assume for uncovering corrupt practices by a company's officers and forcing disclosure when he found out about them?

Although Peterson did not know it when he joined 3M, the company's story was to become a classic in the history of American business. It would provide a case study of the techniques used by some corporations to bypass the nation's campaign funding laws. And, it also would reveal much about the climate in which otherwise honorable and successful businessmen violated the law, and in the process, destroyed their careers.

As for Peterson's role in unraveling the 3M tale, while it did not bring him any particular distinction, at least it did not cover him with shame. And, even though he balked at discussing it, an examination of the facts in the case made it clear that it would take many years for 3M to live down this episode in its history.

For executives of 3M, the growing seriousness of the situation had been dramatically reinforced on a snowy day early in January 1975. Shortly before noon on that day, the assistant attorney general of Minnesota, flanked by two sheriffs' deputies, strode unannounced into the headquarters of the giant Minnesota Mining and Manufacturing Company, hurried to the fourteenth floor, and handed a search warrant to Harry Heltzer, the company's $400,000-a-year chairman.

Minutes later, the law officers seized a set of bulging manila folders labeled "Political Contributions" which contained explosive information on 3M's half-million-dollar illegal slush fund. They were there to finish what the special prosecutor had begun.

Richard Allyn, the legal officer who led the extraordinary raid, would later comment that it was just like "searching some house for drugs."

But, of course, it wasn't. Raids on corporations of any size are far from commonplace. Furthermore, 3M was not just another company. It was one of the nation's industrial behemoths, with about 80,000 employees and annual sales of nearly $3 billion.

Over the years, its Scotch-brand tape had become a household word. It enjoyed an exemplary reputation in Minnesota and its political clout was enhanced by the fact that it helped finance the campaigns of a number of the leading politicians in both Minnesota and the nation.

The raid on 3M headquarters, which Heltzer later characterized as "highhanded," was the single most dramatic event in a series of devastating blows to the company's reputation. The evidence that was unearthed by the assistant attorney general and other investigators revealed that hundreds of thousands of dollars in corporate funds were laundered in Switzerland by paying phony lawyers' fees and insurance premiums, then returned to a safe in the office of 3M's chief financial officer. The cash was later doled out to scores of state and national politicians in a blatant disregard by 3M for the law.

As a result of the illegal contributions, 3M was bombarded with law suits and government actions that rocked the company and sent morale plummeting.

In addition to seriously eroding 3M's once-shining reputation, the rapid-fire series of suits and charges devastated the company's executive suite, wiping out virtually the entire top echelon.

In the most startling development, Heltzer, 3M's sixty-three-year-old chief executive, resigned under fire, after vowing for months that he would remain in his job. He continued as board chairman until his term expired, but immediately gave up his decision-making powers.

Another high official, Irwin R. Hansen, who was sixty-one, resigned in November 1964 from his position as chief financial officer. He continued to serve 3M as a "consultant" and maintained an office at the company, but he, too, did not seek reelection to the board in May.

Finally, Bert S. Cross, who had been chairman and chief executive of 3M from 1966 to 1970, and board member thereafter, left the board where he had served as chairman of the finance committee.

What was it that precipitated the spate of legal actions and the exodus from 3M's top ranks?

A federal grand jury indictment handed up late in January alleged that during the early and mid 1960s, Cross, then chairman, and Hansen, the chief financial officer, had funneled cash into 3M's secret slush fund by withdrawing money from a corporate bank account.

The company money had been transferred to a Swiss bank

account, and Burgess F. Geib, a deceased former partner of the accounting firm of Haskins & Sells, had allegedly conspired to cover up the transactions. The grand jury said Geib authorized the acceptance of phony insurance premiums, and verified the amount of cash that was secretly returned to the safe in Hansen's 3M office in St. Paul.

Another method of building up the fund, the indictment said, was a series of spurious payments to Dr. L. Gutstein, a Swiss attorney, for foreign legal services that were never rendered.

Dr. Gutstein allegedly returned the cash to Hansen, and false bookkeeping entries again concealed the true purpose of the payments.

To illustrate how the scheme worked, government investigators traced one specific series of transactions involving the slush fund. It allegedly took place in August 1963, when Hansen was said to have wired $115,800 of 3M funds to the company's Swiss bank account, which carried the number 782.900.01 M.

The transaction later surfaced when the company claimed the $115,800 as a deduction in its 1963 federal income tax return, identifying it as an insurance expense.

Then, during 1964, according to the indictment, Hansen made six currency withdrawals, totaling $67,200 from the same Swiss account, placing the cash in the safe in his office. During 1964, he allegedly disbursed at least $33,800 from the safe "for the purpose of making political contributions."

The grand jury also charged that in 1968 or 1969, Hansen personally went to Switzerland and collected $50,000 in cash from Dr. Gutstein.

The Securities and Exchange Commission on January 30, said that about $489,000 in cash from the slush fund was ultimately contributed to political campaigns, "in violation of, and circumvention of federal campaign laws which prohibit corporate contributions."

Late in December 1964, in a financial document filed with the SEC, 3M admitted publicly the extent of its wrongdoing.

"Between 1963 and 1969," it said, "the principal sum of

$634,000 was transferred from corporate sources to the fund.
. . . The last year in which corporate money was transferred to the
fund was 1969; in 1973 the fund was dissolved. A balance of
$167,500, which included the remainder in the fund and contribu-
tion refunds of $31,500 was entered as income on the company
books."

The company also admitted that it faced possible claims for
additional federal and state taxes, penalties and interest, which
could amount to $11 million. The figure was subsequently revised
to $9 million.

How was the money doled out? A report issued by the Minnesota attorney general said that Wilbur M. Bennett, 3M's director of civic affairs, "screened the requests and sought the approval
of the chairman of the board.

"From 1963 to 1970," the report said, "the chairman was Bert
S. Cross, and after 1970, Heltzer. If the chairman approved of the
contribution, Bennett took the request to Hansen, who was the
custodian of the fund. Hansen gave Bennett cash from a safe in
his office. Bennett disbursed the money to the political candidates
and committees."

In some instances, Bennett allegedly obtained a personal check
from a 3M executive, forwarded that check to a political candidate
or committee, then gave the executive cash from the slush fund
to cover the amount of the personal check.

One of the executives who was said to be reimbursed by Bennett
was Harry Heltzer, 3M's chairman. According to an internal
memorandum from the Minnesota attorney general's office,
Heltzer admitted to the state's legal authorities that he sometimes
participated in such exchanges.

Heltzer told the investigators that he was under the impression
at first that the money in the slush fund was from "private
sources," but later began to suspect that it was not.

"He candidly admitted that he had some suspicions beforehand,
but he did not pursue them, because he was afraid of what he
might find out," the memorandum said.

Heltzer later said that he regretted what he called both an
"error" and a "mistake in judgment."

"I should have been a lot smarter than I was," he said. "The minute I was first exposed to the fact that the thing [political fund] was there, I should have done something about it. By just not asking the proper questions at the time, I kind of fell into what seemed to be the practice of the times."

According to Allyn, assistant to Minnesota's attorney general Warren Spannaus, much of the evidence relating to the secret slush fund was obtained during the January raid on 3M headquarters.

"We found the big thing we were looking for," he said, "and that was the pages from a big ledger book kept by Bennett that had every contribution made from '63 on." The ledger also contained entries for some of the laundered money that was handled by Hansen, Allyn said.

The first illegal 3M contribution to surface had been a $30,000 gift to former President Nixon's reelection campaign in 1972. That gift was collected personally by Maurice H. Stans, who, like Peterson, had been a secretary of commerce under President Nixon. In 1972, he was serving as chairman of the Finance Committee to Reelect the President.

Stans accepted 3M's invitation to fly to Minnesota in a 3M plane, and to stay at the lavish 3M suite in the St. Paul Hilton. He collected the money and was honored by his friends at 3M and other local institutions at a special dinner at the Minneapolis Club.

In a "dear Harry" letter to Heltzer before the visit, Stans said, "We will take advantage of the transportation plans that you outline in your letter." He added that "Kathleen and I will also enjoy the suite at the Hilton where I remember staying two years ago."

Although the contribution to the Nixon campaign was the most dramatic of the 3M gifts, it quickly became clear that the pattern of illegal donations had stretched back for a decade and had crossed party lines.

According to 3M's files, most of the contributions were for a few hundred dollars, but an occasional gift of $10,000 to $15,000 was offered to organizations like the Minnesota Republican Party

$100-a-Plate Dinner Committee or the state's Republican Finance Committee.

Democrats like Representative Wilbur Mills and Senator Hubert Humphrey also received donations, and in 1971, $3,000 was given to the Democratic Incumbents Dinner.

By the time Herzog had become chief executive, a stream of law suits and government actions had created a steady outpouring of adverse publicity. They included:

(1) Criminal charges by the state of Minnesota that 3M made a number of illegal political contributions with the cash coming from a corporate slush fund containing nearly $635,000. 3M pleaded guilty and was fined $5,000. Hansen, its chief financial officer, pleaded guilty and was fined $3,000.

(2) Criminal charges by the Watergate special prosecutor that 3M and Heltzer, its chairman, made an illegal contribution of $30,000 to former President Nixon's 1972 reelection campaign. Both pleaded guilty. 3M was fined $3,000 and Heltzer was fined $500.

(3) Civil charges by the Securities and Exchange Commission that 3M, Heltzer, Hansen, and Cross, former chairman of the company, violated federal securities laws, partly by disguising illegal political contributions as bona-fide business expenses for prepaid insurance premiums and legal and consulting fees. 3M and its officials "consented" to the SEC action, in effect pleading nolo contendere. They also agreed to appoint an outside agent to examine 3M's books.

(4) A civil law suit by Judith Bonderman, the 3M stockholder who sought reimbursement by 3M officials of company funds illegally donated to politicians. Five key 3M figures agreed to settle the suit by paying the company $475,000. They were Heltzer, Hansen, Cross, Bennett, and William L. McKnight, another former 3M chairman. The largest settlement was made by McKnight ($300,000), although he was not named in the suit.

"These men [Heltzer, Hansen, Bennett and Cross] don't have the same kind of money I have, so I agreed to assume $300,000 of the settlement," McKnight later said.

(5) Indictment by a federal grand jury of 3M, Hansen, and Cross on federal income tax charges arising from the illegal fund. If convicted, Hansen faced a maximum eleven-year jail sentence and fines totaling $20,000, and Cross faced a maximum five-year sentence and $10,000 in fines. Both men pleaded innocent.

As for current political activity, Bennett said it had been sharply curtailed. "As you can well imagine," he said, "everything is sort of in limbo. Requests still come in and I review them, but our activities in this area have gone down to practically nothing."

For 3M, the string of charges and accusations was extraordinarily painful. The company had a long history of paternalistic operations including pleasant working conditions, community involvement, and such amenities as a country club for its employees.

One reader of the *Minneapolis Star* expressed the views of many when he wrote in a letter to the editor that the actions of a few 3M executives had caused the entire corporation to be "publicly pilloried."

"I'm not trying to whitewash the few 3M execs who erred in judgment," he said, "but I am suggesting that the actions of a few should not reflect in a malignant way on the reputation, integrity and innocence of thousands of 3Mers."

The company clearly concurred. "Certainly morale has suffered," said John J. Verstraete, a 3M vice-president. "We don't claim the wounds are merely superficial, but neither are they crippling. The healing process will accelerate as employees recognize that corrective measures are in effect."

3M officials pointed proudly to the long and successful past of the company, which was founded in 1902 to exploit a vein of ore on Minnesota's north shore. 3M initially had concentrated on manufacturing sandpaper and other abrasives. In the late 1920s, Scotch-brand tape was developed and along with reflective roadside signs, became an important product, as did magnetic recording tape, office copiers, and a host of other consumer and industrial products.

As a result of the scandal, however, the company's performance came under close scrutiny by the financial community. Sales and profits had slipped. In the fourth quarter of 1974, 3M's net earnings had dropped nearly 18 percent to 56 cents a share, from 68 cents a year earlier.

The company's stock had slid from a high of more than $91 in 1973 and $80 in 1974, to an early 1975 price of about $55. The company had earned $2.66 a share in 1974, up from $2.62 a share in 1973, but many analysts believed it would earn 15 cents or 20 cents a share less in 1975.

Despite the muted financial outlook, 3M's new management seemed determined to rise above the mistakes of the old. Early in 1975, the company announced that it was replacing Haskins & Sells with another, as yet unnamed, auditing firm.

"We did the last bit of putting the [campaign funding] thing behind us with our action on the auditors," Herzog said. "As far as I'm concerned that ends the political part. The people who were involved in it are now gone. We have done our surgery and it's been pretty brutal, but it's done."

Meanwhile, as Herzog told the *Minneapolis Tribune,* "You can't run down all the good things this company has done over fifty years because of one mistake. All of a sudden, 80,000 people don't become louses."

By the time the 3M scandal erupted, seventeen American companies and fifteen high-ranking business executives had pleaded guilty to federal charges of making illegal political contributions. Included were such corporate giants as American Airlines, Goodyear Tire and Rubber, and Gulf Oil.

The convictions were made possible largely through the existence of a White House list of corporate contributors that was discovered in the custody of Rose Mary Woods, former President Nixon's private secretary. The list was obtained by the Watergate Special Prosecutor and triggered an intensive investigation.

Until the flurry of government prosecutions for illegal contributions, businessmen had been virtually immune from such legal action. Although it was widely known in political circles that corporate funds found their way into campaigns, there was little impetus for a crackdown on such behavior. Consequently, prosecutions were rare.

A few of the convicted executives discussed the reasons why they flaunted the law, mostly citing pressure from political fund-raisers. But, for the most part, the question of why otherwise honorable businessmen, often with long and distinguished careers behind them, knowingly made illegal contributions, went unanswered.

Several executives who were close to the 3M case, but were not themselves implicated in criminal activity, however, speculated about such contributions.

Joseph W. Barr, director of 3M and chairman of a sub-committee appointed by the board to investigate the illegal contributions, said, "This company was put together by Mr. [William L.] McKnight and a group of gentlemen who all became enormously rich, and I mean *enormously* rich. Mr. McKnight's wealth is in the hundreds of millions of dollars, maybe a billion dollars."

When the company's founders were asked for a political contribution, Barr said, they could write a personal check for $50,000 "without missing it."

In the 1960s, however, 3M management shifted "from the men with enormous wealth who had built up that little company" to professional managers. "It sounds funny to people," Barr said, "but a man making a quarter of a million a year is paying out close to $100,000 in taxes. He has $150,000 left over. He's supporting his wife and children and trying to build up an estate."

Such men, Barr said, "can't write a check for $10,000 when somebody like Mr. [Maurice] Stans comes around, or any political fund-raiser, Democrat or Republican, and says, 'Hey, look boys, you used to give us a quarter million. What's happened to you?' "

Barr said the only explanation he could think of for 3M's illegal behavior was that the "big, big money" that individuals formerly could contribute to political parties was not available under a system of "very high taxes."

Wilbur M. Bennett, 3M's director of civic affairs, who handed out political contributions after they had been approved by the company's chief executives, said, "The groups that are probably the most effective in the whole country, and have almost unlimited ability to do a job, are the unions. Yet no one has conducted an investigation of how they put their money in, how they throw people into an election from their national headquarters to any congressional area they want."

Politically speaking, Bennett said, management was in the "first grade" and the unions were in "graduate school."

"It's paradoxical," he added. "Most businesses would like to say 'the hell with it. Let's run the business and forget it.' We'd rather try to make new products, sell Scotch tape and be successful."

However, he said, business has to deal with government and is simply "putting its head in the sand" if it doesn't.

Basically, what business was seeking with campaign contributions, he said, was the chance to "open some doors to be heard."

William L. McKnight, president of 3M from 1929 to 1949, and chairman from 1949 to 1966, said, "I was very sorry that it happened. It was somewhat of a surprise to me, but I don't know why the [3M] company was singled out for so much publicity. They were not the only ones. A large number of companies made illegal corporate contributions. I don't know that 3M did anything different than a great many other companies did."

While some of those arguments were persuasive to many Americans, others were not. What, for example, of the claim that 3M's executives could ill afford to give personal funds?

The fact was that 3M's top executives, virtually all of them career men, became wealthy as a result of their salaries and stock options at the big midwestern manufacturer. Clearly, as the campaign funding scandal unfolded, the officers of 3M had much to fight for. In addition to their reputations, they had earned handsome livings from the company and were eager to hold onto their jobs. Even those executives who were forced to resign by the political funding scandal that swept the company carried with them lavish retirement benefits and millions of dollars in 3M stock.

Harry Heltzer, for example, earned $407,087 in 1973, and had accumulated retirement benefits of $125,000 a year. Because he resigned early, at the age of sixty-three, it was estimated that his retirement pay has been scaled down to slightly more than

$100,000 a year. Heltzer's holdings of 3M stock a year earlier were worth over $2 million.

Another top 3M executive, Bert Cross, the sixty-nine-year-old former board chairman, received a lump sum settlement from 3M when he retired from full-time duty in 1970. In 1974 he owned more than $6.8 million in 3M stock. In 1973, he was paid $82,000 by the company for his duties as a director and committee chairman.

McKnight, who was eighty-seven, had sold one million shares of his 3M stock for nearly $50 million. After the sale, he still owned 3.7 million shares, worth over $200 million. He also headed a family trust and was co-executor of the estate of his late wife, which gave him "ownership of record" of another 1.7 million shares of 3M stock worth $92 million.

Hansen, who spent thirty years with 3M, was paid nearly $180,000 in 1973. His retirement benefits were estimated at about $73,000 a year. In 1974, Hansen owned 3M stock worth $1.2 million.

Ray Herzog, the new 3M chief executive, earned about $290,000 in 1973. He owned 3M stock worth $1.7 million.

An inside look at the company's response to the scandal was provided by Barr, an executive who shuttled back and forth between government and private sector positions.

In July 1974, even as he was scrambling to keep the beleaguered Franklin National Bank afloat until a buyer could be found, Barr was making a sworn statement to Alan B. Morrison, a Washington attorney associated with Ralph Nader, the consumer activist.

Morrison represented Judith Bonderman, the 3M stockholder who was suing to force reimbursement of the illegal contributions to the company. His work in the case was widely credited by government officials for spurring a number of official actions against 3M.

Barr had been a member of 3M's board of directors since 1970, and after the campaign funding scandal exploded, had been named chairman of an internal committee of the 3M board to investigate and recommend a course of action.

The other members of the committee were Peterson, who had joined the 3M board in August 1973; James Binger, former chairman of Honeywell, Inc. and husband of McKnight's daughter; and John G. Orway, Jr., a trustee of the Ordway Trust, which held millions of shares of 3M stock. Ordway had been on the board since 1972, and Binger since 1973.

The committee was created in November 1973. Its mandate: Make sure the corporation structured itself so there would never be a repetition of the illegal donations. Secondly, consider what action should be taken in connection with the officials who had been involved in the gifts.

The committee held two meetings, the first in January 1974, lasting several hours; the other in February, extending through a Sunday afternoon and most of the following Monday morning. All four members of the committee were present at both meetings, and several outside attorneys for 3M attended as well. The attorneys presented the facts, as they had been established by their firm, and reviewed in detail the tax aspects of the case. The same attorneys also had been presenting the facts to the full board, starting in late 1973.

Barr later admitted that his committee did not make any independent investigation of the illegal contributions. Nor, he said, did the committee issue any report on the matter.

According to Barr, there was never any question of whether the company had broken the law. Clearly, it had. The debate centered on whether the top echelon of the company should be asked to reimburse 3M for the illegal contributions, and the likelihood that they would feel they had to resign under those circumstances.

The posture that Barr struck in his sworn testimony was that the company might fall apart if the committee forced the resignation of Heltzer, Hansen, and Cross. He said that Ray Herzog, 3M's president, was asked whether he could hold the company together.

"His answer was he did not think that he could, or he could do it only with great difficulty—but that certainly the best interests of shareholders and employees should be drastically affected by such action, in his opinion."

The officials in question did, of course, leave, and the company subsequently took a more reassuring stance.

Ironically, in mid 1974 Heltzer was asked by a ninth-grade student in St. Paul, during the taping of a classroom conversation, what would happen to 3M if he were absent. Heltzer responded that he had once been out for about a month because of surgery, and it had caused "hardly a ripple."

According to Barr's testimony, Peterson argued for stronger action than the rest of the committee. He said Peterson suggested at one point that the officials involved in the illegal contributions should repay the company for the amounts involved.

It was concluded, however, that such a request would be denied by the individuals, because they would, in effect, be admitting guilt, and thus opening themselves up to private litigation.

At the onset of the committee's deliberations, Peterson and Barr retained a lawyer of their own, Mortimer Kaplan of Washington, a former commissioner of Internal Revenue. Barr said that both he and Peterson knew the issue was an explosive one, and they wanted to be sure their own actions would stand up later.

"Mr. Peterson felt he was in a very sensitive position as head of Lehman Brothers, and he should be very careful," Barr said. "I knew Morty. I was in the Treasury when he was commissioner of Internal Revenue, and he was very good with SEC matters and tax matters of this sort. Pete [Peterson] felt, and I concurred, that [Kaplan] could be helpful to us here."

Barr also said that he relied heavily on 3M for help in the investigation. "When you're an outside director of a company as big as 3M, you try to get your arms around it, but you have to depend very heavily on the judgment of the inside directors and officers," he said. The most persuasive argument, Barr said, was the advice of high company officers that they could not survive the exodus of three principal officials.

"Maybe they were wrong," he said, "and maybe we were wrong."

Indeed, it seemed that at times the committee was more concerned with protecting its flank than with ferreting out the truth and acting on it. After Peterson and Barr hired Kaplan as their outside counsel (with 3M paying the bill), it appeared that some of his tough advice was at least partially ignored.

In his deposition, Barr refused to disclose what Kaplan had recommended. Peterson, however, who was the sole board member to vote against the resolution ultimately fashioned by the committee, said that his "special counsel" had confirmed his views.

At the end of its investigation, the committee offered its resolution at 3M's February 1974 board meeting. In effect, it deplored what had happened but recommended that no action be taken by the company against the officers involved.

Although the resolution was a lengthy one, it contained two key statements. The first said: "It is the judgment of this Board of Directors that the best interests of this Corporation, its stockholders, and employees are best served by the forbearance of any action to recover possible damages from any director, officer, or employee who may have been directly or indirectly responsible for the unlawful expenditure of corporate funds for political purposes. . . ."

The other pronouncement said: "This Board of Directors hereby declines to institute proceedings of any kind against any director, officer, or employee in connection with the unlawful expenditure of corporate funds for political purposes."

Only Peterson voted against the resolution, and against a companion resolution which sharply limited the company's public disclosure of illegal campaign contributions.

Although Peterson declined to discuss the reasons why he voted against the board's whitewash, Barr did mention it later. "I admire old Pete," he said. "I think it [his vote] makes us look much better. The fact that this was not a unanimous decision does indicate that we agonized over it for days and months. Too damn many boards act as rubber stamps. This was no rubber stamp board." Despite Barr's disclaimers, however, it appeared that with the exception of Peterson, the 3M board was very much of a rubber stamp.

Later, of course, after the housecleaning had taken place, the board would put on a show of vigor. "I am now able to tell you," Peterson wrote after the board meeting in March 1975, "that every director nominee on the new slate (you will recall that Messrs. Cross, Hansen, and Heltzer are not nominees) have or will have signed statements saying they did not have knowledge of illegal corporate political contributions prior to July 1973.

"Quite beyond the integrity of the men involved, I remind you that the company is operating under an SEC consent decree that requires full and accurate disclosure. Thus, anyone signing such a statement, if it were not true, would be doing so at a large personal hazard since the statement that none of the director nominees had prior knowledge of political contributions will appear in the new proxy.

"Thus, I think it is fair to say that the company has, in recent months, taken vigorous action on a variety of fronts to ensure that the ongoing management group was uninvolved with the political contributions matter."

What Peterson did not say, of course, was that it clearly had been the initiative of the special prosecutor's office, the SEC, the Minnesota attorney general, the IRS and the Nader lawyers, that had spurred 3M's board to clean house. It had patently not been the whitewash resolution of the special committee on which Peterson had served.

As the 3M case faded from public view, succeeded in the headlines by political funding revelations involving Gulf Oil and Phillips Petroleum, Peterson moved quietly back into his world of black limousines, carpeted foyers, paneled offices and powerful industrialists. He had played his role, spent a brief and unwanted moment in the spotlight, and then returned to doing business as usual. To some, it seemed that the old dictum of the investment banker had once again been proven. The sage Wall Streeter can get out in front once in awhile, but not too often and never too far.

11/ The Stock Scammer

While most investment bankers work in lavish Wall Street offices, and transact their deals in the corporate headquarters buildings that line Manhattan's Park Avenue, the profession also has another side that treads a darker street. It is composed of the "scammers," the fast-buck operators who wheel and deal in stolen stock. Like their law-abiding brethren, they circle the globe in private jets, vacation in mansions outside Rome or Paris, and ride in chauffeured limousines. The stocks they handle rest in the vaults of some of the nation's largest and most prestigious banks, and are used in multimillion-dollar real estate and franchise transactions. The difference is: they're stolen. This is the story of one scammer, Frank Peroff, known in the trade as "Miami Frank."

If Frank Peroff had been born a Lehman, or a Loeb, a Goldman, or a Morgan, he probably would have ended up working for one of the big, respectable investment banking houses on Wall Street. He would have lived in Purchase, New York, summered abroad, married a Radcliffe or Wellesley girl, and enjoyed the baronial life that a six-figure income can buy.

But Peroff was born in the Bronx. His father was in the dry cleaning business, and he literally fought his way through public high school in New York City. For as long as he could remember, he had been a scammer—the underworld term for someone who wheels and deals on the shady side of the law.

At the age of seventeen, Peroff's family had moved from the Bronx to Miami, the "scamming" capital of the Western world. By the time he was in his twenties, he was known as "Miami Frank," and was on his way to a career in illegal finance that would transport him to the center of underworld securities crime, then plunge him into near poverty and fear for his life by the time he was thirty-seven.

Essentially, at the pinnacle of his particular career, Peroff was an investment banker. He made it possible for businessmen to expand their operations, to buy new plants and equipment. He made money available for developers to build hotels, motels, and car washes. He filled the classic textbook definition of an investment banker. Only there was a difference. He did it with stolen stocks. Rather than following the traditional investment banking route of raising money from the public by selling them shares of stock in an enterprise, then making that cash available to businessmen for expansion, Peroff reversed the procedure.

He fenced stocks that had been stolen from the public, and used the securities to obtain money for businessmen. Nothing as mundane as lifting stocks from Wall Street back rooms, or hoisting mail bags from airport cargo sheds into a waiting station wagon for Peroff. Instead, he acted as a middleman. He received stolen stocks, and, in some cases, commissioned the theft. Then, when the stocks were in his hands, he marched into a bank with the "hot" stocks, had a brief discussion with his friendly banker, and walked out with a massive loan that had been secured by the stolen securities—a feat that only a few dozen men in the country have the talent and the wherewithal to successfully carry off.

"I would say that I have actually disposed of, in other words safely passed, $15 million or $20 million worth of stock," Peroff once said. "That doesn't include certificates of deposit, or time deposits or anything like that. I'm talking about stock."

By the time Peroff moved to Miami, he already had gained some experience in making easy money. In his New York high school, he had sold exams to his fellow students. When he was fourteen he was making $120 a week on the side by teaching English phrases to German immigrants at a tool and die plant in his neighborhood.

"It wasn't that I had to have the money," he said. "My people had a business. It was just a thing that I had. I was always making money. When I went down to Florida, I went into this business. I had some partners and we did it on a shoestring. The whole thing collapsed. But right there I got my first real education, because the guy who was doing the teaching was a man who controlled a big bank in Boston. He's dead now, but he helped give me my first real good piece of financial education and my first bleeding ulcer.

"I was charged in that particular deal," Peroff said, "the only federal charges I ever had—with five counts of bankruptcy fraud. I got a directed verdict of not guilty. The judge said I wasn't a crook but I was a lousy businessman. Maybe if he had stopped me then, I wouldn't have gone on, but what I got out of that was a license to keep going."

At the age of twenty-one, Peroff participated in a counterfeit chip deal in Las Vegas.

"I went out there for a mob guy in New York, and passed these chips," he said. "I got caught, and they broke my fingers with a big glass ash tray. I ended up having to go down to Puerto Rico for a couple of months to recover."

While he was in his late twenties, Peroff was associated with a company that manufactured materials used in the construction of large buildings. In his first major deal, he signed a $100,000 contract in Washington, D.C.

"I supplied the insides of a lot of buildings in Washington," he said. "I also got involved directly and indirectly in actual building. I think what turns on most stock people, one way or another, is real estate, because that's where there's the most need for stock. Nearly everybody I used to run into always had that same need. Some still looked at it like dreamers, hoping they were going to find somebody to help them mortgage out, based on what they had. But the rest knew they couldn't, and were looking for the other."

Peroff said his new acquaintances in Washington moved him quickly into big-time action. Until that point his dealings in stock were peanuts, he said. "But during that same period of time, I met a man in Washington who turned me on pretty heavily. He had an unlimited source of stock. In fact, he was a supplier to me in countless deals. That coin turned over, too. There was a period of time when his sources dried up and he couldn't get it, and was coming to me for it. By then, I was an accomplished manipulator. I had my own sources. When I started dealing with this particular guy, I was paying three-quarters of what I'd sell it for. When I sold him the stock, I did it on a friendship basis, and really didn't make any money. I sold it to him for a third of what he used to sell it to me for, because I was buying it that cheap.

"You don't get into it overnight. It takes a long time. But usually, no matter what I was doing at the time, I always had a little going on the side. Then I moved out. I started going into other, bigger things. I started playing with the jets. I started going over to Europe. I developed good contacts over there, and pretty soon, I got big."

As Peroff's career in stolen securities developed, he found that hot stock could be used to finance real estate deals. Curiously, many of them were sound investments, and as the loans that made them possible were paid off, the hot stocks were retrieved and the banks that had accepted them as collateral did not lose a penny.

"Eventually the money is returned," Peroff said, "especially because there are an awful lot of people who make use of [stolen] stock who happen to be upstanding citizens in the community. To them, it's a paper crime. What they're doing is aiming for money.

They need collateral. They fully intend to pay the bank back and they will. But they're doing it knowing it's hot stock."

One use for such stock, Peroff said, was in financing hotels and motels. In such deals, it was possible to keep the stock, which was used as collateral, from surfacing—as long as the loans based on it were outstanding. "They're just going to be pushed deeper in a drawer," he said. "It's going to be just like a certain hotel in Miami. At one point, it had twenty mortgages on it. They just kept making another mortgage to keep the old one from going bad. It's that simple. If you run the bank, and you don't want a bad loan to surface, it's not going to surface. You make another loan, and another loan, and it can go on for years."

Peroff said one well-known motel chain had been financed largely with stolen stocks. "I would venture to say that every hotel they've ever built has been on that basis," he said. "A lot of their financing has come from mob money. People who build a hotel get it running, show a heavy profit on paper, and then sell to another group. By then, all the paper that was used to build the thing is recovered. I would say that 80 percent of the whole south of Spain and Majorca were built on [stolen] American stock. And, I'm speaking from personal knowledge."

The financing of that construction, Peroff said, involved the transfer of stolen stocks to banks in countries such as Luxembourg and Liechtenstein, with letters of credit from those banks then being used to obtain loans from institutions in Switzerland, Sweden, Britain, and West Germany.

Although most of Peroff's major dealings involved real estate transactions outside the United States, he was, for a time, a major manipulator in the car wash business in Florida. "I built car washes," he said, "I sold the equipment, and I promoted them. I was even given the Chamber of Commerce award by Donald Nixon at Arnold Palmer's club for designing car washes. I was involved in the first car wash that Standard Oil ever got into, and I was indirectly involved in the car washes that have gone into Disney World. The point I'm trying to make is that I know my way around the car wash business.

"Now stocks figure into it this way. A man may save $25,000 to $50,000 and want to get into a business. The car wash business did a lot of work in franchising presentations. They made it look pretty good to a man who has that kind of money. The only problem was the lending institutions. That $25,000 to $50,000 didn't count enough. A good full-service car wash—from A to Z —sold in the neighborhood of $300,000. It doesn't seem like it would be that high, but it was. The distributor, the man who's building the thing, naturally wants the car wash to flourish. The profit to the promoter or broker of these things could be between $50,000 and $100,000. The commission, just on the equipment, is a third to the distributor. Then, depending on how well he can manipulate the land, the lease, and everything else, he can move himself up close to $100,000.

"Now, the deal worked this way. Leasing became very big to the finance companies. Basically, the reason was that it gave them license to get usury. There's no question about it. I mean, you could go to the bank and borrow money at 9 percent or 10 percent at that time. It was cut and dried and that was it. But in leasing, if you examine all the charges, everything that happened in the lease, you'd find that it went over 20 percent. The only thing that's really necessary in the lease was from three to five payments in advance. That would be no more than, say, a maximum of about $15,000. Now the balance of the money that the man has would be used for a down payment on the land and on a sign. I put up a car wash in Orlando and the sign alone cost something like $45,000. It was a huge thing. But that's what car washes have to have."

The financing process, Peroff said, involved leasing or finance companies working with the manufacturers. "They're all in the same boat," he said. "They're all operating hand-to-mouth, and it's a feast or a famine business. So, there's a lot of manipulating going on behind the scenes. I sold bad stock directly to one of the biggest car wash manufacturers in the country, because he had to meet some notes, and I guess he used that for collateral on a loan. In this particular case, I even met with his banker.

"What usually happens, though, is there's a contact man in the finance company who works with the manufacturer or the distributor. There's a lot of preliminary work that you have to go into to prepare the initial package. You would prepare it as though you were building a hotel or anything else. You've got to come up with a profit and loss projection. In other words, it's a pro forma. You get this done. You pick out a site. You try to get your permission from the oil company, because the oil company is a participant, money-wise, under the table. Very few people realize that they actually will pay cash to get in on the deal—heavy cash.

"The point I'm trying to make is that everything has to make sense, otherwise there can be no deal. But this is paper. In other words, I can write a pro forma. But the pro forma's never checked out. I'm the expert. If they ask me, 'Is it right?,' I'm going to nod my head 'yes,' and that's about as far as the checking goes.

"The next thing they come to is, 'Let's see the man's statement.' Now I'd say in about 25 percent of the cases, the statements are absolutely legitimate. The man has enough money, enough real estate. Usually what the financing houses look for is about two-to-one. If you're trying to borrow $200,000 or $300,000, for instance, they'd want you to have $400,000 or $500,000 in assets. I think you'll find a man who's worth a legitimate half million has got more than $25,000 or $50,000 in cash reserves."

In another 40 percent of the cases, the assets were dubious but acceptable, Peroff continued. In some of those cases, it was necessary to exaggerate the value of the land a man holds, or to lend him a little collateral to beef up his statement, but that was possible without too much difficulty.

That left, however, about 35 percent of all the investors who were without the necessary funds to carry out their part of the bargain. "The margin between what the finance company wants and what the man really has is too wide to lie about," Peroff said. "It's too wide to lend him a little bit, so what you do is put real collateral in the man's name. You can buy it or rent it. Here's a case where renting collateral works. And, it's not always stock. It can be bad land. You know stock is just one tool, but land with bad title is used in finance the same way bad stock is.

"But, let's go the route with stock. You would go ahead and buy or rent stock. A lot of people going into the car wash business fall into this category."

The financing was done with a leasing company, Peroff said. "The point is that everybody makes money here, all the way to the top. There are kick-backs from the manufacturer. It's to everybody's advantage to get the deal through. A public company can't make bad loans, or do anything that can come back to them later, so all they want you to do is provide them with the tools they need to put one over on their own company, and they'll do it."

Peroff said the individual putting up the car wash, although he might have had no intention of doing anything illegal at the outset, could be trapped into such activity.

"Let me put it this way," he said. "He doesn't come looking for it, but he gets educated real fast. What usually happens is that he's put into a trap, because the guy who's manipulating the franchise first takes his money and then guarantees him the moon. The guy's probably put half of everything he's got in the world in somebody's hands. This guy is supposed to be on his side, like his attorney. Most of the time, there's not even an attorney at that stage. But the contracts that he's used are so beautiful—they're so technical looking and they're so real—the guy is completely snowed and he puts his money up. Then, all of a sudden, you start running into problems, and he starts getting turned down by a couple of legitimate [financial] houses. What is he going to do? He either walks away from it and shoots himself, or he turns around and goes to the guy and says, 'What am I going to do?' and the guy says, 'Well, maybe I have an answer. Can you get me another five or ten grand?' And, the guy will say, 'Well, I don't have it, but somehow I'll raise it.' And, he says, 'I'm going to rent you some collateral; we're going to beat this.' That's the way it works. It's extortion, you know, as far as the guy is concerned, but that's how franchising works."

Peroff said the same individuals who were active in car wash schemes often surfaced in other types of franchises as they become popular.

"It's a very small world," he said. "You'll run into a guy who was selling car washes two years ago, and now he's selling movie theater franchises, or he's selling fast food franchises—whatever is going good."

One car wash deal he was involved in, Peroff said, resulted in disaster, but contained many of the elements that had come to pervade the industry's financing.

"This was a multi-car-wash deal," he said. "They had a lot of franchisers already who had put down the money. It wasn't only a car wash, it was half car wash, half analyzer and tune-up operation. The whole idea was you'd be able to go in a tunnel, and by the time you came out, you got your oil changed, filter changed, this and that—at the end, it would be washed and you'd have a beautiful looking car.

"They did a lot of publicity on it. And, they went through exactly this bit with the stock. Statements were built up. The statements really became crucial with the franchisers—the people who were putting the money up. But it became a strangulation kind of deal. The projected cost in the beginning was around $300,000. I don't know why or how, but after the first load of car washes for this project went out on the railroad tracks to be delivered, all of a sudden they found that the cost was going to run over half a million per.

"Now, a lot of people had put out cash and they were caught in the kind of a deal where you can't get your money back. There's no way. The money's spent in promotion. The car washes were already on the railroad tracks. I don't understand why the thing never blew up into a national scandal. The only thing I can think of was the manufacturers involved in this particular deal have got to be the sharpest manipulators around.

"His [the manufacturer's] situation is this. When he puts a car wash on the railroad track, he gets half his money. When his distributor sends in a signed contract, he can go to his bank and get an additional third. When it's delivered and picked up by the final user, he gets his balance. So, he's really got better than 80 percent of his money already. He's not risking that much.

"Now, I believe there were about eight car washes on the railroad tracks already. That's a lot of money. At that point, he isn't about to give it back. I think it was his maneuvering that stopped the thing from becoming a real crisis."

Peroff said the people who put up their money initially, lost it. He bought some of the car washes himself, at 50 percent of their cost, he said, and used them in other deals. "That deal was loaded with bad stock," he said, "and it never came to the surface. People took their losses and walked away. It's the same as someone cheating on his income tax. How is he going to scream?"

Peroff was asked if he had been involved in any of the bad stock in that particular deal.

"Indirectly I was, yes. I helped one of the people putting the deals together. That's who I gave the stock to."

How?

"This man was on the payroll of the manufacturer. It was his job to work with distributors around the country, put together these packages, and help them over the rough spots. Well, they found a bunch of rough spots, and this was a guy who at that time was propositioning me to 'be my partner.' He came to me because he needed stock. I got him stock. I know where the stock went and I paid cash for it."

How much?

"I'd say it was a total of about half a million dollars."

Where did you get it?

"From a guy who was a partner of mine in the business. I'd done a lot of transactions for him. I actually picked up the stock in Freeport."

What did you have to pay for it?

"Like most of the deals with this man, it was 50-50 of what I got for it. I believe I made twelve points, that much. And, for hot stock! A real inside man will only have to pay anywhere from 1 to 3 [percent of face value] for hot stock, but the market for a guy that needs it can run anywhere from 10 to 20."

What did the man you sold them to use them for?

"He resold them, or rented them in beefing up statements for these deals. I've been in a lot of action with this guy. He is, by the way, an ex-aide of an ex-congressman. The only reason this thing never really surfaced, I'm sure, is because the manufacturer bought it out everywhere he had to. But, it would have been a bad scene. These things never come to the surface unless, number one, there's an investigation, or number two, you rob a bank. No bank got robbed, only individuals. An individual is not a threat. In this case, individuals got burned but not the finance companies."

For Peroff, the progression from trying to pass counterfeit chips in Las Vegas, to car washes, to complex multimillion-dollar real estate deals led him ultimately to Europe and Scandinavia. One such scam involved a young Swedish millionaire whose holdings were estimated by Peroff at nearly $30 million.

"He had eight banks under his control. But the guy only made about $40,000 a year. Sweden is unique because whether you're the director of a bank, or the street cleaner, you pay 50 percent income tax. He was making forty grand and only keeping twenty grand.

"When he became director of this bank, his family lived sixty miles from the bank, so he didn't move them right to that town. He stayed in town and used to go home weekends or every other week. But, then he found himself a nineteen-year-old girl, a good-looking Swedish broad and he fell in love with her. But she was systematically, with the guidance of another guy, setting him up and cleaning him out—putting him in debt. He broke. He became a crook, at first for this other fellow. But he couldn't make connections. He was afraid. When I got up there it was all set up. The people who put me on to him in Switzerland knew what he was looking for, and they knew I was the one who could do it. So all of a sudden I flew up there one day in a private jet and he met us at the airport. It didn't take him fifteen minutes to proposition us in a deal.

"I took over where this other guy left off with the banker. I not only moved stock, but also a tremendous amount of counterfeit [securities]."

Perhaps the most dramatic deal Peroff ever encountered was one that never came off. It took place on an island that has become a household name to vacationing Americans.

"There's a farm in ———," Peroff said. "In fact, the largest farm there. This was the idea of the deal. The farm was supposed to be revitalized. It was a dead farm, but it had a landing strip. It had a school on it and it had stores. It was a big place, a tremendous place. The prime minister was a partner in the deal. A lot of heavy people were partners. They were going to permit farm items, produce and just about everything else, to be smuggled into the farm. From there, it would be shipped out as though it had been grown on the farm. This did two things. Number one, it eliminated the 33⅓ percent tariff on imported goods. Also, all the existing hotels, and everybody else, would have been contracting with this farm. So, you probably would have cut out 90 percent of all the shipments into ———. A cash investment of $3 million was needed to start it off, and I was propositioned to be a partner in it and live on the farm, with my own airplanes and boats.

"Right during the negotiations, I packed my family up and moved to Europe. I was getting a reputation, and certain things happened in Florida that made me certain I was about an inch away from getting on the governor's list of going bye-bye. In other words, I think I would have reached a point where I definitely would have ended up in jail, and this is something that I'm not willing to do, even for all the action I did."

By this time, Peroff was cutting a wide swath in the secretive world of stolen securities. He had made the major leagues where reputation counts for everything, and where a nod or a word in the right place can put a man in the middle of a complex deal that involves bankers and institutions in a half dozen countries.

"I'd say probably 80 percent of all the stock deals I've ever done have come in the last couple of years," Peroff said. "Because when you're up there, you swing. When you start dealing in the big numbers, a lot bigger people start taking notice and I knew that it was just a question of time before I was going to be on that list of no return. So many of the people that I have dealt with are either in jail or awaiting trial."

Still, for a time, it was a heady life. Peroff bought a $100,000 house in Spain, and from there moved to Italy, where he paid $1,000 a month to rent a villa in Rome. Before that he had maintained an apartment in Rome that he said cost him $1,500 a week. "I even kept the apartment while I took a three-month cruise to Sardinia and Corsica in my own boat," he said.

The boat had cost Peroff $85,000, but appropriately, he bought it from another scammer and paid for it with stolen stock. In Rome, Peroff had a brother-and-sister team of servants, and was driven through the city in a Fleetwood Cadillac. He traveled Europe in private jets.

For two years Peroff sat at the top, at one point coming within a whisker of buying a major movie studio. Once he had seventeen corporations in his name. In Europe, Peroff had the faint hope that he could make a heavy killing and get out. "I tried this when I went to Europe," he said, "but the stigma follows you, because it's a small world and somehow people find out. I wasn't hiding under any other name or anything like that, but I was definitely not looking for trouble."

One deal that Peroff said disturbed him involved counterfeit money that he believed came from Communist sources. "Maybe it's a false kind of patriotism or something," he said, "but I dealt with this money, and as soon as I found out that there were Chinese who were printing it, I didn't want to do it. It's a double standard I guess, but it's true. Corny as that may sound. To me, it made a big difference whether it was an Englishman who was printing it or a Chinaman. I helped the government dump it."

After that Peroff began to work periodically as an informant or undercover agent for various federal agencies. In one such arrangement, he heard of an organized crime deal involving over $1 million in Canadian treasury bonds. "When I was told about this, I let the Mounties know," he said. In another instance, Peroff worked with the Drug Enforcement Administration, a United States agency that keeps an eye on illicit drug traffic.

Peroff discussed one narcotics deal in which he had worked as an undercover agent, believing a well-known securities thief was involved. "His money came from paper," Peroff said, "from crooked security deals. He stole money. He made all his money out of paper, and yet here he was doing a narcotics deal. The return is heavy. He may have a lot of money. They say he stole millions. But, I'd like to see how much cash he's got. I don't think his money is anywhere near that amount. No crook's money ever is. You know, it leaves you on top. If I told you how much money I made, it would stagger you. But, I don't have a pot, because it costs you money to operate. You keep going into the next one and the next one. Somehow, if you make $1 million, you spend a million and ten. This has been the situation in my case; I think it's the same in his. I don't think he's got any choice. I mean what he has to go through to just survive is costly. He's put a tremendous amount of money into two losing pots—the Bahamas, which is definitely not a money-making deal, and Costa Rica, which just about breaks even. I know those markets and know them well. So that costs, you know. I don't know how much he's got left, but I don't think it's nearly what people would like to think he has.

"Now, if he had done this deal—he was putting out $300,000 —and, if he was getting half in return on the wholesale value, he would have gotten close to a million and a half. That's a helluva good return in two or three weeks."

Peroff's involvement with organized crime figures traced back to his activities as owner and operator of a small airline charter service. That brought him into frequent contact with underworld figures, and for a time, he said, authorities were calling his operation "Air Mafia." One of his customers was a Canadian named Conrad Bouchard, leader of an underworld group.

In 1971 Bouchard had been arrested in Canada on charges of preparing a huge heroin smuggling scheme. For two years, Peroff had no further contact with the Canadian, but they came together to do business again early in 1973. Peroff was living in Rome at the time, and had been asked by underworld contacts to move nearly a half-million dollars in counterfeit American fifty and one hundred dollar bills.

Instead, Peroff turned the money over to U.S. agents in Rome, who told him that the couriers were dealing not only in counterfeit money, but also in narcotics. Subsequently, with Peroff's help, the French police arrested eight smugglers and seized twenty-five kilos of heroin. That was only a precursor, however, to a far more ambitious plan. At this point the United States Bureau of Customs, Narcotics Intelligence branch, had persuaded Peroff to come back to the United States and penetrate the group that operated out of Canada. From time to time, Peroff was provided with a Lear jet, which he could claim he had leased himself. Unknown to Peroff's underworld contacts, one of the pilots of the leased plane was a federal agent, and the plane and its occupants were kept under constant surveillance.

By this time, Peroff had moved his wife and five children from Europe to Puerto Rico, where they lived on the outskirts of San Juan.

After weeks of surveillance, the undercover work began to pay off. Peroff told his agents that the plane he controlled was to fly to Europe, pick up a load of heroin, then fly back to either the United States or Canada. The American agents, of course, were anxious for the plane to land in the United States, so they could seize the conspirators.

As spring turned to summer, a new and dramatic element suddenly entered the picture. In the final days of June, a name that was familiar to Peroff, but had not heretofore been mentioned in the Canadian deal, surfaced for the first time. It was Robert L. Vesco, the fugitive financier from the United States, who was under indictment along with two former cabinet officers of the Nixon administration on charges that involved a secret campaign contribution of $200,000 for Nixon's reelection campaign of 1972.

After Vesco's name was first mentioned by the Canadians, Peroff began to tape record his conversations. In one such conversation, according to Peroff, Bouchard implicated Vesco and a Canadian named Norman LeBlanc, who was one of Vesco's close associates in the operation of the Bahamas Commonwealth Bank in Nassau.

In mid July, Peroff returned to New York at the request of the Drug Enforcement Administration, which had taken over much of the work of the Customs Bureau in drug enforcement matters.

There was a problem, however. Peroff had become distrustful

of the way he was being treated by the drug agency, and he wondered if the entry of Vesco, who had connections with the Nixon family, had not caused the change of heart. For example, the DEA now refused to provide him with a plane and a pilot so he could proceed with the arrangement he had worked out with Bouchard. By this time, the plan called for him to fly to San Jose, Costa Rica, to pick up the money to finance the drug deal, then fly to Europe to meet Bouchard and pick up the heroin before flying back to North America.

"They said, why didn't I fly down commercial," Peroff said. "Don't they know that would get me killed? They think some guy is going to give me $300,000 in a suitcase and let me try to walk it through security searches and Customs? If I got no plane when I get to San Jose, I get no money. That would mean a bullet in my back. No question about it. There is no way I could bluff it.

"When I came back to New York in July, right after this had happened, my mind was bad. I didn't know where the hell to go. I had two choices—either get on another plane and go back to Europe, and at that point I'm in debt. Or, I could turn around and make this thing honest, which is what I tried to do. I didn't want to call the newspapers. I didn't want to blow it up. Naturally, if I did that at that time, the deal's dead right there. So, I decided to call two people. Buzhardt [J. Fred Buzhardt was President Nixon's White House counsel] and the guy who was handling Vesco for the Justice Department. That's exactly what I did."

From the Hilton Inn at Kennedy Airport, Peroff made and received more than a dozen telephone calls to and from the White House, calls that were later verified by Senate investigators, despite White House denials that Peroff had contacted them.

How many times had Peroff talked to them?

"Altogether, between fifteen and twenty conversations with the White House over a period of four days, starting around the 18th of July [1973]. I talked to a Peter Grant [a Secret Service agent]. I talked to a guy by the name of Phelps. I talked to a guy by the name of Meyers. I talked to a guy by the name of—I'm not sure of his name, but it was something like Andrews or Andros, or something like that. And, I talked to Buzhardt twice. They called me back six times."

Peroff tried to read to Buzhardt a fifteen-minute statement outlining his undercover work. "I got maybe a third of the way through it and he stopped me and had his own list of specific questions. But I managed to tell him the whole story. In other words, the fact that I wanted the deal to go down."

The Secret Service knew from prior checks that Peroff was wanted on a fugitive warrant issued against him in Florida in 1972, over some checks written by a company of which he was a part-owner. Earlier, government agents had accepted his explanation that the checks were issued during his absence after having been presigned. However, at noon on Sunday, July 22, four days after he started calling the White House, Peroff was picked up by two New York detectives on the old fugitive charge and was jailed. Three days later, he was out on bail, having been released at the request of federal agents who said he was a witness in a narcotics matter involving Vesco. Peroff said the federal agents then instructed him to go to Canada and try to create problems about finance and other details that would wreck the narcotics smuggling plan.

To Peroff's surprise, Bouchard accepted the stiff new conditions he laid down, and said that at noon the following day he would have the arrangements made. Again, the deal went awry. The Canadian Mounties told Peroff to pack up and leave, then put him on a plane without a chance to call Bouchard. Later, when he tried to contact Bouchard, he found his telephone out of order. When he finally reached Bouchard, Peroff found him outraged "because he thought I had run out on him." To stall Bouchard, and to provide a plausible cover story, Peroff said his Lear jet had been repossessed by a leasing company.

Now Peroff had to decide what course to follow. Upset by the turn of events, he had the feeling that his role was being sandbagged and that it was related to the entry of Vesco's name in the drug deal. He had the feeling that Vesco, who employed President Nixon's nephew, Donald A. Nixon, and who had never before been linked with a drug case, was being protected. But, what to do about it? His calls to the White House, he felt, had only served to get him arrested. Now he was suspect, both by the crime figures in the deal, and by the government agencies.

Early in August, Peroff moved his family into a residential hotel in Manhattan. He began quarreling with the drug agency and Customs over the money he felt was due him. Then, he took a second major step. He contacted the Senate Permanent Subcommittee on Investigations and told his story. The staff of the subcommittee was intrigued. In recent years, it had been able to demonstrate the link between organized crime and stolen securities, but this provided the opportunity to carry that link one step further, to demonstrate how stolen securities helped to finance drug traffic.

For Peroff, the pace again picked up. His career in stolen securities, and his government undercover work, were culminating in a frenzy of activity. Toward the end of October he was approached by the Royal Canadian Mounted Police from Montreal and offered a payment if he would again help penetrate the Bouchard group. He introduced an undercover policeman into the group, and subsequently Bouchard was arrested on counterfeiting charges on Sunday, November 4. That job completed, Peroff returned to New York and was assigned security guards from the U.S. drug agency, who lived with his family for the next ten days.

Until this time, Peroff's role as an informant and undercover agent had not been publicly revealed. However, on November 6, a Mounted Police constable, testifying at a bail hearing held for Bouchard in Montreal, identified Peroff as a source of information. The secret was out.

"That made me as hot as a man can be," Peroff said. He quickly contacted the drug agency, which offered to give him $500, and suggested that he relocate. He refused, and his guards were withdrawn. He was on his own, with the uneasy knowledge that his life could be in jeopardy. Peroff quickly left New York for Washington, where he began telling his story in detail to the Senate subcommittee staff, hoping for immunity and the chance to change his identity and begin a new life. To help buttress his case, he granted newspaper interviews, and the outlines of his story appeared in the press. Finally, the Senate subcommittee decided that his story was credible, and gave him the protection he had been seeking.

What still had to be established was the alleged Vesco involvement. Was he really a backer in the heroin deal? Or was his name merely being used to make the deal sound more important? Why did the White House deny that Peroff had contacted it? Was influence used by the administration to sabotage the drug deal once Vesco's name had surfaced? And was Peroff caught in the middle of that tricky business? The Senate subcommittee hoped to sort out the answers, although it was by no means certain that they would ever be totally clear.

Peroff said he could show a definite link between stolen securities and hard crime. "They've already proved that organized crime is involved in securities," he said. "But what they haven't shown is that the same pot [cast of characters] that's used for narcotics is used for paper. Now you take the guys I've been involved with up in Canada. They're the primary importers of heroin into North America and they're also the heaviest manipulators of paper there are. I'd say it [stolen securities] is probably directly involved in half the action in narcotics."

As happens with legitimate investment bankers, Peroff's career brought him into contact with dozens of famous people. One Southern banker, the brother of a well-known politician, was a frequent and knowing recipient of stolen stocks, according to Peroff. In late 1969 and early 1970, Peroff said, he took three batches of stolen stocks to the banker, valued at $125,000, $85,000, and $60,000. The banker paid Peroff 18 percent of the face value of the securities for the first batch, 15 percent for the second batch, and 10 percent for the last. Before the transactions were completed, however, Peroff said he faced real trouble. He was asked about it:

Q. Describe the deal.

A. I sold stock to him on several occasions.

Q. Hot stocks?

A. Yes.

Q. He [the banker] knew they were hot?

A. Yes. He tried to punch me out one time. I had to shove him down on the couch in front of people in his office.

Q. Why did he punch you?

A. He didn't have the money and he didn't want to pay me, so I started grabbing the stock. He came at me. He tried to hit me. He's nuts. He shouted. He's got some crazy temper you know. I left the stock with him because after that little incident, he promised to pay me at a certain time. And I got it.

Although the deal with that particular banker involved "hot" or stolen stock, there is yet another deal that involves illicit securities. It is classified by the underworld as "cold" stock.

Cold stock is by far the most desirable, and rarely surfaces because such transactions are difficult to arrange. It is stolen at a very high level by an officer of a brokerage house, at a time when the stock has just been inspected and verified in the firm's vaults. Because the certificates are not normally scheduled for inspection again for another six weeks, they can be removed without fear of detection for at least that long. In other words, the theft will not be reported for over a month, so the securities will not be listed as stolen by various reporting agencies.

"This is stock that gives you a grace period of four to six weeks," Peroff said. The gross yield on that stock is split up. "Approximately 30 percent of that goes to an attorney and to the broker who resells it. They both usually know what kind of a transaction it is, and they're the ones who have to face the law when it surfaces. The way it's done is this: The stock isn't stolen until everybody's ready for it. The attorneys create a third person —a man, an actual body [a fictitious name, represented by a hired imposter]. They make sure the secretary sees him. They actually walk this man into the brokerage house. He usually talks to several salesmen, people who see him and can describe him. This is a man who came in to see the attorney to sell some stock. It's usually bearer stock or street name stock.

"So what happens is that the stock is stolen. It goes through the attorney. It goes through the broker. It's sold [again] a week later. You get your money and they're gone. Now, four to six weeks later, that stock is going to turn up missing in the [securities] house. The house is going to turn around and lay it on the insurance company, and the police are going to be involved, usually the FBI. The FBI starts tracing it. It comes back to the broker. The broker says, 'Yes, we handled that stock. It was brought in by his lawyer.' They go to the lawyer and look at his file. Everything is in order, and that's the end of it. There's no other door to go to."

Peroff said "cold" stock usually is sold for 40 percent to 50 percent of its face value, but that costs of completing the deal would average 20 percent to 30 percent, leaving little margin. Nonetheless, because cold stock deals were so simple and safe, they were highly desirable. Moreover, because they required high-level participation from brokers and bankers, they seldom occurred.

"I've only seen cold stock surface twice," Peroff said. "I saw some cold stock in the office of Al ———— in Florida. He's a heavy real estate man and mob guy. The other was up in Canada. The stock was brought up there by Jimmy ————. He was a *consigliere* in New York. Those are the only two places I've seen it, and let me tell you, I am not a novice in this business. It's just that hard to get."

The major type of stock deal for scammers is hot stock, Peroff continued. "Hot stock can be gotten in a lot of ways. It can be stolen privately. It can be taken at a bank. That requires that somebody in the bank go along with it—just gone, you know, boom. A lot of it is stolen out of airports. A tremendous amount is stolen from messengers. But the problem with hot stock is that ten minutes after you steal it, everybody knows it. It goes on a list.

"There is some hot stock that is preferable to others, depending on who the transfer agents are. This is a very technical thing. In other words, if the transfer agent is a bank, for instance, like the Chase, which has world-wide communications instantaneously, you've got a problem. You can buy stock like that for maybe one or two percent [of face value]. Or, you can rent it. Hot stock is always for rent."

Peroff would buy hot stock cheaply, and then, by using his connections, sell it for 50 or 60 percent of face value. What made it easy, he said, was that virtually every major bank in the country had one or more crooked loan officers who were willing to participate in a hot stock deal.

"It doesn't boil down to the bank," he said, "it boils down to the individual. Just think of a bank like National City or Chase. You've got a tremendous number of loan officers. One guy could be making himself a million dollars a year on the side. You get a friendly banker. That's all it takes."

Peroff named two of the biggest banks in New York. "More hot deals go through there than anywhere," he said. "You know what the point is? What rules can you bend?"

Peroff explained how such a loan is handled. You bring in some hot stocks to use as collateral for a loan. The banker has a choice of either checking the stock, or making the loan without verifying the authenticity of the securities.

"Every loan officer has his own limit, depending on how high he is in the bank, where he doesn't have to go to the loan committee [for approval]. If it falls within that limit, there's no problem. Even if it doesn't fall within that limit and it's important enough to him—if he's going to make enough money out of it—he can go to the loan committee and get you approved without stating what your collateral is, except that you said you're going to give him $100,000 or $200,000 worth of New York Stock Exchange blue chip stocks. The loan committee will either say yes or no, based on your delivering that amount.

"He can go to the loan committee using this kind of approach. Say you want to borrow $100,000. The loan committee may turn around and say, 'Let him put up $200,000 of paper.' He'll say, 'My man needs $100,000, but he can only come up with $150,000 worth of paper.' He'll make a big issue over the amount of collateral, rather than what the collateral is. Now, he's got his approval from the loan committee. That's all done. He gets the paperwork done and you come in with the stock. He doesn't have to go back to the loan committee with the stock. They never know what it was."

The banker frequently skimmed 20 percent off the top of such a deal for himself, Peroff said, either in cash, or as a piece of whatever was being financed. "He could end up with part of the deal, you know, either through himself or through a straw [a representative used to conceal his identity]. If somebody ever took a good look around, they'd find that a lot of these bankers don't stay that long. Their careers are usually short-lived."

The secret, according to Peroff, lay in connections. Just as investment bankers like Lazard Frères and Goldman Sachs have close connections with important financiers and government officials around the world, so do individuals like Frank Peroff know intimately the underbelly of the financial world.

"It can't be done without the banker," he said. "It just can't be done. A strange guy coming off the street, walking into a strange bank. He's going to go through the wringer. He's going to get checked out. It's impossible. I mean, even if the banker gets to know you, and you build yourself up and do some business with him for five or six months, and he knows you're straight and everything else, he still by law is supposed to check that stock out. That's the name of the game. Sure, there's a certain amount of discretion there, but he's obligated to check that stock out through a transfer agent. In New York that's as easy as picking up a telephone."

There is a degree of risk in holding hot stocks, Peroff said. At one point, while he was living in Italy, he lit a tremendous bonfire, with stolen securities serving as the fuel. It was the summer of 1973, just after Peroff had illegally shipped his furniture to a home outside Rome, and he became worried that the police would search his premises because he did not have a residency permit that allowed him to live there.

"They have the right to walk in your house at any time without warrants or anything like that," he said.

Peroff said if he had been able to move the hot stock, it might have brought him $3 million to $4 million.

In Peroff's view, it would be simple to guard against stolen stock deals, if the nation's financial institutions wanted to clean up the situation. Part of the answer rests with better administration, particularly in cold stock deals, he said.

"For cold stock there's only one way. The stock is stolen for a specific deal. That deal's made before the stock's even taken out of the vault and sold. It becomes hot a couple of months later, and then you've got a brick wall. The trick is to find out who took it out of the vault. They shouldn't scatter vaults. The stock should all be kept in one place and there should be a federal outfit there, so when any stock was removed, the numbers, the names, and the man who's got it in his hand would have to be registered. It's that simple, really, because then if it's stolen, and if it comes back, they have something to go back to, to find out who actually carried it out. Even if this man used a dummy to take it out, the dummy's going to say who told him to. That's the only way you're going to stop it. There's no other way."

For hot stock deals, it would be even easier to prevent thieves from using stolen securities, Peroff said.

"Hot stock is as simple as a reporting service. If they passed legislation forbidding the banks from taking any stock without a check first, and a certificate to go with it that it's been checked, that would do it." Second, said Peroff, a central computer could be used to keep track of stolen stocks. "If they do it with credit cards now, why can't they do it with stocks? It's so much more important, money-wise. If a man is able to put the numbers into a machine, it wouldn't hold the deal up. It could take less than five minutes to come back with a response."

Peroff said he believed there was resistance to such simple solutions because the financial community did not really want any central repository of information.

"When you're going through one central outfit, everybody knows everybody else's business right then and there," he said. "You know, money is secrecy. Nobody wants anybody else to know what's going on.

"So, all right, if that isn't the right answer, then you could require every brokerage house to have their own [computer]. Why can't they have a computer that lists every piece of paper in that vault? And, if it's stolen, let the computer know it's stolen."

As Peroff waited to find out what his fate would be, he talked about his family, about the circumstances that had cast him in the role of a securities con man, instead of an investment banker. Appropriately, he had met his wife, a former beautician, during one of his scams.

At the time, Peroff had been trying to get a license from the state of Florida as a make-up man so he could transfer the license to New York and peddle a beauty program in the Catskill Mountain resorts. "There was no intention of me doing any make up," he said, "the whole deal was being able to move this stuff."

A large man, over six-feet-one, Peroff shifted his 275 pound bulk in his chair, and spoke of his five children, the oldest thirteen and the youngest, six. What did they think of his career? "Well, of course, they know now. It's hard to keep it from them. My oldest ones understand, my youngest don't. My oldest ones understand that I was a scammer, and that now for the last year or so, I've been working at undercover."

For Peroff, the main difference between a legitimate securities dealer or banker, and someone like himself who operated on the other side of the law, is fear of getting caught.

"Here's a funny thing," he said. "They all know what's going on, and would love to take part in it. The only reason they don't is fear. They're afraid to go over that line. I'm sure they all steal in their own way. You know, they may rob somebody, or short-change them, or something like that, but they won't take the big step."

What about the people he has bilked out of their life's savings?

"You talk about a guy who saved all his life, comes up with this money, and gets robbed. At this point, naturally I feel for this man, but I can see a hundred ways where this guy should have covered himself by getting good advice."

Then the scammer in Peroff took over. He could hardly stop relishing his con-man abilities. "I can tell you about situations where a guy would go to an attorney, for the attorney to steer him right and make sure it was legitimate," he said. "Hell, I've turned around and bent the attorney. I went right around the other door and made my deal with the attorney."

On September 18, 1973, Philip R. Manuel, one of the most knowledgeable men in the nation on the subject of securities frauds, stood before the U.S. Senate's Permanent Subcommittee on Investigations. As an investigator for that subcommittee, Manuel had spent more than thirteen years tracking down scammers like Frank Peroff.

What did he think was the role of the securities swindler? How widespread were their operations? Were they expanding? Were they real, or merely the figment of some overzealous television or movie producer's imagination?

"There is," Manuel told the senators, "and has been developing for some time, a burgeoning group of professional confidence men and international swindlers who are, to a great degree, closely knit and interlocking. They cooperate rather openly, each promoting the fraudulent schemes of the other for mutual benefit and profit."

The thieves operated, Manuel said, virtually without fear of legal restraint, despite the fact that most of them had been exposed by various government agencies.

"This group has conceived and has applied sophisticated corporate principles to the age-old art of swindling. Their forte is that they know 'how to use bad paper' and in so doing, are limited only by their own ingenuity.

"This group of swindlers comprise in themselves an organized criminal group who form a natural alliance with those organized criminals who control the theft and distribution of securities and on whom their supply of this paper depends."

Their frauds touched every part of the country, Manuel said, from New York to Los Angeles, from Las Vegas to Chicago, but flourished particularly in the Miami–Fort Lauderdale area.

Their modus operandi: "Stolen, counterfeit, or basically worthless securities can be safely represented as legitimate assets in corporate financial statements, provided the spurious nature of the paper can be effectively hidden."

The fact is, Manuel said, that "the swindler is not limited to any boundary. Therefore, the regional, national, and international scope of the operations has precluded any single jurisdiction from effectively detecting and curtailing these crimes. With the modern speed and effectiveness of both transportation and communications, the swindlers can, for example, live in Fort Lauderdale, headquarter their companies in the Bahamas, place their assets in Switzerland or Panama, and victimize persons anywhere else in the world."

Investment bankers. Manuel never used the term. But it was clear that in his own way he was describing the vast nether world of investment banking, a world where the stocks were hot and profits enormous.

12/ The Wrist Slappers

*N*ot since the marathon antitrust suit presided over by Judge
Harold Medina in the 1940s has there been a major investigation of the investment banking profession. As a result, securities
violations flourish and criminal prosecutions are rare. One government agency, however, keeps a close watch on Wall Street. The
Securities and Exchange Commission and its tenacious enforcement chief, Stanley Sporkin, bring a steady stream of civil and
administrative actions against the malefactors of the securities
world—from the mighty Merrill Lynch to such tiny firms as Cohen
Goren. Unfortunately, the penalties more often than not are merely
slaps on the wrist. Thirty-day suspensions and forced agreements
never again to violate antifraud laws are typical punishments for
firms that bilk investors out of millions of dollars.

In March 1974, the business community of the United States had plenty to think about besides securities fraud. The nation was suffering through an energy crisis and corporations were spending 50 percent more for fuel than they had a year earlier. The stock market was struggling to break out of an extended depression. A busy New York investment banker, scanning his newspaper on Saturday, March 23, would have been confronted with dozens of signs of this turbulent economic age. In Great Britain, he would have read, the government was trying to stem inflation by ordering major retail food companies to reduce their profit margins. In West Germany, the government was denying that it planned to revalue the mark. In Maine, the state attorney general had filed a civil suit against the giant Exxon Corporation, charging it with misleading the public. In Tokyo, a 62 percent increase in the price of petroleum products had added to the country's already soaring inflation. In Philadelphia, trustees of the Penn Central Railroad had once again told a federal district court that the bankrupt road's future was gloomy.

It was business as usual across the world economic scene. But for Wall Street investment bankers, there was one bit of news that Saturday morning that caught their eye and made them pause. Investors who held Douglas Aircraft bonds had won a law suit. A careful reading of the story indicated that a district court judge in Manhattan had at last ruled in one of the most closely watched law suits affecting investment bankers in recent years.

Eight years earlier, Douglas, the big aircraft company, had sold $75 million in debentures to the public. Unusual? Not at all. Little attention was paid to the sale. Later it was revealed that the Douglas Aircraft Company had been in deep financial trouble— a good deal deeper than a careful buyer of the debentures might have gathered from reading the prospectus. Believing they had been misled, the investors filed a number of law suits, alleging, among other things, that they had been cheated because Douglas had failed to disclose a loss of $7.5 million. And even though the prospectus had said the company's income for the next year was expected to be "nominal," the suits argued, the company was, in fact, to sustain a $52 million loss.

Judge Constance Baker Motley, who studied the evidence for five months after the trial ended, concluded that the charges were well founded and ruled in favor of the issue's purchasers. Although she did not immediately say how much money they would get, it was anticipated that it could run to millions of dollars.

Why was the case so important? Primarily, because Wall Street investment bankers and corporate fund raisers live on an ill-defined perimeter of the regulatory world. By law, they are not allowed to tout securities, so they must rely on a document called a prospectus which, in theory, tells a prospective investor what he needs to know to make a sound investment decision. The prospectus is often written with the help of the investment banker from information provided by the company. However, by its very concept, it presents its drafters with a problem. On the one hand, an issue is sold to raise money, and no investor is going to buy a company's stocks, bonds or debentures if he doesn't think it is a wise investment. That means the prospectus must present pleasant prospects, not gloomy ones.

On the other hand, most companies have a skeleton or two hanging in the corporate stockroom, and the question arises: How many of the skeletons ought to be trotted out for public viewing? The government insists that "material" information, that is, information which could have a significant impact on a company's future, be it good or bad, be passed along to prospective purchasers. However, there are differences of opinion as to what sort of information is material. Some companies and investment banking firms bend over backwards to make sure that everything is included in a prospectus. Others are less careful. But, regardless of the size or reputation of a company, a securities house, or an investment banker, there are few who have not at one time or another run afoul of the Securities and Exchange Commission or of the federal courts.

SEC action is considered an irritant by most offenders. It is the prospect of a private law suit that really chills them. SEC actions have traditionally served as devices to intimidate violators. Penalties are minimal—a thirty-day suspension from securities activity; a fine of a few thousand dollars. Usually there is one quick blast of bad publicity when the charge is filed by the SEC, followed by a consent agreement the same day by the company or firm being charged. Even the consent is hedged. A defendant is allowed to agree to the sanction without admitting that he is guilty of the charges.

Sometimes SEC actions are filed against the companies making an offering and sometimes against the investment banker who has underwritten the securities. In many cases, both are involved. Similarly, as with private law suits, there can be a variety of defendants.

Most feared by big companies are class action law suits, actions in which one stockholder represents all the stockholders in similar circumstances. Such suits are an extraordinary part of American law, analagous to a case where an alert shopper discovers that he has been short-changed because a twelve-ounce box of cereal contains only ten ounces. In addition to giving that one customer a refund, under the class action concept, the cereal manufacturer is required to give a similar rebate to every purchaser of that type of cereal, whether or not he discovered the discrepancy himself.

The Douglas Aircraft case, a class action shepherded by Abraham L. Pomerantz, an aggressive and experienced New York attorney who specialized in such actions, was brought by a bondholder named Lawrence J. Beecher on behalf of all the purchasers of the $75 million issue. As with most class action suits, the identity of the litigant was relatively unimportant. He served mostly as a figurehead, but because he bought the questionable securities, he was a necessary part of the procedure.

At about the same time the Douglas suit was brought, a similar suit had been filed against Merrill Lynch, Pierce, Fenner & Smith, Inc., the world's largest securities house, which was the leading underwriter of the $75 million bond issue.

In that suit the U.S. Court of Appeals ruled that Merrill Lynch, too, was liable for damages arising out of the Douglas offering. Judge William H. Timbers said that Merrill Lynch, seven of its vice-presidents, and a number of other defendants had violated the antifraud provisions of federal securities laws and therefore were liable for damages to five customers who had filed suit.

Still to be decided, however, was what the damages should be, and whether the suit would be allowed as a class action on behalf of all the other shareholders who had sustained damages.

In addition to the adverse decision by Judge Timbers in the private law suit, Merrill Lynch already had felt the sting of SEC sanctions. In November 1968, the Commission had charged that the big investment banker and a number of its officers and employees had committed fraud. In its announcement, the SEC laid out the unsavory details of the case—details that alleged the misuse of inside information and the giving of preferential treatment.

In 1966, the SEC said, Merrill Lynch, in its position as managing underwriter of the Douglas offering, had received private information from Douglas management about its earnings, specifically that Douglas would report earnings for the first six months of its 1966 fiscal year that were sharply lower than the eighty-five cents per share reported for the first five months; that it had sharply reduced its estimates of earnings for the 1966 fiscal year, and was expecting to show little or no profit for the year; and that it had substantially reduced its projections of earnings for the following fiscal year. In short, it revealed a significant deterioration in Douglas's prospects.

The SEC said some of Merrill Lynch's favored customers sold Douglas stock they held and made short sales, the two actions totaling more than 190,000 shares on the New York Stock Exchange "prior to public disclosure of the information and without any disclosure of such information being made to the purchasers."

While the adverse information was being disclosed to large customers, the SEC said, Merrill Lynch "did not disclose this [same] information to other customers for whom it affected purchases of Douglas stock." In other words, the world's largest brokerage house was taking care of some of its favored customers at the expense of some of its smaller customers.

Merrill Lynch decided not to contest the charges, and in the language of securities law consented to the fraud findings "without admitting the allegations." The penalty amounted to a slap on the wrist. The firm's New York institutional sales office and its West Coast underwriting offices were suspended for twenty-one and fifteen days respectively. Ten of the firm's employees were censured, and seven of them were suspended for periods ranging up to sixty days. Not much of a penalty, but at least it showed the Wall Street sharpies, the dignified investment bankers, and the bell-bottomed mutual fund swingers that somebody out there was watching.

There were many honest men on Wall Street in the 1970s, but there were also many with a touch of larceny in their souls. Frank Peroff, the self-admitted scammer who dealt in stolen securities, believed that a lot of men on Wall Street would like to take the plunge into overtly illegal activity but were afraid. Part of the reason for that fear was the threat of a class action law suit that would strip them of their cash and their reputations. But often the deterrent was the SEC, where the enforcement division was headed by a forty-two-year-old bulldog of an attorney named Stanley Sporkin.

Sporkin was viewed with distaste by many investment bankers. The son of a Philadelphia judge, he had spent thirteen years at the SEC. With a law degree and a background in accounting, he was not easily fooled by the high-priced attorneys and accountants who represented their blue chip clients before the SEC.

Arriving in Washington in 1961 to participate in a special study of the securities markets that was being undertaken in the wake of a series of scandals that rocked the American Stock Exchange, Sporkin switched quickly to the SEC's enforcement staff. He worked his way up from branch chief to chief enforcement attorney, and then from assistant director to associate director, deputy director, and finally, in the winter of 1974, director of the enforcement division. One of his jobs was to keep a close eye on investment bankers, the big ones and the small ones.

Sporkin's major concern with large firms was to see they exercised "due diligence"—a lawyer's term meaning that the investment banker should conduct a major inquiry into his client's affairs before selling his securities.

Another thing the SEC watched for was whether the offerings of the big investment bankers were simply a "best effort" or whether they were firm commitments. In the first instance, the firm would simply do the best job it could, and if some of the securities remained unsold, the company that issued them was stuck, not the seller. In the second instance, the selling firm actually bought the securities from the issuer, so if he couldn't sell them, he took the loss.

A persistant problem for the SEC, Sporkin said, was the small over-the-counter firm that helped underwrite a speculative issue and found itself in trouble when the issue failed. In recent years, a number of underwriters had been stuck with large inventories of marginal issues at high prices, pushing them into bankruptcy. Not only did they go under, but many of their creditor firms also failed.

Another problem that cropped up in such cases, Sporkin said, was that the securities being sold were sometimes placed in the hands of a nominee, a third party such as the underwriter, who would hold the stock under his own name for the true owner. Such a method was often used to conceal the true ownership of the securities. However, it also served a more underhanded purpose. If the market for a new issue was strong, the firm could sell to the public out of its nominee accounts, earning for itself the difference between the high after-market price (the value of a stock any time after the day it's first offered) and the initial cost. The hot-issue market of 1968, in which the public knowingly bought all kinds of third-rate securities because they were almost certain to sky-rocket in price, had been riddled with such devices.

"Here's the problem with a hot issue," Sporkin said. "There would be a great demand for the issue and it would rise precipitously, usually right after the public offering—sometimes tripling or even going to four or five times the public offering price. A tremendous speculative fever was involved. The stock would come out at say $5, and sometimes go as high as $50 or $60. Power Conversion went from a few dollars a share to around $50.

"There may be other things involved besides just the fact that people were buying. There could be a holding down of the supply of the security by various techniques. One is the use of nominee accounts. Another is to require that people who want to buy your stock make equivalent purchases in the after-market. In other words, if you let them buy 1,000 shares of the initial underwriting, then they have to agree to go out and buy 1,000 shares in the after-market, which, in effect, fuels the fire.

"The best way to describe it," Sporkin said, "was that when the hot issue market went into high gear, the 'bigger fool' theory operated. The hot issue investor believed there was always a bigger fool who would buy him out at an ever-higher price. Of course, more often than not, the bubble burst."

One thing that especially disturbed Sporkin was the underwriter who was more interested in placing an issue than he was in serving his customers. Some underwriters, for example, habitually placed marginal issues in their customer's discretionary accounts.

"My personal view is that it's inappropriate unless the issue is discussed with that person—that he is told everything necessary for him to know, and that there be his knowledgeable approval."

Discretionary accounts presented a particularly vexing problem, Sporkin said. Securities in such accounts could be traded by the broker, some bought and others sold, without the specific permission of the customer whose money was being spent. The conflict of interest problem Sporkin raised was an intricate one, but one that lay close to the heart of the broker's relationship with his individual clients, and to the underwriter's relationship with his corporate clients. If a firm was acting as both broker and underwriter, did it owe its allegiance to the individual client whose discretionary account it maintained or to the company whose securities it was trying to sell? Should it be permitted to sell the stock it was underwriting for a corporation into the discretionary account it was handling for individual investors?

"You are really not supposed to deal in a fiduciary relationship on a so-called principal basis. You are supposed to be dealing with the individual client strictly as an agent. And, in underwriting, you're on a principal relationship. In my own opinion, it's wrong, although it's being done."

There also were problems, Sporkin went on, when underwriters had few, if any, discretionary accounts for their new issues. In such cases, the danger was that the underwriter, in talking to his clients, "might overstate the issue in order to get the stock sold. You find a lot of that."

What about the fact that investment bankers sat on corporate boards? Over the years there had been enormous criticism that such a widespread practice could and did lead to serious abuses. Investment bankers became privy to new or critical information about that particular company which they could use to guide their own and their customers' investment decisions. Responsible investment bankers made a deliberate attempt to avoid misusing such inside information, which is a violation of securities law, but others were not so careful or so scrupulous.

"My own view is that being on a board is a problem," Sporkin said, "and I think you will see more and more people trying to sever these connections, not serving on the boards of companies that are being underwritten."

One case brought by the SEC against several over-the-counter securities firms illustrated the type of "hot issue" dealings that Sporkin was particularly concerned about.

On May 24, 1972, a registration statement offering 125,000 shares of the Logos Development Corporation at $10 a share, became effective. A firm called Cohen Goren Equities, Inc. of New York was the underwriter. Later on the same day the stock was first offered, it was trading as high as $22 a share, and it subsequently reached a high of $26 a share. A simple turn of good fortune? Hardly. SEC investigators later charged that Cohen Goren, two of its officers, another brokerage firm called L.M. Rosenthal & Co., one of its vice-presidents, and several other smaller firms and their principals had defrauded the public by manipulating the offering of Logos stock.

According to the SEC, here's how they did it: Cohen Goren and others withheld from sale and placed in so-called nominee accounts "a substantial portion" of the Logos shares that were supposed to be sold to the public. They also "induced the purchase" of the stock by representing that it was a "hot issue" and would open at a premium far in excess of the $10 public offering price.

Cohen Goren and some of its officers and salesmen then required their customers to buy shares of Logos stock in the after-market at artificially inflated prices in order to obtain shares of the stock in the public offering at $10 a share. Furthermore, Cohen Goren allegedly sold the Logos stock that had been withheld from the public offering into nominee accounts at artificially inflated prices far in excess of the stated public offering price, "thereby reaping undisclosed and excessive profits, while inducing their customers and others to purchase such stock."

As if it weren't enough, the firm and some of its officers and customers failed to pay for some of the Logos shares they purchased in nominee accounts until the shares had been resold and payment for them had been received.

What all this amounted to, the Commission staff charged, was that Cohen Goren and others had "initiated, maintained, dominated, controlled, and manipulated a market for Logos stock at artificially inflated price levels."

There also were some peripheral actions that came under the SEC's scrutiny. For one thing, the Commission staff alleged that Cohen Goren and several other firms had deliberately created the illusion of a free and independent market for the Logos stock when, in fact, they were buying and selling the stock with guarantees against loss and for a profit. Furthermore, the SEC investigators continued, they quoted the price of the stock, and bought it, at "artificially inflated prices" without regard for its investment merits or the legitimate supply and demand of the securities. They added that some Cohen Goren salesmen received extra compensation for Logos stock that was bought by their customers and received no commission at all on shares of Logos stock sold by their customers in the after-market. Normally, stock salesmen get equal commissions on both purchases and sales.

What the firm also did, the SEC staff said, was arrange for its customers to buy Logos stock from other brokers in the after-market, that is, after the original sales, thus creating the misleading appearance of widespread demand for the stock.

All this, according to the SEC investigators, amounted to an almost classic case of "hot issue" manipulation. As a result, Cohen Goren lost its license to deal in securities and some of the firm's principals were barred from the business.

Another case that illustrated the SEC's policy toward the misuse of inside information developed in the late 1960s. It involved a precious metal company called Spiral, and a small investment banking firm called Van Alstyne, Noel & Co.

As SEC investigators related the details of the case, here is what happened: In November 1967, the Van Alstyne firm was the prospective underwriter of a public offering of Spiral stock. In February 1968, it also was a prospective purchaser of $1 million of Spiral's convertible debentures, which it hoped to place privately. Spiral's plant had been burglarized in late 1965, and its facilities had been partially destroyed during a fire in mid 1966. Therefore, for the fiscal year that ended on March 31, 1967, Spiral had reported pretax earnings of only about $90,000 on sales of about $3 million. The company desperately needed money to build additional electrolytic cells for refining silver.

Van Alstyne's managing partner, James A. Russell, concluded that additional cells would substantially increase production, sales, and income, without increasing either overhead or wages by very much. In fact, he believed that $3 million in new capital, to be raised through a public offering of Spiral stock, would increase annual earnings to over $1 million after taxes.

So, in November 1967, Russell helped Spiral obtain an increase in bank credit from $500,000 to $2 million, and Spiral began construction of the additional cells. Spiral needed still more money, however. So, acting on Russell's suggestion, it decided on a private placement of $1 million in convertible subordinated debentures. Before making a firm commitment to place these debentures, Russell had Spiral retain an independent engineering firm, selected by the investment banker, to evaluate the company and report on whether an additional $3 million would improve Spiral's financial position.

On March 21, 1968, Russell received a "confidential" preliminary report which disclosed among other things, that Spiral's pretax earnings for the nine months ending December 31, 1967, were almost five times greater than its pretax earnings for its entire fiscal year ending March 31, 1967, and that the favorable trend had continued into the first two months of 1968. The report also contained projections which showed that an additional $3 million in capital would result in pretax earnings of over $2.4 million.

Less than three weeks later, the Van Alstyne firm proceeded with the $1 million offering of debentures, buying $700,000 for itself through a wholly owned subsidiary, the largest single investment it had ever made, and placing the remaining $300,000 with nine favored customers and associates.

According to the SEC, prior to any public disclosure of the favorable developments at Spiral, however, officers and employees at Van Alstyne had begun buying up shares of Spiral stock for themselves, their families, and their customers. Between April 4 and June 3, David Van Alstyne, Jr., the firm's senior partner, bought 12,500 shares for his family and family trusts, at prices ranging from $11.50 to $24.50. The stock would later shoot up in price after the favorable developments became known, hitting $44 by January 1969. Beginning on April 18, Van Alstyne also bought about 37,000 shares for his customers at prices ranging from $14 to $30.25.

On April 18, Russell bought 500 shares for a personal charitable foundation at just over $14, and between April 4 and May 13, he bought 3,000 shares for customers at $11 to slightly over $16. Meanwhile, three brokers at the firm had learned of Spiral's good fortune during discussions with Russell and Van Alstyne. One of the brokers bought 800 shares for himself at $16.25; another bought 400 shares for himself at $25.50 and $26.50; and all three of them bought more than 13,000 shares for their customers at prices ranging from $16.25 to $29.75.

What is especially disturbing about buying on inside information is that for every share of stock that is bought, there must be a seller. That seller, someone who bought the stock at an earlier date in hopes that it would increase in value, does not get a fair chance to make a profit. It is an accepted American tradition for businessmen and investors to try to outsmart one another. But it also is a tradition that the deck must not be stacked, and when stock trades are made on the basis of inside information, the deck is clearly stacked. If an investment banker reaps a $100,000 windfall because he bought a stock at the right time, nobody is hurt and more power to him. But, if he buys the stock because he knows something about the company that the person who sold the stock doesn't know, and that action constitutes a violation of federal securities law, then the game has been fixed.

"It is clear," the SEC said after it concluded its investigation of the Spiral case, "that because of registrant's [the Van Alstyne firm's] special relationships with Spiral, registrant, Van Alstyne and Russell were entrusted with nonpublic material information which they used for their own advantage and that of their customers."

The result? A minimal disruption. The SEC suspended the activities of the firm's retail sales department for twenty business days, and its underwriting department for fifteen days. It also ordered that David Van Alstyne, Jr., be "dissociated" without pay from the firm for ninety calendar days, and that James Russell and the three brokers similarly be dissociated for twenty business days. Most startling of all: The profits they reaped were theirs to keep.

One of the most complex court cases brought by the SEC in recent years involved the Seaboard Corporation of Beverly Hills, California, a company that acted as investment adviser and principal underwriter for a variety of investment companies.

The case involved the public offering by Seaboard early in 1970 of over 500,000 securities units, each unit consisting of two shares of Seaboard common stock together with one warrant with which to buy an additional share of Seaboard common stock.

The SEC charged that Seaboard, with the aid of other financial houses, had manipulated the offering in a variety of intricate ways and milked some of its subsidiaries to help make the offering succeed.

The case, according to the SEC, began to develop late in 1969, when the big New York securities house of Hayden Stone Inc., then known as Cogan, Berlind, Weill and Levitt, made a private placement on behalf of Seaboard, of 60,000 shares of Seaboard stock to the firm of Arnold Bernhard & Co., Inc.

It was not an uncommon type of deal, but it gave Bernhard an option to sell the 60,000 shares back to Hayden at $5.25 a share, if they were not sold in a public offering later in 1970. The existence of the 60,000 shares soon became a problem, and Hayden Stone informed Seaboard in January 1970 that it had not been able to find a buyer for the shares. If a buyer could not be found, it said, the big scheduled public offering of 543,100 units would have to be reduced accordingly.

That didn't sit well with Seaboard, so a private investor was contacted and asked to buy the 60,000 shares at $5.75 a share. As an inducement, three of the top officials of Seaboard said that if necessary they would later buy the shares from the investor for $6.00 a share. No risk for him, and a guaranteed profit, so the deal went through. Meanwhile, the three Seaboard officers entered into a secret agreement among themselves that if it became necessary to buy back any of the 60,000 shares, it would be Seaboard as a company and not themselves as individuals that would be made responsible for the repurchase.

Seaboard continued preparations for its big public offering. The registration and prospectuses were prepared, omitting, however, the secret facts about the 60,000 shares. Ironically, one of the three Seaboard executives involved, Peter Landau, counsel to the company, and later its chief executive, was a former employee of the SEC. At the time of the offerings, Seaboard and its related companies were his major client, and accounted for about $250,000 a year in legal fees.

On the day of the offering, Landau visited the SEC offices in Washington to deliver the final amendment to the registration statement. He did not disclose the secret agreement that had just been made on the 60,000 shares. Meanwhile, as an added inducement for the single private investor who bought the 60,000 shares for $345,000, Landau and the other Seaboard officers agreed to pay the interest costs in connection with the investment. Even as those events were taking place, there was other work being done to prepare for the big public offering.

Hayden Stone, which was to underwrite the offering, was having a difficult time locating prospective buyers and underwriters to come in on the deal. The immediate problem was the poor financial condition of Seaboard. Even more threatening, however, was the declining price of Seaboard stock. The slump meant there was a possibility that the underwriting would have to be abandoned, or that the funds raised would be insufficient for Seaboard to go ahead with a planned acquisition. What's more, it was thought that abandonment or substantial reduction of the underwriting might cause the immediate financial collapse of Seaboard.

Faced with such a dire possibility, Seaboard quietly approached some of the officers and employees of the securities firm of Cantor, Fitzgerald & Co. in Beverly Hills, and asked that they find buyers to purchase Seaboard stock in the market *prior* to the public offering, with the understanding that such buyers would be protected against loss.

The SEC would later charge that undisclosed arrangements were entered into "to have a series of transactions effected in Seaboard's securities during the period from on or about January 16, 1970, to on or about January 28, 1970, for the purpose of (a) creating a false and misleading appearance with respect to the market for said securities; (b) maintaining and raising and manipulating the price of said securities; and (c) facilitating the distribution of Seaboard securities."

The manipulation was accomplished, the SEC said, by causing purchases of 93,800 shares of Seaboard stock to be made in the market during that period immediately preceding the public offering. Furthermore, it went on, the price of Seaboard stock began to fall after the offering.

The SEC said one investor bought 30,000 shares for $195,000, and as part of the consideration for his purchases, he received an option to resell the shares to two officers of Seaboard at cost. A second 30,000 shares, it said, were purchased with $195,000 that was misappropriated from Seaboard by three of its officers. The remaining 33,800 shares were allegedly purchased by Cantor Fitzgerald, with 20,000 of them later being resold at $5 a share to a nominee of two officers of Seaboard who had obtained a bank loan to purchase the stock; that loan was later paid off by Seaboard.

"As part of the scheme," the SEC said, "the books and records of Seaboard were falsified, false legal opinions were given, false documents were filed with the Commission, and Seaboard was forced to pay fictitious consulting fees to Fran Daniels (president of Norton Daniels & Co., a Los Angeles-based financial public relations firm)."

Meanwhile, the problem of the original 60,000 shares that had been sold prior to the big public offering also surfaced. After the offering, with the price of Seaboard stock dropping, the buyer of the block wanted to exercise his option to sell at a profit. As a result, the SEC said, three officers of Seaboard, Irwin Solomon, John A. Coe, Jr., and Peter Landau, as well as others, began to misappropriate assets.

In two instances they allegedly caused investment companies managed by Seaboard to pay out a total of $175,000 in fictitious finders' fees to nominees of the three men, with the money used to buy a portion of the 60,000 shares. In another instance they allegedly caused a real estate investment trust to pay a fictitious real estate commission of $45,000 to a nominee who used the funds to buy a portion of the 60,000 shares. And, in four instances, a total of $83,250 was misappropriated from Seaboard to purchase additional portions of the 60,000 shares, and Seaboard's books and records were falsified to mask the time and purpose of the payments.

In the course of its investigation, the SEC also alleged that the investment companies managed by Seaboard had lost at least $9 million as a result of "mismanagement, negligence, fraud, and outright conversion." The major count dealt with a scheme to defraud the funds (investment companies) carried out primarily by three California securities executives. The SEC said the officials caused the investment companies to make large purchases of thinly traded over-the-counter securities after they themselves had purchased the same security. Then, after the purchases by the investment companies had caused the price to rise, they would sell their own holdings to them at a large profit.

The scheme earned them over $800,000 and resulted in losses of more than $4 million to the funds, according to the SEC.

Also in the course of its investigation, the SEC found that Hayden Stone had failed to disclose certain facts to purchasers in the big Seaboard offering, and had improperly sold some of the securities to its discretionary accounts.

The complexities confronting the SEC were illustrated in charges brought separately in New York by the Commission against Hayden Stone, and against Marshall Cogan, a Manhattan resident who was an officer, director, and principal stockholder of the firm.

Most disturbing was the allegation that during the course of negotiations with Seaboard, prior to the securities offering, Hayden Stone had obtained from Seaboard a commitment to recommend a Hayden Stone subsidiary to be the investment adviser for a firm that Seaboard was planning to buy. This raised the spectre of further private deals going on concurrently with an offering, and inducements that the prospective buyers of the Seaboard securities knew nothing about.

The final straw for the government investigators was the disclosure that Hayden Stone had sold 42 percent of the Seaboard securities to its own discretionary accounts and to accounts managed by its subsidiary, Bernstein Macaulay, Inc. Some of those sales, the SEC said, were effected without obtaining consent from the accounts. And, to add insult to injury, the sales were made even though Hayden Stone's corporation finance department had prepared a report questioning whether the current market price of Seaboard stock was justified, and whether a sophisticated institutional investor would find Seaboard stock an attractive investment.

As a result of the SEC probe Hayden Stone was required to establish a fund of $300,000 to be paid to purchasers of the Seaboard offering, and was suspended from managing registered underwritings for sixty days. Cantor Fitzgerald's institutional trading department received a ninety-day suspension, but it was waived because the firm paid $265,000 in profits to the court.

The Commission also asked for "disgorgement of illegal profits" from the three Seaboard officials charged with looting the funds. And it asked that Seaboard and the other twenty-eight defendants be enjoined from further violations of the federal securities law. In addition, court-appointed receivers were sought for Seaboard and the four registered investment companies formerly managed by Seaboard subsidiaries.

Here was a big case, involving thousands of man-hours of investigation by the SEC, yet the penalties seemed astonishingly light in terms of the millions of dollars lost by unwary investors.

Another recent example of how the SEC worked to ferret out fraud also involved Hayden Stone. The case revolved around $5 million in debentures offered on behalf of an ailing toy company called the Topper Corporation. Essentially, it concerned the sale of debentures by Topper and its investment banker at a time when the toy company's finances were in dismal condition and, according to the SEC, Hayden Stone either knew or should have known about it.

There were a number of tip-offs to Topper's plight, the SEC said. For one thing, in December 1970, the company had announced an astoundingly liberal marketing program to give its sales a boost during what was normally a sluggish period.

Topper had offered its customers the right to return merchandise for cash, free storage of merchandise they had ordered in public warehouses, extension of due dates of whatever money they owed to Topper, and extended payment terms for as long as eight months from the time their toys were shipped.

Although big sales to toy departments by manufacturers are unusual in December (the toys arrive too late for Christmas buying), Topper recorded sales of $16 million that month, a substantial part of its sales for the entire year.

Under ordinary circumstances, such a program might go unnoticed by a company's investment bankers, but during the entire period two officials of Hayden Stone were sitting on the Topper board of directors. They were Roger S. Berlind and Sanford I. Weill, chairman of Hayden's executive committee and chairman of its board respectively.

Two intriguing facts about the year-end program emerged. First, about $14 million of the product sales in December 1970 carried extended credit terms. The comparable figure for the previous year was only $2 million. Second, there was no mention in Topper's financial reports of the souped-up program to attract year-end business.

An investigation by the SEC also turned up other information that cast doubt on Topper's financial health. For one thing, two Topper officers, Jack J. Rosc, the senior vice-president for finance, and Frederick C. Pierce, the vice-president for sales, unloaded in succeeding months thousands of their own shares of Topper stock. For another, Topper's customers were flooded with merchandise they couldn't resell. And, because the vast bulk of the sales were on credit, Topper's accounts receivable mushroomed.

At this time, Topper's primary source of funds was a group of banks that made daily advances to the toy company, based on its accounts receivable. However, in the spring of 1971, Topper began to have difficulty collecting those accounts. By July, about half of them were past due, $7 million in merchandise was being stored by Topper for customers in public warehouses, and about 38 percent of Topper's accounts payable were at least ninety days past due. In addition, Topper by now had loans outstanding with banks that exceeded the entire value of its accounts receivable collateral. Finally, in mid September, Topper got a $7 million loan from a single institutional investor.

In late September, confronted with this dismal situation, Topper and Hayden Stone went ahead with their sale of over $5 million in Topper debentures. Hayden Stone, through a subsidiary, recommended to some of its accounts with which it had investment advisory agreements that they buy the debentures.

The prospectus used in selling the debentures, which Hayden

Stone had helped prepare, stated that Topper's pretax profits (before extraordinary depreciation) were expected to increase from $6.7 million, in 1971, to an estimated $24.7 million by 1975. It also predicted that a large cash surplus would be generated in 1971, which would allow Topper to pay down its short-term indebtedness by the end of the year. For its role as agent in negotiating the terms of the debentures and in selling them, Hayden Stone was paid $207,500 by Topper.

What actually happened to the big toy company differed substantially from the rosy scenario painted in the prospectus. Far from improving its performance, Topper went bankrupt. As for Hayden Stone, it shrugged off the debacle. Its legacy from the Topper deal was a charge of fraud by the SEC. "Hayden Stone knew or should have known," the SEC said in its formal complaint, that the statements made in the memorandum and prospectus, and by its employees directly to customers, were "false and misleading." As a penalty the firm was enjoined from engaging in fraud. Translation: Don't do it again!*

Although the modern regulatory atmosphere for investment bankers springs largely from SEC actions, and in a broader, more benign sense from the Medina trial of 1950, there was a dramatic precursor. In 1913, Arsene Pujo, a Democratic congressman from Louisiana, headed a subcommittee that conducted a broad investigation into investment banking. The resulting report alleged that six banking institutions—J.P. Morgan & Co.; First National Bank of New York; National City Bank of New York; Lee, Higginson & Co.; Kidder, Peabody & Co., and Kuhn Loeb & Co.—had been the nation's "most active agents" in fostering the "concentration of control of money and credit."

Pujo gave the name to the famous "money trust" that was to dominate the public view of Wall Street until Judge Harold R. Medina reported a dramatically different view years later.

---

*Early in 1976, Shearson Hayden Stone, Inc., the successor firm to Hayden Stone, settled for a total of $1.7 million three private lawsuits filed by holders of Topper notes.

Furthermore, as Vincent Carosso pointed out in Harvard University's *Business History Review,* Pujo's findings had a major impact on the bitter controversy over compulsory competitive bidding for securities that "raged on through the 1940s." They also were instrumental in convincing the Justice Department to file its 1947 antitrust suit against seventeen of the country's leading investment banking firms, he said.

More than a decade before Sporkin arrived in Washington to begin his career at the SEC, and thirty-seven years after the Pujo report was written, Judge Harold R. Medina officially gaveled into existence the longest and most celebrated trial ever to involve the investment banking profession.

Later it would become known simply as the "Medina trial," and would be looked on benignly by investment bankers. But in November 1950, when it began, with no clear indication of how or where it would end, it was viewed with apprehension by most of Wall Street. After all, the United States Government was charging seventeen of the nation's leading investment banking houses with conspiring to monopolize the securities underwriting business—a serious, perhaps devastating, accusation, if the charges were sustained.

More than twenty years after the marathon trial ended, Judge Medina reminisced in his chambers on the twenty-fourth floor of the Federal Courthouse on lower Manhattan's Foley Square. His eighty-six years sat lightly on him, as he occasionally fingered his white moustache and touched the gold Phi Beta Kappa key that dangled from a chain across his vest.

What about the conspiracy, he was asked? What about this trial that consumed nearly three years; that cost the government almost $3 million and the defendants $7 million? What about the 108,000 pages of written evidence that were entered into the record? And, of course, what about the grand conspiracy alleged by the government?

Judge Medina said what surprised him most was that at the outset he thought the government had a watertight case, and was certain to win. His opinion began to change, he said, as he discerned that some of the very things the government was using to try to prove conspiracy actually contributed to the competitiveness of the industry.

"I was satisfied," he said, "that if you ever saw a bunch of cutthroats getting after one another, it was these investment bankers. There wasn't any doubt about that in my mind when I got through with the case. All the time the government was saying 'Oh no, they wouldn't compete. They had these formulas and they bowed and scraped to one another.' Whereas, the truth was they were fighting like tigers."

The characters who appeared at the trial, or whose testimonies were read by the attorneys, varied widely. They ranged from Harold Stanley of Morgan Stanley, described by Judge Medina as a man of great integrity, to Otto H. Kahn, a Kuhn Loeb official who "would talk one way out of one side of his mouth, and all the time he was getting in some good licks behind their backs."

Finally, in September 1953, Judge Medina dismissed the case without ever hearing the side of the defense. If he had not taken action when he did, it could easily have dragged on for another three or four years.

Although Judge Medina concluded that investment bankers were a relatively honest and fiercely competitive breed, there is another, less generous school of thought on Wall Street.

Consider, once again, the practice of investment bankers sitting on boards of directors of large corporations. Not everyone believes they do it simply because their firms underwrite the securities of those companies and it helps to have insight into the plans and operations of the client. There also is a more sinister possibility, and one that many Wall Streeters believe is more realistic.

Abe Pomerantz, a class action attorney, takes a particularly jaundiced view of the gathering and misuse of inside information. "Why do people of great wealth serve as directors of large corporations for $500 a year?" he asked. "Social service? Nonsense. I think the answer to that somewhat rhetorical question is that there's gold in them thar hills."

Referring to the celebrated Texas Gulf Sulphur case, where

some of the company's executives bought stock on the basis of an unannounced mineral discovery, Pomerantz cited the prevalence of similar, if less publicized actions. "For every Texas Gulf case," he said, "you'll find 103 cases of the unrecorded telephone call. If I can say to you in the quiet of my office, I want you to buy 1,000 shares of the XYZ Corporation, there's no record. Nobody is doing it carelessly today. It's the kind of crime where you don't leave fingerprints."

"It's perhaps the biggest problem there is," said Hans R. Reinisch, a natty, self-appointed watchdog for small investors who frequently testifies before congressional and regulatory bodies. "If a director learns at a board meeting that a secondary issue is in the making, he knows there will be a dilution of earnings and the stock will decline. So, the minute a director learns that, he may tell his own director of research, 'Let's change from a hold to a sell.' I would say very many brokerage firm partners do that, and I speak from personal experience."

Another common practice is the leaking of vital information to big customers before the small investor ever hears of it. In fact, it is so common that Wall Streeters joke about it privately. The managing partner of one of the country's biggest and most successful investment banking houses confided to his dinner companions one night that, of course, the firm's important customers get a telephone call from him a day or two before the company's investment analyses are released for public consumption.

"I think it's a fairly widespread practice," said the research director of another Wall Street securities house. "There are many firms that regard the commission business they get as payment for that first phone call. There are guys in the wire room of the big trading houses who are trading on the information that's going out to customers the next day. It sure raises the point that the little guy who deals in one-hundred-share lots doesn't get the same information."

Sometimes arcane techniques are used to conceal the fact that trading action is based on illegal use of inside information. Take the case where an investment banker learns through his connection on the board of directors of a large corporation that a pending action would influence the price of a stock. What if he then tips off his analyst who covered that industry?

"Say I learned something material," said one analyst. "I couldn't put that out to my clients without breaking the SEC rules, so I might go to our firm's chartist and say 'don't the technical market factors seem to be saying that this stock is going to go down?'

"He'd put out a report saying the stock would soften on a technical basis, and I'd get on the phone to my clients and say that for very general reasons I didn't like the outlook. I'm not trying to flaunt the SEC, but here's a chance to be of real service to my client and to my company."

What does SEC Commissioner Irving Pollack think about all this? In mid 1973, while still head of the enforcement division, he was a panelist at a meeting of the Bar Association of the City of New York. For awhile he listened impatiently as a securities industry attorney complained that the reason investment banking firms were charged so often by the SEC with violations was because the law was too vague. "There's another alternative," Pollack shot back, "and that's greed."

Pollack was not the only government figure to express doubt about the purity of investment bankers. In a massive investigation of conglomerate corporations by the House Antitrust Subcommittee in the early 1970s, the staff turned up stacks of evidence of the enrichment of investment bankers for their role in fostering the conglomerate movement.

The staff's overall consensus was that "financial considerations and not productivity goals were dominant motivating forces in the postwar merger movement.

"Participation by operators in the money and securities markets in mergers and takeover attempts was a characteristic of the acquisition programs of each of the companies in the subcommittee's sample [companies like ITT, Gulf & Western, LTV, Litton]."

In other words, money flowed and wallets were fattened. Investment bankers got rich. Corporate executives increased their power. And competition suffered.

The unhappy fact is that starched white-collar crime on Wall Street still risks little more than a managing partner's or a firm's good name. In virtually every other type of serious crime, law enforcement officials employ a huge arsenal of weapons ranging from undercover surveillance and court-ordered wiretaps to interception of mail. For white-collar criminals it is a different world, consisting of polite interrogations—mostly at the convenience of the suspect, with his Wall Street attorney at his side. For white-collar criminals the risks are minimal, particularly when weighed against the rewards of a successful crime. So the public bilking goes on, less flagrant than it was in the "bucket shop" days of the 1920s, but nonetheless real. And when the SEC occasionally strikes, you swallow hard. You take your lumps. And you go back to business as usual.

EPILOGUE:
The Yo-Yo Years

Investment banking in the mid 1970s faced an unsettled future. The merger boom and hot-issue markets that had earned millions of dollars for its partners had faded. Offerings of stocks and bonds went begging. Firms were collapsing in a sea of red ink. Public skepticism about businessmen and financiers was rampant. The result was that investment banking firms were retrenching. Some went out of business. Others shored up their traditional activities and tried to stay solvent. Most eyed the new pool of Middle East money that sprang from skyrocketing oil profits. But for many, the months ahead would provide a serious challenge to their ingenuity even after the stock market began to surge upward in late 1975.

What then of the future? How was investment banking changing as the nation rushed through the 1970s? With the public playing an ever smaller role in the securities markets, would it remain an important adjunct to the nation's financial structure? Would its primary function, the raising of capital for growing businesses, continue? And what of the firms? Would they continue to reap high profits and make millionaires of the bright young men who joined them?

To many of these questions there were no certain answers. The securities industry was in turmoil. However, one fact seemed relatively sure. Barring a total collapse of the nation's economic system, some form of investment banking would survive. As long as companies or governments or institutions needed capital, they would turn to investment bankers for the know-how to extract that money from the public. The financiers would not vanish.

For the investment bankers still around who had been active in the early 1900s, the changes seemed immense. Financiers like Walter Sachs spanned an era in which investment banking had literally moved out of the horse and carriage age into jet aircraft.

At the beginning of the century, the general partners of the big securities houses had been related. Most of them were of Anglo-Saxon or German-Jewish origin, maintaining their firms as closely knit family units for as much as half a century. Then in the late 1920s and early 1930s, men from diverse backgrounds began to find their way into some of the more progressive firms. They often started as messengers and a few of them made their way to the highest seats of power in the financial community.

That avenue of advancement changed too, and in the 1940s, investment banking houses began hiring returned veterans from World War II. As G.I. Bill college men, these ex-soldiers offered early maturity as well as brains. By the 1950s, the industry had turned to the graduate schools, the Harvard Business School being the favored source of young investment bankers.

Just as the types of partners employed by the investment banking firms changed during the twentieth century, so did their clients. In the beginning, most of the industrial concerns and business establishments that needed to raise capital had been small in size with small capital needs. That was fortunate because during that period there had been no vast supply of savings squirreled away by prosperous wage earners. There had been neither the need for much risk capital nor the availability of such capital within the boundaries of the United States.

As the century progressed, however, industry grew and its capital needs expanded. Concurrently, excess cash began to accumulate in the nation. That opened up opportunities for investment bankers, and those specialized money purveyors of the financial world soon were channeling billions of dollars each year into new or expanding enterprises.

In the profession's early years, investment banking was virtually unregulated. Until the mid 1930s, there was no Securities and Exchange Commission to look over the field. As a result, many buyers of stocks and bonds were fleeced. Those who were wise soon learned that virtually their only safeguard was to buy shares in big, well-established companies—preferably from a securities house with an impeccable reputation. Then the basic premise was that an investor had to take a sizeable gamble if he wanted to make a considerable profit. Investing in a railroad or utility might be safe, but it wouldn't double your money overnight. On the other hand, investing in a speculative silver mine usually meant tossing your money out the window.

In those days there was no such thing as a prospectus. Investment bankers were usually given access to a company's balance sheet and profit and loss statement, but investors had to take the word of the investment banker that the company was sound.

As the twentieth century wore on, the public became more active in the securities market. In the 1950s and 1960s, millions of Americans converted their extra dollars into stocks and bonds. They became conscious, for the first time, of the money-making possibilities of a booming stock market. By the middle 1960s, the institutions had begun to dominate the market. The dollars of individual speculators still were invested by way of the institutions, but were once removed. They were the dollars that labor unions had bargained for—dollars that would be put away for pensions in the years ahead—or dollars invested by mutual funds.

In 1961, the individual investor accounted for more than 60 percent of the dollar value of public trading on the New York Stock Exchange. The rest was done by the big institutions. Then, for the next decade, the institutions steadily gained in strength and importance. By the early 1970s, individuals accounted for less than one-third of the trading value. What did all this mean to the investment banker? Simply this: After decades of attempting to build up large chains of retail selling offices, the investment bankers began discovering after the 1940s that a different type of service was necessary. In the 1950s and 1960s, a new type of investment banking service that catered to large, institutional clients began to predominate and some flashy newcomers began to put the older, more staid firms in the shadows.

Three partners named Donaldson, Lufkin, and Jenrette made their fortunes when they recognized the importance of the institutional investor and catered to him. The Weedens prospered when they realized that the over-the-counter markets and negotiated deals were becoming an increasingly important part of the securities business. Jack Dreyfus recognized that millions of Americans would welcome the chance to have a professionally organized mutual fund pick their stocks for them. William R. Salomon saw that he could fill a need and earn a fortune by instantly "crossing" huge blocks of stock for the new trading institutions.

There was another movement in the business world that also had an enormous impact on investment bankers. It was the conglomerate boom of the 1960s.

Companies like ITT, LTV, and Litton Industries grew from modest beginnings into vast conglomerate giants. For the most part, their parts had no relationship to the original enterprise. ITT sold bread, rented hotel rooms, built houses, rented cars, tried to buy a television network—all from a base as a telephone and telegraph communications corporation. The managers of these conglomerates liked to talk about synergism, two and two adding up to five, but more often than not, prosperity hinged on their taking skillful advantage of accounting principles rather than management adroitness.

Nevertheless, the conglomerate boom continued, fostered by a steadily rising stock market. One giant company after another traded its own inflated stock for the stock of a smaller company. If the big company gave away an inordinate amount of stock for the smaller company, shareholders acquiesced as long as profits climbed. Sitting in the catbird seat as this conglomerate-building went on was the investment banker. Often, it was the investment banker who brought the small company to the big company, or the big company to the small company.

The investment banker determined the appropriate exchange of securities. He floated the issue, often after taking care of his own best clients first. At every stage of the process, the investment banker was standing in the wings, whispering cues to the principals. And, while most of the conglomerates ultimately fell on hard times—their stock prices severely depressed, their earnings down, their shareholders disgruntled—the investment banker collected his fees, earned his commissions, took care of his friends, then moved on to other pursuits.

The conglomerate movement in this country, one financier said, was carried out more for the benefit of the investment bankers than for the businessmen who ran the giant companies, or for the public that bought their securities. Mindful that some conglomerates lessen competition, that many of them are inefficient, that many businesses declined after they were acquired by a conglomerate, the investment banker got in, got his, and got out.

By the mid 1970s, the securities industry had been transformed and investment bankers were changing as fast as their customers. The merchants-turned-investment-bankers of the early 1900s would scarcely have recognized their successors. Times had changed. Rules had been reversed. Big corporations were buying up their own stock rather than selling new securities. Companies that had gone public a few years earlier were going private. Corporations were financing more of their capital needs with the cash they generated from the sale of their own products. Companies were eschewing traditional offerings of straight debt and equity and were seeking innovative ways of raising money.

As the attractiveness of stocks and bonds ebbed and flowed, investment bankers were moving into other areas—options, real estate investments, commodities, gold. The merger boom that had sustained them was dormant for several years before it revived somewhat in 1976. The hot-issue markets that had made them heroes to their clients had vanished. And, just as investment banking was changing in substance, so was it changing in form. Once a profession dominated by closely held partnerships, investment banking by the mid 1970s consisted almost entirely of incorporated firms, many of them publicly held and traded on the stock exchange.

The partners of the newly restructured firms no longer faced paralyzing personal bankruptcies if they failed. But they did have to make more information available to the public, thereby shedding some of the air of mystery that had always surrounded the old partnerships. As disclosure increased, so did the government's scrutiny. By the 1970s, regulation was tighter than ever, and the SEC was bringing a steady stream of cases against both large and small investment banking firms. Although the penalties were light, responsible firms had to think twice before they again flouted the nation's securities laws. As for giving investors information, that, too, had changed. Long prospectuses spelled out in great detail the financial performances of the companies issuing the securities. They were even forced to tell of any important legal actions pending against them. And if the prospectus didn't tell all, the SEC was ready to step in.

While the investment banking industry was being transformed in the mid 1970s, it also was being squeezed by a slumping stock market. In 1973, the nation's investment bankers and brokers suffered their worst year since World War II, with net losses of nearly $50 million in aggregate. In other words, business was so bad that after the losses had been subtracted from the profits, the industry was $50 million in the hole. One firm after another closed its doors in the face of higher costs and lower earnings.

313

The number of new securities issues plummeted. In 1973 alone, the number of new bond offerings declined to 248 from 470 the year before. And the number of new stock offerings dropped from 1,460 to 440. Furthermore, a large number of the offerings that were made in 1973 were for public utility companies that had no choice but to go to the market to meet the growing demand for energy.*

Why the drastic decline? It wasn't that the investment bankers didn't want to bring out new issues. And it wasn't that the industrial companies of America didn't need the money for expansion. The simple fact was that nobody wanted to buy new issues. The market had gone dead. Securities firms were going broke. Between 1955 and 1965, fifty-one firms either merged or went out of business. From 1966 to 1970, forty-nine more firms disappeared. From 1971 through early 1974, an additional thirty firms vanished.

One reason for the decline was the steady disappearance of the small investor. He was the individual who had to decide whether to put his extra income into a savings bank, a mutual fund, tax exempt bonds, real estate, paintings, oil wells, or stocks sold on the New York Stock Exchange. Unhappily for investment bankers, the small investor stayed on the sidelines during the mid 1970s, although by 1975 he had begun to return. In 1972, for the first time in nearly a generation, there was a decline in the number of Americans owning shares of stock. It decreased by about 800,000, a shocking development in a country that has made a fetish of growth and expansion. The decline triggered loud alarms from the investment banking community.

To compound the problem, many senior investment banking partners, disturbed by the trends of the seventies, decided to withdraw their capital from Wall Street firms and put it into

---

*In 1974, the decline in equity issues by nonfinancial corporations continued, plunging from $7.2 billion in 1973 to $3.5 billion in 1974. By 1975, however, the outlook had improved sharply, with equity issues more than doubling (in terms of dollars) during the first third of the year. Late in 1975 the stock market also began a spectacular recovery.

safer investments, such as real estate, thereby hastening the very disaster they feared. In a sense, the investment banking community was caught in a self-fulfilling prophecy. At the same time, many banks, insurance companies, and other large institutions decided that it was too risky to loan their money to marginal investment banking firms. The result? The ability of investment banking firms to compete was eroded and the very weakness that might have been prevented by a stronger capital position predictably showed up.

By 1973, the total net worth of the industry had dropped to $3.6 billion from $4.2 billion in 1972. Some $49 million of the decline was attributed to losses, and some to changes in the market value of capital. A good deal of it, however, resulted from withdrawals of capital from the firms themselves. And even those figures did not tell the whole story, because aggregate borrowings by investment banking firms went up some $16 million in 1973. Capital, by all accounts, remained the most persistent problem on Wall Street in the mid 1970s. The irony was not lost on many businessmen who wondered how investment banking firms were to fuel an entire economy with money if they couldn't even take care of their own capital needs.

Internal financial controls and management by objective became the bywords of the mid 1970s. It was not surprising that a premium was placed on computers and the men who knew how to use them. The profile of a typical investment banker began to change once again. Polished, hard-driving young men with slide rules began to replace those who were wine experts.

One such newcomer, Frank Zarb, a thirty-nine-year-old Brooklyn native, climbed the investment banking ranks and then burst into prominence in Washington late in 1974.

Zarb's dominant characteristic was energy and a willingness to step on toes if necessary to get the job done. From the time he earned his graduate business degree from Hofstra University and went to work for Goodbody & Company on Wall Street, he was usually found in front of the pack. At Goodbody, Zarb had a first-hand look at how an investment banking firm's back office should not be run. In 1970 Goodbody collapsed amid a welter of paperwork and only a dramatic rescue by Merrill Lynch saved it from bankruptcy. Zarb later ran the back office at Hayden Stone.

He left to become an Assistant Secretary of Labor in the spring of 1971 and quickly became a part of the cadre of hard-nosed young managers who served as troubleshooters for the Nixon White House.

He served in both the Federal Energy Administration and the Office of Management and Budget. Late in 1974, Zarb was selected by President Ford to head the FEA, replacing William E. Simon, himself a former investment banker and currently Secretary of the Treasury. Zarb accepted the assignment even though he already had been slated to become executive vice-president of the Export-Import Bank, an export-financing federal agency headed by William J. Casey.

Associates of the hustling young Brooklynite gave him mixed reviews. Some felt he could not escape responsibility for the collapse of Goodbody & Company, while others said he had not been in a position to save it. At any rate, his career served as a model for ambitious young investment bankers on how to get ahead on Wall Street with an occasional detour to Washington.

As an investment banker, Zarb had been earning $110,000 a year. His salary was not unusual for successful partners on Wall Street. For industrialists, money was an impartial arbiter, a measuring stick they preferred and understood. It made sense to them that a good investment banker could earn up to $500,000 or even $1 million or more in a single year, and that most of the successful ones were millionaires by the time they reached middle age. Indeed, it was part of the investment banking philosophy that if you were to deal successfully with millionaires and the great business executives whose salaries ran to the high six figures, then you had to look like them, talk like them, and act like them.

Despite the money and the possibility of national fame, investment banking by the mid 1970s was beginning to lose some of its luster. For decades the big investment banking houses of Wall Street had been able to attract the best business talent available from the college campuses with promises of money, luxurious surroundings, a chance for young men to rub shoulders with former high-government officials and legendary millionaires, in an exciting, ever changing field. With the possible exception of consulting work, investment banking held the greatest attraction for budding young businessmen who had the skill, the brains, and the polish to make it.

But increasingly, as the seventies wore on, the bright young men coming out of the nation's business schools or completing their Rhodes Scholarships found attractive alternatives. The commercial banks, for example, were encroaching on traditional investment banking preserves: selling stocks; making investment plans available. Commercial banking recruiters were blunt about their competition. Avoid the investment banks, they told the students. Come where the action is.

The investment bankers had only one rejoinder. We've been in trouble before and weathered it, they said. After all, somebody has to provide the capital that industry will need. In the United States alone, capital demands for industry were expected to rise from $120 billion in 1974 to almost $233 billion in 1985. Even with internal corporate cash producing 65 percent of those capital needs, an awesome amount of money still had to be raised through the bond and equity markets.

Chauncey Schmidt, vice-chairman of the First National Bank of Chicago, stated the problem succinctly. He said he was less concerned about shortages of physical resources that were plaguing the world than he was about the shortage of "wisdom and drive" to produce the world's financial underpinnings. "When we consider the billions of dollars called for by the projects needed to overcome today's and tomorrow's shortages," he said, "it is obvious that much more will have to be done to mobilize capital."

But where would the money come from? Expansion traditionally had been financed from American and West European capital markets. However, in 1973 and 1974 there had been a five-fold increase in the world price of crude oil and the result was a dramatic financial crisis that swept the globe from Iran to Italy, from Saudi Arabia to Japan. The countries that produced oil had money. And those that bought oil didn't. Suddenly the brass ring that investment bankers sought was the petrodollar—the dollar paid by oil-importing countries to the rich oil-exporting nations of the Middle East.

Financiers and investment bankers became entranced with the new possibilities. Some, like Peter Peterson of Lehman Brothers, rushed to the Middle East to explore business opportunities. Others stayed at home and explained the significance of the new world of petrodollars.

"Of all the obstacles confronting us today," said Henry Kaufman of Salomon Brothers, "the international kind are the most mind-boggling." At the heart of the problem, he said, was the transfer of wealth from oil-consuming countries to oil-producing nations. Such a transfer would inevitably increase the living standard of the recipient and reduce that of the transferrer. Furthermore, the creation of debt to finance oil deficits would generate sticky problems.

"Oil producers probably recognize that as they become huge creditors of oil consumers, the well-being of their newly acquired financial assets depends entirely on the well-being of their oil customers," Kaufman said. "Exchanging real assets for financial assets forces the new creditors into more of a dependent relationship, financially and economically."

For the oil-producing nations, it didn't take long before the accumulated petrodollars had to be spent. In the first nine months they invested $27 billion of their surplus funds in the United States, Britain, and Western Europe. But that was only a start. It was estimated that for the entire year the oil-producing states would have an estimated surplus of $60 billion.

Much of the money was invested in traditional reserve assets such as U.S. and British government securities. However, some was invested in other types of holdings ranging from property to private enterprise. In one week, late in 1974, reports surfaced that Iran was negotiating a major investment in gasoline stations operated by the Shell Oil Company on the eastern seaboard of the United States, and that Kuwait had bought a 15 percent interest in the West German company that made Mercedes-Benz automobiles.

Earlier in the year, Iran had bought 25 percent of the Krupp Steel works in Germany, and it also had signed agreements with West Germany to build two oil refineries and a petro-chemical complex.

The Kuwaiti government also had made a cash bid of $248 million for the St. Martin's Property Corporation, an English company that owned buildings in the London financial district; and it invested $14 million in Lonrho Ltd., a group with diversified African holdings ranging from gold mines to sugar plantations.

For those who had been watching the investment bankers act and react for decades, it seemed unlikely that they would not somehow slice off a piece of the Middle East action. As long as pools of money existed in one area, and a need for that money existed in another; as long as intermediaries were needed to bring together working partners; as long as investors had cash which they were ready to invest in the nation's future, it seemed likely that the financiers would be around working their unique blend of science and magic.

SOURCE NOTES

Introduction

Particularly useful as a source for background material in the introduction were the books *Investment Banking in America* by Vincent P. Carosso (Harvard University Press, 1970) and *The Merchant Bankers* by Joseph Wechsberg (Little, Brown & Co., 1966). Professor Carosso provided additional information in an interview. Also helpful were a number of accounts of trends in investment banking which appeared in various issues of *Corporate Financing* and *Institutional Investor.* Valuable statistical tabulations came from *Finance* magazine and from records maintained by the Securities and Exchange Commission.

Specific details of William Simon's career in Washington and on Wall Street came from contemporaneous accounts in *The Wall Street Journal,* the *Washington Post* and *The New York Times,* as well as from personal observation of Simon. Material attributed to the investment banking industry was provided in a brochure entitled *A Profile of Investment Banking,* published by the Securities Industry Association. Details on the careers of Peter Peterson and William Donaldson came largely from personal interviews and observations but also from newspaper and magazine accounts. Donaldson's early departure from Washington is chronicled by Leslie H. Gelb in an article in *The New York Times* (May 9, 1974).

Alan Silverstone's unusual switch from investment banking is described by the *Los Angeles Times,* Fairchild News Service, and *Mainliner* magazine in articles appearing in 1973. Additional information was obtained by interviewing Silverstone. A detailed article on investment bankers switching firms, by John Thackray, was in *Corporate Financing,* November/December 1972 issue. Details on the career of Richard Coons came from interviews with the subject.

Chapter 1

Much of the material for Chapter 1 came from lengthy personal interviews with Charles Allen and his associate Howard Holtzmann, who described the events surrounding the purchase of Syntex. Allen seldom gives interviews, so the insights he provided were particularly helpful. Other information about Allen and his firm came from articles by Stanley Penn in *The Wall Street Journal* (August 4, 1970) and by Robert Sheehan in *Fortune* magazine (May, 1954). Allen & Company provided me with numerous file copies of Syntex annual reports, proxies and prospectuses. Other material was collected from the files of the Securities and Exchange Commission, and from contemporaneous accounts in financial and general newspapers and magazines. A colorful description of the trading of Syntex stock on the floor of the American Stock Exchange was given by Frank Graham during an interview. Other interviews about Allen's methods of operating provided important information and insights, but the individuals who gave them asked to remain anonymous. An exception was H. Ross Perot who willingly discussed with me his dealings with Allen.

Chapter 2

Interviews with Robert Baldwin of Morgan Stanley, John Scanlon of AT&T, Asher Ende of the Federal Communications Commission, Richard Rosenthal of Salomon Brothers, and Lee Arning of the New York Stock Exchange provided much of the material for Chapter 2. Baldwin was particularly forthcoming about the events surrounding his firm's mobilization of the investment community. Willard Nelson of AT&T also gave me some insights into the mechanics of the $1.6-billion offering.

An exhaustive 202-page report by the FCC on AT&T's request for a rate increase (issued

July 12, 1971) was valuable, as was Allan T. Demaree's article "The Age of Anxiety at AT&T" in *Fortune* magazine, May 1970. Also helpful was a copy of the testimony of Baldwin at an SEC hearing on November 4, 1971.

A variety of background documents, including a 19-page presentation by AT&T that was used to interest brokers in its big offering, proved useful, as did annual reports and prospectuses from AT&T, and SEC filings by Morgan Stanley. Various Wall Street executives agreed to assess the importance and degree of success of the offering.

Chapter 3

I covered much of the floating-rate story for *The New York Times* during the summer of 1974. In addition to almost daily conversations with the principals, I maintained regular contact with the agencies and associations objecting to the issue. I was also present in the meeting room at First Boston when the documents formalizing the issue were signed, and spent some time that morning in the First Boston trading room watching the action. Also valuable for this chapter were follow-up interviews with Walter Wriston and Donald Howard of First National City Bank.

While most of the material in the chapter is the result of personal observation and interviews, I also used material from prospectuses and registration statements on file at the Securities and Exchange Commission. Also valuable was correspondence between Louis J. Lefkowitz, attorney general of New York State, and Ray Garrett, chairman of the SEC, and between Wriston and various government and regulatory officials.

The death of Thomas Sanders was described by Michael T. Kaufman in *The New York Times* (February 3, 1975). Contemporaneous accounts of the floating-rate issues of Citicorp and other institutions were contained in the *American Banker*. The *Institutional Investor* published an excellent account of "The Launching of Floating Rates" in its September, 1974 issue. An assessment of the notes was published by the Argus Research Corporation in the "Argus Capital Market Report" of July 9, 1974.

Chapter 4

Interviews with Richard Coons, Roger Tamraz, and George VonPeterffy, all major participants in the Intra Bank salvage, provided much of the material for this chapter. In addition, Terry Decker of Kidder Peabody provided many original source documents of the firm's study, including some confidential analyses written on the scene by outsiders. Also helpful were contemporaneous accounts that appeared in such publications as *L'Orient,* the *Beirut Daily Star, Reuters, Business Week, The New York Times* and *The Wall Street Journal.*

For descriptions of John Ehrlichman's dealings with Robert Vesco, I am grateful to Robert E. Dallos of the *Los Angeles Times* and to Philip Greer of the *Washington Post.* The article on petrodollars that was co-authored by Robert Roosa appeared in the January, 1975 issue of *Foreign Affairs.* David Lilienthal's comments about the article were recorded during an interview.

For the history of Kidder Peabody, I relied partially on Part II of the 424-page *Corrected Opinion of Judge Medina in USA versus H.S. Morgan et al* published on February 4, 1954.

Chapter 5

Since the most important source of information on the sale of Hughes Tool—that is Howard Hughes himself—was not available, I relied heavily for my account of the transaction and the meeting between Hughes and his investment bankers, on information provided during an interview with Julius Sedlmayr of Merrill Lynch. Other important details of the transaction came from a prospectus filed with the Securities and Exchange Commission.

Particular insights into the personal and professional activities of Hughes were provided by a variety of contemporaneous accounts in books, newspapers and magazines, and especially by Wallace Turner and Robert Cole of *The New York Times.* Additional details of the sale of the tool company in 1972 came from the July/August 1973 issue of *Corporate Financing,* the November 1972 issue of *Fortune,* and the October 17, 1972 issue of *The Wall Street Journal.*

Chapter 6

Much of the material for this chapter came from contemporaneous interviews with the principal financiers who worked to keep New York City from defaulting. They included Felix Rohatyn of Lazard Frères & Company, Wallace Turner of Merrill Lynch, Pierce, Fenner & Smith, Frank Smeal of Morgan Guaranty Trust Company, Thomas Labrecque of Chase Manhattan, and Edward Palmer of Citibank.

I also had the opportunity to participate in group interviews with Mayor Abraham Beame and Governor Hugh Carey.

John Darnton, Fred Feretti, and Steven Weisman, colleagues who reported on the city's financial crisis, also were generous in sharing their insights. A number of Wall Street brokers and investment bankers also gave me their opinions but asked to remain anonymous.

Members of the Emergency Financial Control Board who provided information included Albert Casey of American Airlines and David Margolis of Colt Industries. Professor Edward F. Renshaw of the State University of New York at Albany shared his knowledge, as well.

Most helpful, however, was the experience of living through New York City's fiscal crisis for nearly nine months and writing about it almost continuously during that time.

Chapter 7

The financial collapse of the Penn Central was the most intensively investigated business event of the twentieth century. For anyone seriously interested in learning the intimate details of that collapse there is a wealth of material. Among the documents I found most helpful were an exhaustive two-volume staff study by the Securities and Exchange Commission (August 7, 1972), a staff report by the House Committee on Banking and Currency (December 1970), and a staff report by the Senate Committee on Commerce (December 1972). Together, these three reports provided more than 1,400 pages of material gathered by scores of investigators who conducted thousands of interviews. The SEC study was particularly helpful because of the detailed presentation of the securities aspects of the collapse.

While few of the principals involved in those events were willing to be interviewed because of continuing litigation, one of the major figures did agree to a lengthy background session on the condition that he not be quoted directly. Also helpful in preparing the chapter was *The Wreck of the Penn Central* by Joseph R. Daughen and Peter Binzen (Little, Brown and Company, 1971). In addition, valuable insights were given by Robert Bedingfield, the transportation writer for *The New York Times*.

Chapter 8

Information about Goldman Sachs's involvement in the sale of Penn Central commercial paper came from a Securities and Exchange Commission staff report on the Penn Central (August 7, 1972), from court filings in the cases of "SEC versus Goldman Sachs," and "Welch Foods et al versus Goldman Sachs," and from various contemporaneous accounts. Although Gustave Levy agreed to an interview, he refused to discuss the Penn Central case because it was being litigated.

For information about the early days of Goldman Sachs, I relied heavily on the transcript of the Medina trial of the late 1940s and early 1950s, particularly the testimony of Walter E. Sachs taken in May 1951. Mrs. Sachs later provided additional information on behalf of her husband.

For insights into the personality and business methods of Levy, I am particularly grateful to some of his business associates who spoke candidly about him, and to "Gus Levy Answers 132 Questions About His Firm, His Business and Himself" by Gilbert E. Kaplan (*Institutional Investor,* November 1973). Many of the details of the Sears Roebuck $250-million offering came from a prospectus dated October 22, 1970.

Chapter 9

Few companies in modern times have been the subject of as much litigation as ITT. Court filings, including complaints and depositions, provided much of the information for this chapter. Also valuable were government documents like the transcript of hearings before the Antitrust Subcommittee of the House of Representatives (November 1969), and the 110-page memorandum of March 6, 1974 from the Internal Revenue Service's national office to its district director in Manhattan. Other valuable documents used to research this chapter included the original contract between ITT and Mediobanca dated November 3, 1969.

Lengthy interviews with Felix Rohatyn and other financiers provided considerable material. Also helpful in preparing the history of Lazard Frères was a privately published sketch of "The House of Lazard" dated October 1926, which was given me in confidence.

A number of government officials and public interest attorneys provided information, particularly Reuben B. Robertson, III, a Nader lawyer. Also helpful was the former ITT executive who first alerted me to the potential scandal of the Mediobanca affair. He must go nameless.

Chapter 10

In addition to interviews with most of the principals in this chapter, including Peter Peterson, Joseph Barr, Harry Heltzer, Wilbur Bennett, and William McKnight, I relied heavily on court documents for information. Especially helpful in describing the role of the special committee was a 119-page deposition by Barr, given in Washington on July 17, 1974. Other important details came from confidential memoranda and internal reports prepared by the office of the attorney general of Minnesota, and from an indictment handed up by a Minnesota Grand Jury. Securities and Exchange Commission documents also provided valuable information, including a complaint against 3M and its leading executives dated January 30, 1975. Assorted proxies, prospectuses, and amendments also were useful.

Important details were provided in an exchange of private correspondence between 3M officials and Maurice Stans, who raised funds for former President Nixon, and in various documents from a private law suit against 3M and its former chairman. Alan B. Morrison, a Nader attorney in Washington, provided materials and insights.

The 3M company gave me some material about its history, which was supplemented by an account written by Arthur W. Baum, "How to Run a Sticky Business" (*Saturday Evening Post*, July 18, 1959). Much of the material in this chapter appeared originally in an article I wrote for *The New York Times* (March 9, 1975) although I have expanded on the role of the investment banker.

Chapter 11

I met Frank Peroff in a hotel room in Washington, D.C. He was hiding from his former business associates, waiting for the Government to give him immunity and a new identity. Later, he relocated under a new name after he had told a Senate subcommittee what he knew about stolen securities. This chapter is Peroff's. We spent many hours together with a tape recorder, and the result was a 62-page transcript. While I independently verified with outside sources only portions of what Peroff told me, his basic credibility was affirmed by investigators in Washington. In cases where libel would be a problem, I omitted the names of the individuals he discussed.

The chapter concludes with remarks by Philip Manuel. His insights, given during numerous personal discussions, were invaluable. A complete account of his remarks can be found in *Organized Crime—Securities: Thefts and Frauds,* published by the Senate's Permanent Subcommittee on Investigations following hearings on September 18 and 19, 1973.

Chapter 12

Interviews with Stanley Sporkin, Irving Pollack, and Irwin Barowski, all of the Securities and Exchange Commission, Judge Harold Medina, Abraham Pomerantz, Vincent Carosso, Hans Reinisch, and numerous Wall Street analysts and brokers who asked for anonymity, provided much of the material for this chapter. In addition, I obtained the SEC complaints and court papers that had been filed in each of the cases mentioned. Also useful was Professor Carosso's article "The Wall Street Money Trust from Pujo through Medina" (*The Business History Review,* Winter 1973).

Epilogue

Although discussions with numerous financiers helped shape this chapter, I found particularly useful Henry Kaufman's "Financial Roadblocks to a New Economic Expansion" (November 22, 1974); Chauncey Schmidt's "A World Dilemma: Deficiency in Capital Investment" (January 16, 1974); and New York Stock Exchange chairman James J. Needham's "The Threat to Corporate Growth" (February 1974). Also helpful was a projection prepared by the Securities Industry Association: "Crowding Out and the Outlook for Underwriting Revenues" (May 30, 1975).

For background, I used a number of publications including Raymond P. Kent's text, *Money and Banking* (Holt, Rinehart and Winston, Inc.) and a treatise on "U.S. Investment Banking" by the Stanford Research Institute. Details on Frank Zarb and his Wall Street employers came from his present and former associates, and from Securities and Exchange Commission documents, as well as from contemporaneous accounts of his Wall Street activities.

ACKNOWLEDGMENTS

I am indebted to my colleagues at *The New York Times* for sharing both research materials and insights. My appreciation goes to Truman Talley for his shepherding of this project from conception to fruition, and to Ann Elmo, my agent, for her wise counsel; also to Margot Forbes who typed the manuscript skillfully, to my wife, Janie, who edited with a keen eye, and to Barbara Machtiger, who performed the final polishing.

Above all, my thanks go to Janie and our children, Heidi and Mike, for giving up countless weekends, evenings, and vacations that rightfully should have been theirs, and instead were devoted to *The Financiers*.

INDEX